# Women at the Top

# Women at the Top
## Powerful Leaders Tell Us How to Combine Work and Family

Diane F. Halpern and Fanny M. Cheung

A John Wiley & Sons, Ltd., Publication

This edition first published 2008
© 2008 Diane F. Halpern and Fanny M. Cheung

Blackwell Publishing was acquired by John Wiley & Sons in February 2007. Blackwell's publishing program has been merged with Wiley's global Scientific, Technical, and Medical business to form Wiley-Blackwell.

*Registered Office*
John Wiley & Sons Ltd, The Atrium, Southern Gate, Chichester, West Sussex, PO19 8SQ, United Kingdom

*Editorial Offices*
350 Main Street, Malden, MA 02148-5020, USA
9600 Garsington Road, Oxford, OX4 2DQ, UK
The Atrium, Southern Gate, Chichester, West Sussex, PO19 8SQ, UK

For details of our global editorial offices, for customer services, and for information about how to apply for permission to reuse the copyright material in this book please see our website at www.wiley.com/wiley-blackwell.

The right of Diane F. Halpern and Fanny M. Cheung to be identified as the authors of this work has been asserted in accordance with the Copyright, Designs and Patents Act 1988.

Wiley also publishes its books in a variety of electronic formats. Some content that appears in print may not be available in electronic books.

Designations used by companies to distinguish their products are often claimed as trademarks. All brand names and product names used in this book are trade names, service marks, trademarks or registered trademarks of their respective owners. The publisher is not associated with any product or vendor mentioned in this book. This publication is designed to provide accurate and authoritative information in regard to the subject matter covered. It is sold on the understanding that the publisher is not engaged in rendering professional services. If professional advice or other expert assistance is required, the services of a competent professional should be sought.

*Library of Congress Cataloging-in-Publication Data*

Halpern, Diane F.
   Women at the top : powerful leaders tell us how to combine work and family / Diane F. Halpern and Fanny M. Cheung.
     p. cm.
   Includes bibliographical references and index.
   ISBN 978-1-4051-7105-2 (hbk. : alk. paper)   1. Work and family.   2. Women executives–Family relationships.   I. Cheung, Fanny M.   II. Title.
   HD4904.25.H354 2009
   306.3'6–dc22

                                                                                    2008018527

A catalogue record for this book is available from the British Library.

Set in 10.5 on 13 pt Sabon by SNP Best-set Typesetter Ltd., Hong Kong
Printed in Singapore by Fabulous Printers Pte Ltd

1   2008

# Contents

Preface                                                                    vi

Chapter 1   For Women at the Top:
            How's the Weather up There?                                      1

Chapter 2   Learning from Mothers, Mentors, and Others                      21

Chapter 3   Saving and Spending Time                                        47

Chapter 4   Happy Homemaker, Happy Marriage:
            The Female Executive Edition                                    73

Chapter 5   Cherished Children: Tales of Guilt and Pride                   106

Chapter 6   Work–Family Spillover:
            From Conflict to Harmony                                       131

Chapter 7   Culture Counts: Leading as the World Changes                   154

Chapter 8   Leading as Women:
            Styles, Obstacles, and Perceptions                             183

Chapter 9   How to Lead a Dually Successful Life                           208

References                                                                 231

Appendix: Biography of the Women Leaders                                   246

Index                                                                      278

# Preface

Sometimes, it is difficult to know what is fair and what is discrimination. In 2000, Diane received two e-mails from Hong Kong, on the same day. At the time, she didn't know anything about "the case." It was the first time that the recently formed Equal Opportunities Commission (EOC) had sued a government department, and both sides wrote to her on the same day asking her to be their expert witness and consultant. It was a sex-discrimination case, but unlike most of the cases that are very common in the US, this one concerned the educational opportunity of sixth-grade girls.

Hong Kong had a complex system of allocating places in secondary schools. The system allowed sixth-grade students (actually their parents) to choose which secondary school they would attend within their geographical district. Not all of them could get into the school of their choice. So, all of the students rank-ordered the schools they wanted to attend, and those students who had better academic results had priority in the allocation. The students were grouped into five categories (bands) according to their academic results. The top 20 per cent of the students had priority to choose their first choice, then the next 20 per cent, and so on. So, if your academic results were not at the top, you might end up in a school at the bottom of your list. The academic results that were used for the grouping included the students' grades in three school subjects, English, Chinese, and Mathematics. The students' scores in a public Academic Aptitude Test were used to benchmark the schools because there were large differences among the elementary schools the children attended. In the late 1980s, the Education Department of the Hong Kong government found that, on average, boys were scoring higher on the public test, but girls were getting better school grades. It is a common phenomenon that girls get better grades in school just about everywhere (Halpern et al., 2007). Boys catch up with the girls later on, at least on some educational assessments, but, on average, boys are behind the girls in classroom grades at the end of sixth grade. If grades in English, Chinese and Mathematics alone were used to categorize students, the top 20 per cent group would be more than half girls.

So, the Education Department decided that, in order to be "fair," the benchmarking of the schools should be scaled separately for boys and girls in the same school (producing a boys' norm and a girls' norm); the male students and the female students were separated into two parallel groups for banding; and the admission quota for boys and girls in co-educational schools were set to be about equal. In other words, boys were compared to boys only and girls compared to girls. Though convoluted, this sounded like a fair plan at the time because it resulted in each of the five "bands" or preference groups being half girls and half boys.

When the Sex Discrimination Ordinance came into effect in Hong Kong in 1996, parents realized that their daughters were disadvantaged in their priority banding because, even though some of the girls got higher school grades than the boys in their class, the girls might be placed in a lower band because each band was required to have an equal number of girls and boys. They complained to the EOC. The EOC considered that this system discriminated against those girls who scored ahead of some of the boys in the top bands, because this system treated them unfavorably on the grounds of their sex.

The actual situation was considerably more complicated, but this is the main idea behind the "banding" system that was used to establish preferences for entry into secondary schools. After significant soul-searching about what is fair for girls and boys, Diane decided to work for the government side in this case, reasoning that she would have the biggest effect on the schools if she worked *with* them and not *against* them. In fact, she recommended that they do away with the system of banding and preferences for secondary schools and use a different system for secondary school placements.

Fanny was the founding Chairperson of the Equal Opportunities Commission (EOC) in Hong Kong from 1996 to 1999. She had initiated a formal investigation on this case, which concluded that the government's school places allocation system was discriminatory

(Equal Opportunities Commission, 1999). She recommended that the government review and revise the system in line with nondiscriminatory and modern pedagogic practices. Her successor subsequently brought the case to court, and the EOC won. Although Fanny was not the Chair of the EOC at the time the lawsuit was brought against the government, she and Diane met when they were on opposite sides of a historic sex discrimination lawsuit in Hong Kong. Most people would think that it would be impossible for a deep friendship to take root and flourish under these circumstances, but most people would be wrong. We found that although we were on opposite sides of an intensely heated issue, we actually agreed on almost everything related to the case, including a preference for an amicable resolution instead of a costly, protracted, and bitter legal battle. Over the years since our initial meeting, we have become close friends and great fans of each other's work, despite living on opposite sides of the world and coming from very different backgrounds.

## Fanny Cheung

Fanny came from a traditional Chinese family in which sons had a more favorable status than daughters, but educational achievement was supported and rewarded in all of the children. It was through academic achievement that she developed her self-efficacy, which is a psychological term we explain later in this book. It refers to the belief that with hard work, you can achieve high-level goals. Inspired by the activism she witnessed during her undergraduate studies at UC Berkeley and doctoral studies in Minnesota, Fanny has spearheaded many campaigns on behalf of women since she returned to Hong Kong. She started the War-on-Rape campaign in the late 1970s, set up the first women's center in the local community and the first gender research center at her university in the 1980s, and lobbied the government for the extension of CEDAW (the UN Convention on the Elimination of All Forms of Discrimination against Women) to Hong Kong in the early 1990s. She joined a network of Asian women scholars to promote gender studies in the region. In 1996, she took leave from her university position to serve as the founding Chairperson of the Equal Opportunities Commission, to bring the Sex Discrimination Ordinance into effect. With her background in psychology, she reckoned that it would take more than legal action to change society. She laid a strong foundation in public education and research at the EOC. Through her advocacy at the United Nations CEDAW Committee and her networking of local women's organizations, she successfully lobbied the Hong Kong government to establish the Women's Commission as a central mechanism to promote the advancement of women in 2001.

From her experience of promoting equal opportunities to a public that was uninformed on gender issues and skeptical about the need for the EOC or a women's commission at all, Fanny learned a lot about the biases and myths that need to be dispelled. In particular, the cultural values placed on the family and on harmony are often cited by Chinese men and women to counter what they consider as unnecessary and imperialistic imposition of Western feminism. Feministic values promoting women's autonomy and empowerment are regarded as threats to the family and social harmony. Many women themselves subscribe to these traditional norms and justify the gender gap as a matter of choice that women make voluntarily. If it is an act of free choice, then the gap should not be considered as discriminatory. However, the argument here has missed a fundamental problem – women's choices are constrained by the systemic barriers that are implicit in the norms.

Early studies on the gender gap focused on women's deficit and disadvantages. In highlighting women's problems, women were often studied as victims of their perpetrators and the oppressive system. Less attention was paid to their resilience and agency in defying all odds to overcome the barriers. Recent developments in positive psychology illustrate the value of studying the strengths and assets of people who thrive and succeed in spite of adversity. What factors will bring a positive outcome?

Psychology has also demonstrated the power of social learning, learning from observing role models. So learning from women who succeed in bridging the gender gap despite the barriers would inspire others on what it takes to do so. Having met many successful women leaders through her work, Fanny has been reflecting on these questions. Given the importance of family to women's lives, is it possible for women to have a happy family as well as a successful career? How can women overcome the assumed conflict between the demands of a happy family and a successful career? What can we learn from those women who are leading dually successful lives, with happy, thriving families and occupational success at the highest levels?

When Fanny was selected as one of 31 international scholars in the 2004 Fulbright New Century Scholars (NCS) Program, she decided to take this opportunity to find out the answers from dually successful women leaders. The theme of the 2004 Fulbright NCS was "Toward Equality: The Global Empowerment of Women." In addition to participating in focus groups on shared interests among the NCS scholars, she undertook an individual project on "Work–Family Balance for Women in Chinese and US Societies: Implications for Enhancing Women Leadership." She interviewed Chinese women leaders from Hong Kong and Mainland China, and compared them with women leaders in the United States. The two Chinese societies reflect convergent and divergent trends of development in women's status while sharing the same cultural roots in the concept of womanhood. Hong Kong also serves as a bridge in the contrast between Chinese and American women, being a more Westernized and economically developed society. Fanny included Asian American women as a further cultural link between Chinese and American societies.

In the US, Fanny contacted several state chapters of the International Women's Forum (IWF), with the endorsement of the IWF President at that time. IWF is an organization of pre-eminent women and its mission is to further dynamic leadership, leverage global access and maximize opportunities for women to exert their influence. Some of the interviewees referred other women leaders to the study. In Mainland China, Fanny contacted women leaders in Beijing and Shanghai through contacts at the All-China Women's Federation, the National Congress of Women, the China Association of Women Entrepreneurs, as well as universities and personal networks. In Hong Kong, Fanny knew most of the top women leaders in the public and private sectors through her previous position as the EOC Chairperson and through the Hong Kong chapter of the IWF.

To enhance sensitivity to the American cultural perspective, Fanny approached Diane to collaborate with her on this project from the beginning. Diane and her university hosted Fanny's sabbatical in the US to conduct her interviews with the American women leaders. Over a series of mutual visits, we worked together seamlessly to interpret the findings, tie in the relevant research literature, and write up the book. This collaborative process opened our eyes to the convergent styles that we shared in doing our best for our work and our family. We also recognize the relentless support that both of our husbands have given us throughout the entire process. When Fanny spent her two-month sabbatical at Claremont McKenna College, her husband, Japhet Law, an academic trained in operations research and industrial engineering and a former Dean of Business Administration, took leave to be with her and assist her with her study in the US. He has always been a champion of her cause, and has encouraged her to take up the leadership opportunities that emerged in her career path. He is an integral part of her work and family life.

## Diane Halpern

Diane finds it difficult to write about her childhood. Her early years were spent in one of Philadelphia's poorest neighborhoods. Diane's mother died when she was 8. Although her father came to the United States from Romania when he was young, he maintained traditional attitudes toward the role of women. She recalls her father telling her that there was nothing worse than a career woman. Of course, rural Romania where her father grew up is so different from today's world that it is difficult to know how to judge these attitudes given the time and context. Diane recalls that he was opposed to women being allowed to vote, reasoning that they would vote for the better looking candidate instead of considering the issues.

One of the major turning points in Diane's life came when she was awarded a full scholarship to the University of Pennsylvania. She spent her freshman year in mechanical engineering, a choice that she made while in high school when she was totally unaware that she would be the only female in all of the engineering schools at Penn at the time. She caused a small scandal when, as the only female in engineering, she wrote an article for the Alumni magazine on mechanical birth control devices. Her boyfriend at the time suggested that she sit in on some of his psychology classes that were given by the legendary psychologist Henry Gleitman. She did and she was hooked forever – both to psychology and to the boyfriend who recommended the class to her. Diane married at the end of her sophomore year (at a very young age). When Diane's husband took a job as legal counsel to Federated Department Stores in Cincinnati, she applied to universities in the area. It was her good fortune to enter the doctoral program at the University of Cincinnati where she was mentored by Joel Warm and Bill Dember, two real scholars in perception, which was the area of her dissertation.

Diane and her husband, Sheldon, had adopted transracially and are the very proud parents of Evan, who was 5 years old when Diane began her doctoral program, and Joan (now Jaye), who was 2 years old at the time. Diane had no idea how she would manage graduate school with two young children. Three years later, when Sheldon's job transferred him to the Los Angeles area, Diane was fortunate in finding academic positions, first a temporary position at University of California, Riverside, then at California State University, San Bernardino, and presently at Claremont McKenna College. Their children flourished in the warm California sun. Evan is now an endodontist married to Karen, with two amazing children of his own, Amanda (5) and Jason (4). Jaye is in her third year of law school, married to Danny and mother of a terrific 2-year-old, Belle. Jaye began law school when Belle was 5 months old, so issues of work and family are both personal and professional for all of us.

In 2004, Diane was elected president of the American Psychological Association, one of the largest professional societies in the world. She made the issue of combining work and family one of her central themes during her presidency. Even today, she gets moving letters and e-mails from working mothers in all sorts of jobs thanking her for raising the issue nationally and bringing more psychologists and others into the field. As director of the Berger Institute for Work, Family, and Children at Claremont McKenna College, Diane continued her work in the intersection of work and family issues, where she studied the effect of parental leave on post-partum depression, how family-friendly work policies reduce stress and enhance health, and how families prepare themselves for the new demands of the knowledge economy.

Diane spent three months in Hong Kong, working with Fanny on the manuscript for this book, which took almost two years to complete. Her husband, Sheldon, helped her settle in Hong Kong and supported her separation from the family so that she could complete this book. Diane believes that we owe it to our sons and daughters, granddaughters and grandsons, and the generations that will follow them to create solutions that allow them to live fully – enjoying the richness of a loving family and using their talents and interests in meaningful work. Why should they settle for anything less?

We marvel at rich experiences that our group of women leaders have shared with us candidly. They are all extremely busy women who were willing to take the time to speak to us about so many aspects of their lives. We are most grateful for their participation. We also acknowledge the support of the Fulbright New Century Scholars (NCS) Program administered by the Council for International Exchange of Scholars, which created the opportunity for and funded the major part of this project.

Very few women make it to the top of their profession and among those who do, almost half have no children or other caregiving responsibilities. The message for working women everywhere has been clear: to make it to the top you have to pick one – your family or your career. *Women at the Top* presents a new look at how women can create dually successful lives. Women everywhere are waiting for an answer to the universal question of how to succeed in their profession when they are also wives, mothers, and family caregivers. Using the best psychological research and personal interviews with 62 women with families and prominent leadership positions in the US, China, and Hong Kong, and drawing on the life experience of prominent women leaders with children in Europe and other places around the world, we show women how to combine babies and briefcases for dually successful lives.

In this book, our diverse perspectives come together to create a new vision for dually successful women leaders – leaders whose lives are filled with meaningful work and loving families. In other words, leaders who have it all.

# Chapter 1

# For Women at the Top:
# How's the Weather up There?

"I remember my days on Wall Street when women would go out of their way to behave like a man. They would argue loudly in meetings, just like the men, and I would watch and think that women have a different way of doing business, and it doesn't have to be the man's way. I remember when women executives would boast proudly about not spending any time at home. One woman told me that she went back to work two days after she gave birth. I thought that was so stupid and unnecessary. Why would anyone want to do that? Of course, Wall Street is male-dominated, but the women who worked there didn't help either; they basically played along with the rules of the game that were laid down by men. There are so many misconceptions about how women should behave if they want to be as competitive as men. It is a misconception for young women to think: 'I can't get married, I can't have children because then I will lose my competitiveness.' That is just wrong. So much of women's growth comes from being a mother and a wife. . . . The way for women to lead is as equals with men and to work in the professional world in their own womanly style."

These are the reflections of Zhang Xin, who was recognized by the World Economic Forum as a "world global leader" for her work as Chairman and Co-CEO of SOHO China, Ltd., an innovative real estate firm. She is one of the 62 powerful women leaders whom we interviewed for this book. Each rose to the top of her profession while she was "married with children," or, in a few cases, provided elder care or had other family caregiving responsibilities. These powerful women reveal personal insights into the rarefied atmosphere of "life at the top." How do women with family care responsibilities make it over multiple hurdles to get to the top of their profession and then go home every night to change diapers and read bedtime stories? What can the rest of us learn as we gaze upward into the world of top-level decision makers, politicians, law makers, chiefs of police, university presidents, and CEOs for major manufacturing corporations, to name a few positions these women occupy?

We have two very different stories to tell about women's leadership around the world and, depending on your attitudes toward women in leadership positions, the news is very good or very bad. Let's get one contemporary myth out of the way. Despite the endless blogging and newspaper headlines, women are not "opting out" of the workforce to stay home with their babies. The workforce participation rate of mothers in the United States has dropped by 2 percent since its peak in 2000, but as economist Boushey (2005) demonstrated, there was a similar drop in employment for women without children and all men, which was caused by a general recession from 2001 to 2004. Women, including those who are mothers, are in the workforce to stay. Many prefer to work fewer hours, some will take temporary stop-outs, and almost everyone wants more flexibility in how they work. Not surprisingly, the best educated women are most likely to be working; they invested years of education in preparing for employment, and they have the most to lose in terms of salary and status when they stop out. The best educated are also getting married later, having fewer children, and, consistent with this trend, may be divorcing at lower rates, which could be due to the fact that they are marrying later and hence have fewer years when divorce is possible.

The good news is that women are enjoying phenomenal advances and success in some areas. They now make up almost half of the workforce in the US (46 percent; US Census Bureau, 2007, August 9), China (45 percent; People's Daily Online, 2007, May 18), and Hong Kong (42 percent; Census and Statistics Department, 2007), which are the three societies we focus on in this book, although we include interesting facts from other countries in every chapter. The data on employment are comparable for other industrialized countries. Women are getting more education than ever before; they comprise the majority of undergraduate college enrollments in two of these societies and all other industrialized countries in the world (57 percent in the US, US Census Bureau, 2007; 44 percent in China, Department of Population, Social, Science, and Technology, 2004; 54 percent in Hong Kong, Census and Statistics Department, 2007).

Another way of thinking about the phenomenal advantage women now have in college enrollments is to highlight the growing gap between women and men in the US. Among women in the US between 25 and 34 years old, 33 percent have completed college compared to 29 percent of men (US Department of Education, 2005). The cumulative effect of this sizable difference in college graduation rates is very large. As might be expected from women's higher educational achievement, there will be increasingly more women than men in mid-level management positions, creating an overflowing "pipeline" ready for advancement to top-level executive positions.

Now for the bad news. Despite women's success in education and mid-level management, few women make it to the "O" level – CEO, CFO, CIO, CTO – in the corporate world or comparable top levels in noncorporate settings, such as the highest levels of political office, or top rungs of the academic ladder. In the US, women hold more than 50 percent of all management and professional positions, but only 2 percent of Fortune 500, and 2 percent of Fortune 1000 CEOs are women (CNNMoney.com, 2006, April 17). Comparable data from the Financial Times Stock Exchange 250 (FTSE 250; Singh & Vinnicombe, 2006) show that 2.8 percent of CEOs for the top 250 companies listed on the London Stock Exchange are women. In the European Union (EU), which actively promotes gender mainstreaming, only 3 percent of the large EU enterprises have women as CEOs; women make up 10 percent of the governing boards of top listed companies, and 32 percent of the managers (European Commission, 2006). Of course, there are variations among the EU countries, with the Scandinavian countries leading in the proportion of women in decision-making positions, and Italy and Luxemburg at the bottom of the list.

It has been a half-century since the start of the women's movement, and women have only moved closer to the half-way mark in the corporate world and other organizations; most are stuck in middle management. Women in China and Hong Kong are still far from that half-way mark. In China, women make up 16.8 percent of the heads of government departments and the Communist Party, social organizations, enterprises, and institutions (Department of Population, Social, Science, and Technology, 2004). In Hong Kong, women constitute 29.1 percent of persons employed as managers and administrators (Census and Statistics Department, 2007), but few make it to the top level. However, with the trend of more women obtaining higher education in these societies, they will be following in the similar footsteps of the American women.

A bevy of commentators have suggested that women are better suited for the "New Economy," with its emphasis on communication and interpersonal skills and the rapid loss of jobs in manufacturing, agriculture, and most jobs where physical strength is an asset. Although this may seem like a logical conclusion, there are very few women who have made it to the top leadership positions.

Statistics showing that the most talented women are stalled at mid-level positions are repeated in every career path we examined. A recent survey by the National Association of Women in Law Firms (2006) in the US found that while women account for close to half of all associates (45 percent of beginning level attorneys), they account for only 16 percent of the top-level partners, or about one in six. These numbers get even smaller when you look at managing partners, where the percentage of women is 5 percent. The disparities between women and men in the legal profession are not just a matter of waiting until there is a sufficiently large pool of talented women with the experience to move into partner-level positions, because large numbers of women have been graduating from law schools in the US since the late 1960s. The scarcity of women at the top is not a pipeline problem.

Why are there so few women at the top of the leading organizations or running law firms or heading other major institutions, given the large numbers that are stalled at middle management? An important clue can be found by taking a closer look at the women who have made it into the rarefied atmosphere of life at the top. It is even more disheartening to find that among the small percentage of high-level executives who are women, almost half do not have children. According to a report from the US Census Bureau (2004), the more money a woman makes, the less likely she is to ever have children, with close to half of all women in the US with salaries greater than $100,000 without children. Similar data are found for women who achieve at the highest faculty ranks at research universities, where there have been extensive and eye-opening analyses of the academic success of women with children. Only one-third of all women who began their job at research universities without children ever become a mother, and among those who attain tenure, they are twice as likely to be single 12 years after obtaining their doctorate than their male counterparts (Mason & Goulden, 2004). A McKinsey and Company survey (2007) of middle and senior managers around the world showed that 54 percent of the women were childless, compared to 29 percent of the men; 33 percent of the women managers were single, compared to 18 percent of the men. Hewlett (2002) showed that in America, 49 percent of the "best paid" women in the 41 to 55 age range and making over $100,000 per year are childless, compared to 19 percent of the men. The double-standard is alive and well in the workplace. The presence of children signals stability and responsibility for men, who are assumed to be better workers because of their role as breadwinners. The identical situation for women has the opposite effect. The choice for highly successful women has been clear: you can choose either a baby or a briefcase.

But, what about those women who refused to make a choice and have succeeded at the top of their profession with children and other family care responsibilities? What can we learn from these women who are leading dually successful lives, with happy, thriving families and occupational success at the highest levels? To answer this question, we interviewed 62 women at the top of their profession, with about equal numbers from China, Hong Kong, and the United States. Their ages ranged from mid-forties to early eighties, with the majority in their fifties and sixties. These high-achieving women had all been married and, in most cases, were also mothers or, in a few cases, had some other highly-involved caregiving responsibility, such as caring for a sibling with disabilities or ailing parents. They occupied a wide range of top-level positions including Chairman of Deloitte LLB, President of Old Navy/Gap, Managing Director of China Light & Power, several university presidents, chief of police, Vice-President of IBM Greater China Operations, president of a television station, cabinet member, presidential adviser, state legislator, Supreme Court justice and deputy chairperson of the standing committee of the National People's Congress in China, and President of the Legislative Council and head of the civil service in Hong Kong. The American leaders include white, African-American, and Chinese-American women, several of whom are listed in *Forbes* magazine's (for multiple years) *100 Most Influential Women in the World*. A listing of the women we interviewed, with a brief biography for each, can be found in the Appendix. This cross-cultural group of women leaders helps us to understand the issues women face in a more diverse and global context.

The interviews were conducted as part of a project entitled "Work–Family Balance for Women in Chinese and US Societies: Implications for Enhancing Women Leadership" for which one of the authors (Fanny) received funding as a participant of the 2004 Fulbright New Century Scholars (NCS) Program. The interviews focused on the decisions that Chinese and American women leaders made about their work and family roles, on the strategies they adopted at different stages to address these competing forces, and on the cultural meaning of work–family balance for these women, as well as on their leadership styles.

To ensure diversity of background, we included women leaders from different sectors, including government, politics, business, and the professions. The sample of women leaders was not intended to be representative. To start with, they are not the typical women in the population; they are also not typical of women leaders as few top women leaders are married and have children. Instead, access to top women leaders with family responsibilities who would consent to the interview was the key consideration. We relied on networking for the access.

Fanny conducted all the interviews personally, in the cities in which the women leaders resided, or, in a few cases, during their visits to Hong Kong. The in-depth interview was based on an outline that had been sent previously to the interviewees. Although an outline was provided, the interview was unstructured to allow the interviewees to elaborate on themes that were important to them. We only spoke to the women personally, not any of their family members. Other than a few who requested anonymity, most of the interviewees consented to the use of their identifying information for research purposes.

## Mommy Track versus Career Track

The Mommy Track was first offered as an alternative to the Fast Track by Felice Schwartz in an article she wrote for *Harvard Business Review* in 1989. In that article, she suggested that corporations and other employers offer an alternative career track for women who wanted either to slow down their pace at work or to step out of the world of work for a while to spend more time with their children. Schwartz never used the term "mommy track," but it was used repeatedly in the media frenzy that followed her publication and the term stuck because it succinctly summarized a polarizing concept in the contentious debates about women and work. The alternative and admittedly slower-paced career track Schwartz proposed was intended as a way of retaining talented women who might otherwise leave high-pressure jobs when childcare responsibilities were added to an already overly full day. Schwartz was pilloried by the popular media as being opposed to women's advancement.

The idea that giving birth meant career-death generated emotional responses from all parts of the work–family spectrum. In fact, Schwartz was arguing that corporations, law firms, and other major employers of highly talented women were losing their investment by not providing ways to help women with primary childcare responsibilities succeed at work. Today, we find this sort of thinking in the establishment of what are commonly known as family-friendly work policies. These are policies that are designed to provide more flexibility and more control to individual workers so that they can manage the dual demands of family and work. These organizational policies coupled with tax incentives are well established in the Scandinavian countries, which set high standards in gender equality. Depending on the nature of the position, options may include the opportunity for part-time employment, including reductions in the number of days worked so that parents can be at home when their children have school holidays, flexible start and stop work schedules, job sharing, telecommuting, and almost any combination of alterations in the standard nine to five workday, which in reality can be a standard 8 a.m. to 10 p.m. workday in high-pressure jobs.

One reason why there was such an outcry of condemnation for the idea of a mommy track was that it would be utilized mostly by women, and thus created a second-class citizenship for women in the workplace. It also created an organizational category for women based on assumptions about their ability to remain on the fast track while toting babies and carrying the bulk of the responsibility for care of the home. The concern was, and still is, that the mommy track creates a second-class ghetto for women, and even the most ambitious women who have no intention of reducing or rearranging their work hours will be damaged by being automatically categorized as someone who will never be a high achiever.

With the advantage of hindsight, it seems that both points of view on the establishment of work conditions that help working mothers stay in the workplace are correct. Providing more flexible ways of allowing employees to do their work is good for business and can relieve stress for employees with children or others to care for, but it can also have negative effects on the career trajectories for the employees who use them. There are, of course, other ways to help families combine work and family, but these other ways involve a redefinition of many of our societal roles and rules, and societal changes are much more difficult than changing work policies or passing legislation to protect the rights of employees who are also caregivers. Real reform involves changing the normative roles of mother and father so that both are equally responsible for the family and the home they share. It involves removing the stigma from the users of family-friendly work policies, and arranging the nature of work so that anyone who steps off the fast track is not penalized with lower hourly pay, less desirable work assignments, little chance for advancement, and no way to rejoin their fast-track peers when they are ready to re-enter full-time employment. Real change also requires community support for working families and valuing caregivers. We are a long way from real change, but we are moving in that direction.

The biggest problem with workplace solutions to managing work and family is that they carry an implicit assumption that motherhood is incompatible with life in the executive suite. The opposite assumption is made for men, who are perceived as more responsible when they have children. The default assumptions are that mothers will be less committed as workers and have more absences from work than fathers. While many parents may want more time to catch their breath while also toting strollers and perhaps pushing wheelchairs, not everyone does. The powerful leaders we interviewed make it clear that it is possible to have a highly demanding career and a happy family. We have heard people say that it is not possible to do both, often repeating the trite aphorism that "no one can have it all"; the experiences of the high-achieving women we interviewed and many others clearly show that it is possible for women to combine a commitment to their family with a commitment to a high-level career. Of course, it is not easy to combine a high-powered job with motherhood, but it is also not easy to care for children all day, or to work part-time, with reductions in pay and few opportunities for advancement, while caring for children. Not all mothers will want a job at the top, but it is possible. Our outstanding women leaders tell us how they did it and how they inspired others to do it too.

For Jenny Ming, President of Old Navy/Gap, it was never a question of family or career. For her, these two most important spheres of life create one identity. She told us:

> "I look at my career and my personal life as one. I don't see them as separate. It's one complete circle of who I am. Other people say, 'Now I'm going to put my career on hold so that I can have a family, then once my family's back on track, I am going to go back into my career.' I never looked at it that way. I want them both at the same time. I really didn't want to be a stay-at-home mom because I really like the outside interests. But I didn't just want to be a career woman without a family. For me, career and family have never been separated. It's about having both."

Jenny Ming takes a straightforward approach to integrating work and family. She did not want to be short-changed in life, so she created a dually successful life for herself. No wonder *Wall Street Journal* listed her among the *Top 50 Women to Watch*. When work and family are thought of as separate domains of life, we assign the caregiver-family role to women and the assertive-career role to men, keeping them aligned with traditional sex roles where men are the breadwinners and women are the bread bakers. A recent study found that these stereotypes persist – both men and women believe that male leaders "take charge" while female leaders "take care." These false beliefs reflect a fundamental fallacy. They reveal the underlying assumption that these traits are mutually exclusive so leaders cannot both "take charge *and* take care" (Catalyst, 2006). But the women we interviewed have already proved they can. Psychologists now understand how stereotypical beliefs operate automatically and unconsciously to affect our behaviors. The ideology that work and family are separate spheres of life shapes our expectations and creates an implicit barrier to women's advancement. Leaders, like the rest of us, live one life, not two, and new models of successful living call for success in all domains of life.

## Work and Family Domains

The research literature has traditionally conceptualized work and family as two separate spheres of life and often focuses on the conflicts between them. In a recent study of working executives conducted by the Families and Work Institute (2006), the researchers compared the relative emphasis the executives placed on their work or their family. They called these two orientations "work-centric" and "family-centric." They asked about priorities over the past year because there are momentary differences when one domain will take over the other, depending on a myriad of possibilities – whether the children are home with the flu, or the deadline for the report really is tomorrow, and so on. Not surprisingly, given the group that was sampled, 61 percent were work-centric, which means they showed a tendency to center the activities of their life on their work. By contrast, 31 percent were dual-centric, placing equal emphasis on both work and life. If work and family were actually conflicting roles in the lives of working adults, then we would expect that being equally committed to both spheres of life would be very stressful because it would be very difficult to do both well. Surprisingly, the dual-centric executives were less likely to report that they were stressed than those who were work-centric. Caring equally about family and work reduced stress, possibly because it made life more interesting and there are more opportunities for success. It is not necessarily more stressful to be committed to both work and family. Caring for a family all day is stressful and exhausting work, so it is not as though the alternatives to combining work and family are restful or easy.

It is interesting to note that, in general, women who work outside the home are both happier and healthier than those who do not. In Barnett and Hyde's (2001) review of the literature, they conclude that working women are less depressed and report better physical health than women who are not employed. In their review of the Framingham heart study (a large study of precipitating factors for cardiac-related illness), they conclude that the only group of working women that shows an increase in heart disease that is related to employment is women in low-paid jobs, with high work demands and little control over their work, with several children at home, and little support to help with the children. When we consider the stressful lives of women at the top of their profession, we also need to respect the fact that women in low-wage jobs near the bottom have their own stressors and it is these women who show the negative health effects of long work hours and little support. Women in low-wage jobs have little control over their work lives and often over other aspects of their lives.

Other indicators that combining family and work is not bad for your health come from the finding that the entry of large numbers of mothers into the workforce has not reduced life expectancies for women. One prediction about the entry of women into the paid workforce in large numbers was that they would start dying at younger ages, much like men in general. Women live an average of 6 to 8 years longer than men, a fact that has been attributed to many factors including the fact that they are less likely to engage in risky behaviors, that they are less likely to go to war, and the possible protective effects of estrogen. The gap in life expectancy between women and men is narrowing, but the narrowing is more likely to be caused by increases in male life expectancy than by decreases in female life expectancy. Life expectancy at birth for both women and men in the US, China, and Hong Kong has been increasing. It now reaches 80 for women and 75 for men in the US; the corresponding figures for China are 74 and 71; and those for Hong Kong are 85.5 and 79.4. Having meaningful work is associated with psychological well-being (Arnold, Turner, Barling, Kelloway, & McKee, 2007). Working and caring for a family do not cause ill health or high levels of stress. High stress levels result from lack of support, low wages, overwork, and monotonous work where there are few opportunities for control. Similar conclusions are found in studies with Chinese women (Aryee, Luk, Leung, & Lo, 1999; Tang, Lee, Tang, Cheung, & Chan, 2002).

The importance of having meaningful work in one's life was recognized by Lorna Edmundson, President of Wilson College in Pennsylvania: "We [my husband and I] were well along in our work when we married. I'd also watched my mother ignore her own ambitions by deferring to my father. And I could see that that wasn't very good for her mental health; I didn't want that to happen to me." For Lorna Edmundson the question was not whether having a high-powered job and a family would be too stressful, but whether *not* having a challenging job and a family would be bad for her mental health.

In Chapter 6, we illustrate how our group of women leaders integrate their work and family domains and transform the conflict model of work–family balance into a model of harmony.

## Discrimination and Dissing

The climb to the top of any profession can be brutal, but it really is a steeper route for women, who face multiple obstacles, which require high jumps and belly-crawls. Did you know that it is legal to discriminate against mothers in hiring in many states in the US, because these states have no employment laws to protect mothers? In fact, those who are opposed to providing equal protection for mothers during the hiring process argue that it is their right to decide not to hire mothers. Despite this unsettling situation, many mothers are suing their employers for discrimination under a variety of laws, and winning. Very large verdicts against companies who have gone too far in their discriminatory practices against mothers are making overt discrimination less likely, but implicit or less obvious types of discrimination still occur. Discrimination against women employees who are pregnant or have just given birth is also one of the most frequent complaints received by the Equal Opportunities Commission in Hong Kong.

Most people probably know that women, on average, earn less money than men, but the real difference in wages between women and men is the difference between women with children and women without children. Mothers earn much less than women without children, whose salaries are often close to those of men with comparable qualifications and jobs. Thus, the gender wage gap is really a mommy wage gap – as if working mothers needed the double whammy of more work and less pay!

Dissing (actually dissin') is a common slang word for showing disrespect. Like discrimination, it is often more visible when women rise through the ranks of macho professions, like police departments. Margaret York, former Deputy Chief of Police for Los Angeles Police Department (LAPD), explained that for many police officers, her rise to power was "an assault on their masculinity. When we were in homicide, I was working with a woman partner. This was the first time two women ever worked on the same homicide team, anywhere in the country. And so, we got a lot of notoriety because we were two women. They started calling us 'The Crack Team.' Now, the crack team, what they were giggling about behind the scenes was they meant the crack in a woman's anatomy, which is the vagina. That's what they meant by 'The Crack Team.' But it also is a common term in our vocabulary that means 'good team,' 'you're right on,' and 'you're right on top.' One male detective was interviewed in the newspaper, and he said, 'Oh yes, they are our crack team.' But he said it as, 'Oh yes, they are one of our best teams.' But all the boys were laughing because they knew what he really meant."

Discrimination and disrespect can take many forms. Marjorie Yang, Chairman of the Esquel Group, a global manufacturer of over 60 million shirts a year – virtually every fashion brand name, including Polo Ralph Lauren, Hugo Boss, Tommy Hilfiger, and many more – told us how she handled gender discrimination as she worked her way to the top.

"When I worked at Jardine Fleming (one of the leading international financial investment firms), I knew how to handle verbal discrimination from my bosses. I could handle their teasing because I had a strategy. For example, when they asked me to pour coffee, I did not mind; but I would later ask them to do other similar tasks for me in return. In general, I was able to rein in my negative emotions and avoid anger using this strategy."

Marjorie Yang is now among the "50 most powerful women in the business world," according to *Fortune* magazine.

Kim Campbell, the nineteenth Prime Minister of Canada, was the first female to hold that position. She is also a past President of the International Women's Forum, an organization of pre-eminent women leaders. She reflected on the nature of prejudice against women in high-powered positions and women's prejudice against women leaders:

"As human beings, we begin to learn from birth how the world works. If we live in a world where leadership is masculine, we react negatively to women in that role even if consciously we think we support equality. Our early preconceptions are very difficult to change and this is why many women do not support women leaders. Ambitious women often identify with men because they are the empowered group."

It is hard to read her words without thinking that she must have faced some difficult situations as the first woman prime minister in Canada. She also hits on a central theme that we repeat throughout this book – much of the discrimination and prejudice against women at the top of their profession is unconscious. But that doesn't mean that we are hopeless and helpless pawns doomed to remain prejudiced. There is much we can do to prevent our immediate reactions from becoming actions and to help others recognize their own automatic and unconscious prejudices (Williams, 2008, suggests we use the term "unexamined").

Mary Ma, CFO at Lenovo at the time they were purchasing IBM Personal Computing Division, was identified by Forbes (2005) as one of the most powerful women in the world, and ranked as number 10 by Fortune (2006) in the 50 most powerful women in business. She offers sage advice for handling prejudice and discrimination:

"I always view myself as neutral. Probably people view me differently, but the important thing is whether you view yourself differently. You can view the fact that you are a woman and feel discriminated against, then probably you will feel the discrimination. But if you don't view it that way, then you won't feel anything. If you take it seriously, the impact will be doubled or tripled. But if you take it casually, then you can overcome it."

She suggests that at the individual level, you don't need to think about the daily hassles as discrimination, but just deal with whatever comes along, more like a problem to be solved. Such an approach will keep you from boiling over when asked to bring the coffee or when there is a sexist comment. Next time, ask others to bring the coffee in a spirit of sharing the office tasks, and respond to a sexist comment as you would to any insult.

Reframing the experience of discrimination at the individual level does not mean that it is not confronted as a systemic problem at the collective level. It should be, and the international and national efforts in strengthening antidiscrimination measures should not be relaxed. The disrespect for women in the workplace, especially in positions of power, needs to be addressed, but in a way that does not denigrate the woman. For example, when Hillary Clinton stumbled on a question during one of the US presidential debates, the other candidates rushed in to take the advantage. You are probably thinking, so what – this is what political candidates do. But in making her look ridiculous they "did Hillary imitations, complete with mincing steps and effete hand gestures," as *New York Times* columnist Stanley Fish (2007) described the ensuing events. They ridiculed her by exaggerating female stereotypic behaviors and women's generally higher-pitched voice. Some readers will respond to this as "no news" because political candidates attack whatever they can about their opponents, but by emphasizing to the public extreme female traits, they were subtly reminding voters about negative female stereotypes and why they might not want a woman for a president.

## Earning a Living and Psychic Dollars

A *New York Times* analyst working with data from the US Census Bureau shook our views about how people arrange their lives when he announced that "51 percent of women are now living without a spouse" (Roberts, 2007). These data may be somewhat misleading because they include all women over the age of 15 and few women that young would be expected to be married, and they include temporary separations due to military service or similar circumstances. But even if these data overestimate the percentage of women without spouses, they make a strong point about our contemporary lives – we can expect to live some portion of it without being married. With an aging population, in which women generally outlive men, we also expect a growing proportion of elderly women who would not be living with a husband. In a popular book, *The Feminine Mistake*, which is a clever take-off of the feminist classic, *The Feminine Mystique* (Friedan, 1963), Leslie Bennetts (2007) presents the reasons why women should not rely on husbands for their financial security. She argues that women need to remain in the workforce because even short time-outs have a large effect on lifetime earnings. Given the high rate of divorce, women need to be prepared to support themselves and their family; and even for families with intact marriages, family emergencies can quickly deplete the financial reserves of the single-paycheck family.

## The Earnings Gap

Why do women earn less than men in comparable positions? This question has dogged researchers for decades. Some portion of the difference can be explained by the fact that many women take time out from paid employment to care for newborn children and sick family members, and when they return to work, they are more likely to work part-time or fewer hours in full-time positions than men. Women also tend to select careers and occupations that generally pay less than others that require comparable experience and years of education, such as teaching versus engineering or social work versus working in a financial institution. An analysis of this sticky economic question was conducted by the Council of Economic Advisers (1998) in the US. They found that even after controlling for these variables, "the evidence is that labor market discrimination against women persists" (p. 2). A more recent analysis estimates that approximately 20 percent of the earning gap between women and men cannot be accounted for by occupation, hours worked, and other relevant variables (Government Accounting Office, 2003). The authors of this report also document the finding that jobs that offer more flexibility also offer lower pay and fewer opportunities for advancement, a fact that they took into account when estimating the "unexplained" portion of the pay gap. There is a lingering bias against paying women at the same rate as men. Similar results were found in the analyses of gender earnings differentials in Hong Kong (Lee, Li, & Zhang, 2008). The actual earnings differential widens with age. These economic analyses show that over 90 percent of these earnings differentials from 1991 to 2001 were due to unexplained factors, which may be caused by discrimination or other unrelated factors.

## Earning Respect

Working for pay provides people with "psychic benefits" that go beyond the money earned. In general, women who earn their own money have more power in their marriage or other relationship than those who do not earn their own money.

Nora Sun, Chairman and President of a consultancy company which advises European and US firms on their investment in the China market, and former Principal Commercial Officer for the US Foreign Service, offered advice that is similar to Bennetts':

"Don't depend on marrying a husband and having him take care of you. After I got my college degree and started working, I had a sense of accomplishment I never had before. I felt free that I could do things and I'm competent. Even though my husband was very responsible and took care of us, I did not have self-confidence until I had my college education. There are some women in the US who are overly rude or abrasive, because they want to prove they are also competent. I don't think you need to do that. You can't pretend to be what you are not. If you are competent, you are confident."

With so many women in middle management positions and the substantially higher graduation rates from college, an increasing number of wives are out-earning their husbands. Twenty-five percent of wives in the US and 29 percent in Canada earn more money than their husbands (Bureau of Labor Statistics Current Population Survey, 2005; Statistics Canada, 2006). A survey conducted by the Marriage and Family Society of China in cooperation with the Psychology Faculty of Beijing Normal University found that one-fifth of working women in China earned more than their husbands, but the earning discrepancy was not large (Xinhua News Agency, 2002, July 6). However, while wives who out-earn their husbands gain more power in the family, the reversal of the power structure may pose challenges to the marital relationship. The researchers of this study suggested

Figure 1.1   *Source*: TMS Reprints, Glenview, IL

that when the Chinese husband earned more than his wife, they were most likely to enjoy a harmonious home life. This suggestion reinforces the old Chinese proverb that says a marriage will not last long if a wife is more capable than her husband.

We did not ask the women in our high-achieving sample about income levels because such information is often perceived as being more private than the details of one's sex life or other intimate issues. One reason why people so intensely guard information about their income is that the amount of money people make is implicitly tied to feelings of self-worth. However, some of our interviewees did reveal that they were making more money than their husbands. As we discuss in our closing chapter, having more money does not buy more happiness, and in fact, once essential needs are met, additional money does little to increase happiness (Diener & Seligman, 2004).

However, money is a big factor in discussions of CEOs and people in other top positions. *Money* magazine and other financial publications regularly publish the salaries of top leaders. The average CEO salary for a company listed in Standard & Poor's 500 was 14.78 million; of course that means that half made more. In an article written for *Forbes* magazine, the authors described executive compensation as "paychecks on steroids" (Ozanian & MacDonald, 2005). As you might guess, the steroids were not estrogen. There is a big difference between the salaries of the top one or two people in large organizations and those of numbers three, four, and five. Even a brief reading of the list of CEOs who are top earners will reveal the absence of women's names. So, while more money will not bring more happiness, this is a relationship that very few women will get to test firsthand. But when they need to test it, how to handle this exception to the normative expectation in the marital relationship is a challenge. Some of the women leaders in our sample shared this challenge with us.

## Why the Scarcity of Women at the Top Matters

The G8 is a group of eight countries which exerts substantial control in the global economy via a variety of economic institutions such as the World Bank. In 2007, Angela Merkel, Germany's first woman chancellor, hosted the G8 meeting. This was the first time the G8 had been hosted by a woman since 1984 when Margaret Thatcher was the host. The 2007 meeting was also the first time the issue of women's equality appeared on the agenda. There was also a focus on poverty and women's issues in Africa on the 2007 agenda, which has been credited to Merkel who is an advocate of women's rights. The consideration of these issues by G8 leaders could result in major advances in improving the lives of many people around the world. We do not wish to denigrate the work done by many men who care about poverty, disease, peaceful solutions to conflict, education, human rights, and similar topics that are sometimes called "women's issues," but we do believe that, on average, women's priorities will reflect a set of concerns that have been ignored or perceived as less pressing when only men have been in charge.

As you will learn, the women leaders in our sample created workplace practices that are more supportive of families when they assumed positions of power. The politicians carried what was initially a concern about the education of their own children into office and translated it to education for all children. Kim Campbell, the first woman prime minister of Canada, and one of the women we interviewed, is a longtime proponent of women's rights. She worked on legislation designed to prevent violence against women, which was one of her key objectives as prime minister. When women lead, their leading issues reflect their experiences as working women, mothers, daughters, wives, and caregivers. If there is any doubt that women can also lead during times of war or effectively manage finances, we ask readers to think of the ferocity of mother bears when their cubs are threatened, or the countless women who manage family budgets with limited incomes. There is nothing in women's roles (or nature) that would reduce their abilities in any of these areas.

The need for recruiting more female talent at the top is most keenly felt in Europe where there is a drop in the talent pool with the low birth rate and a shortfall in the active workforce is forecasted. By tapping into the underutilized pool of skilled women, the projected shortfall will be drastically reduced. A McKinsey (2007) study analyzed the relationship between the number of women on the governing bodies and the performance of 101 listed companies across Europe, America, and Asia. The study found that companies with a critical mass of at least three women in an average of 10 members in a governing body obtained better results in organizational excellence and financial performance. In a follow-up study, McKinsey (2007) further found that companies with women in top management out-perform their sector in terms of return on equity, operating result, and stock price growth. So recruiting and retaining women at the top makes business sense.

When leaders are selected from only one-half of the population, you must also wonder about the lost talent from the other half. Any society that is not developing the talent of all of its citizens will find itself losing economic and political ground in the coming decades. We all benefit when the talents of all citizens are developed to their fullest extent. For those readers who are wondering how we can nurture everyone's talents so that everyone can participate in mean-ingful work, and still have a caring society that nurtures and protects its children and those who are disabled or ill, we turn now to the voices of our extraordinary sample of leaders and bolster their com-ments with scientific research findings. The powerful women leaders who shared their life stories with us show us how to combine work at the top of one's career with a happy and healthy family.

# Chapter 2

## Learning from Mothers, Mentors, and Others

How do highly successful women get that way? Many of the women leaders told us that they learned how to succeed from the best. The seeds for their success were sown in early childhood and nurtured by mentors throughout their career. Although a few of the superstars we interviewed mentioned the important role that their father played in their life, the role of their mother was also prominent for many of the women who made it to the top of their profession.

### Mencius' Mother Moved Three Times

There is a classic story about the mother of Mencius that is well known to Chinese children. As any Chinese child can tell you, Mencius was a famous Confucian philosopher from the third century. According to this tale, Mencius' father died when little Mencius was only 3 years old. Although his mother was very poor, she was willing do whatever was necessary so that her young son would succeed later in life. She made their home in a poor hut with sand floors where Mencius learned to write his daily lessons. But Mencius, not unlike contemporary counterparts, fell into bad behaviors. First, he imitated the fighting scenes depicted on the tombstones in a nearby cemetery, so his dear mother moved their home to another part of town away from the bad influence of the tombstones. Their second poor hut was in the market district, where Mencius soon adopted the braggart language of the salespeople. So, Mencius' poor, dear mother moved yet again, this time close to a school so that he would grow into a man with only positive and learned influences on his young life. Mencius later became one of the greatest Confucian scholars and is often acknowledged by the Chinese as the father of learning.

Unfortunately, similar stories about sacrifices that were made for the future success of young girls and women are missing from the fabled tales of most of the world's cultures. But, the women we interviewed supplied their own real life stories about the sacrifices made by their mothers so that they could learn to succeed. The stories they told about their mothers' sacrifices could become as legendary as the story about Mencius' mother, if society cared as much about the real life success of contemporary women and the hardships their mothers suffered so that they could succeed. They also talked about many other strong women who served as role models and mentors for success in work and life.

## Songs My Mother Taught Me

The mothers of the women leaders in Mainland China lived through a historical era of wars and hardships. Their personal stories of survival during the Cultural Revolution and Sino-Japanese War provide a fascinating, private glimpse into a period of history that most Westerners and young Asians know little about. Few of the women who came of age during this repressive period in the history of their country had the opportunity to attend school because education was devalued by the government and many schools were forced to close. However, they learned other valuable lessons, including the importance of perseverance, the need for independence, and the necessity of education for their daughters. In their own ways, the mothers of today's leaders in China became role models for their children, despite tremendous differences in their lives. The generation of women who lived through massive political repression and war are also role models for the rest of us as we strive to understand how these women were able to provide for their families and raise daughters for positions of leadership, despite their difficult circumstances. We get snapshots of their lives through their daughters' words.

Ma Yuan, who retired as the Deputy Chief Justice of the Chinese Supreme Court, wants to write an autobiography with the title, *An Extraordinary Close Relationship between Foster Mother and Daughter*. Ma Yuan credits her foster mother for at least half of her success, reserving the other half for her own hard work. In old China, women had little education, but Ma Yuan described her mother with pride:

"My mother had some simple, though not explicit, ideas on gender equality. When I was a little girl, she sat me up on the table and encouraged me to study hard. She told me that we could not rely on others. She wanted me to become a teacher or a doctor so that I could support myself. Although my family was not well-off, my mother said she would work hard to earn money for my education."

Ma Yuan was born into a family of eight children and was later given to her father's sister, whom she now regards as her mother. Though her mother did not have any status in her family of origin and had little education, she encouraged Ma Yuan to be independent.

"I always said my mother's support and influence changed the course of my life. If I had been raised in my original home, I might have become an elder woman in a rural area, or just die away at an early age. . . . Being feudal-minded, my biological mother made marriage engagements for four of her other daughters when they were 7 or 8 years old, and married them off in their teens. But my foster mother was not like that. She was very smart and had her own opinion about things around her."

Ma Yuan studied very hard because of her mother's influence. When she was a university student, the smoke of the Korean War spread to the Yalujiang River, close to her hometown. She was determined to enlist in the army to protect her motherland. Her decision to give up civilian pursuits for a military career at that time was also supported by her mother. After the Korean War, Ma Yuan eventually returned to Renmin University in Beijing and was assigned to do postgraduate work at the Faculty of Law. Later, as a judge at the Supreme Court, she was promoted to Head of the Trial Panel at such a young age that it was even exceptional among her male counterparts. At a time when age and seniority were very important, she was surprised at her quick promotion, but was later told that she was being continuously evaluated without realizing it. It was during the 1980s when the "Four Modernizations" became an official party directive. The Four Modernizations emphasized knowledge and youth. Ma Yuan believes that she benefited from being an educated young woman at this time in history when these qualities were officially recognized as a valued asset for China. We will return to the effects of sociohistorical influences on women's lives in

Chapter 8, where we will show how culture can determine which path we will follow in life. Ma Yuan was eventually promoted to Deputy Chief Justice of the Supreme Court in 1985 and retired at the age of 65.

Shi Qingqi, Vice-President and Secretary General of the China Association of Women Entrepreneurs and former Director of the Institute of Industrial Development under the National Development and Reform Commission, said she could not talk about her own achievements without mentioning her mother.

> "I had to dedicate everything to my mother. She never complained about her hardship. She was a very independent and tough person."
>
> "My mother believed that women had to study in order to be independent.
>
> My mother had bound feet. She wanted to participate in the Sino-Japanese war, but she could not [because of the physical limitations imposed by her deformed and painful feet]. She sent her son to war; therefore, she wanted me to attain a high level of achievement."

During the war, Shi Qingqi and her mother stayed in their home village while her father and brother went away to fight. Mother and daughter had to struggle to stay alive.

> "Every day, we woke up and made some bread to sell. She saved some money for herself and used the rest for my education. Although I was just 7 or 8 years old, I was mature and I made yarn on Sunday. . . . After selling the yarn, we would buy second-hand paper for writing. Despite these hardships, I always came first in my class. . . . Later, I said I did not want to go to school because I felt my mother was having a difficult time [making the money to pay for my education]. However, she forced me to continue. In fact, at that time, my mother learned that my father had remarried, and even had children. She told me a story about how an abandoned woman brought up her children. Every time I said I did not want to go to school, she would cry. Therefore, I studied very hard. And every day when I got home, my mother would wait until I finished my homework before we would have dinner."

After Shi Qingqi got married, she continued to live with her mother and her mother continued to make yarn to earn money for Shi's studies. When Shi moved to live at the university, her mother did not have much to do. So she sold all of her belongings to set up a nursery. Her nursery had more than 100 children because she accepted disabled children who were not wanted at other schools; she even accepted those who could not walk. She massaged their feet to help them walk again. The children's parents bowed and went on their knees to thank her. And later, the All-China Women's Federation honored her as an "Active Builder of Socialism." This is a compelling story of strength and triumph for Shi's mother, a woman with little education and whose husband abandoned her with a young child who was later honored for her achievements.

Shi Qingqi described her own personality as somewhat masculine during childhood. She was the instructor of the children's corps in her village during the Sino-Japanese War. The children carried little red spears, and they mounted the guard post and checked the approval passes of people coming into the village. In an all girls secondary school, she was very tall and looked like a boy. She liked sports and playing the accordion, both of which were uncommon for girls at that time. In a crowded situation, her classmates asked her to walk in the front to lead them. She was the head of the military and sport section of the student union, so she had early experiences in leadership foisted onto her because of the war, her physical agility, and her height.

Shi Qingqi believes that her experiences in secondary school helped her to develop her values and worldview, which formed a foundation for her adult years. Her secondary school and university experiences trained her to be strong and tough – two traits that she needed in her later professional life. She was also one of the best students in the university. There were few females in her class at the China University of Geosciences where she studied petroleum. At that time, Liu Shaoqi, President of the People's Republic of China, presented a "hunting rifle" to the university as a symbol of courage for the students to act as "peacetime guerrillas" to hunt for "treasures" in support of the post-war reconstruction efforts. She was so impressed with this presentation that she studied petroleum. It was a good choice for her because she liked hunting for "treasures" in rural undeveloped areas where she could sleep in the wilderness like a guerrilla fighter.

However, because of the Communist system of managing intellectuals at that time, Shi Qingqi could not pursue her career goals in petroleum or geological sciences. She said she did not want to become a teacher, but when she was in Year 3 at the university, the Communist Party assigned her to be a teacher of economics in the Political Science Department. Shi described how she felt:

"I was shocked because at that time, we were the Party's tools and had to follow their instructions. We could not voice our own opinions. I was just 21 at the time, still a kid. I finally could not hold back and said that I did not want to go off to become a teacher because I had not graduated. As a result, I was reprimanded for being individualistic and not making the benefit of the larger society my first priority. [After this incidence of insubordination] I was only permitted to study economics and read the *Capital: a critical analysis of capitalist production* by Karl Marx. . . . Since I was a child, I was determined to develop my own career. I did not know what to do when they forced me to change my studies when I thought I was doing so well. The only thing I could do was to work hard and learn the new subject. This was 1960, and for the next five years, I lectured in economics."

Shi Qingqi eventually succeeded in her career as an economist, winning prestigious awards in China and internationally for her research projects. She later became Director of the State Economic and Trade Commission. After her retirement, she took up the position of Vice-President and Secretary General of the China Association of Women Entrepreneurs, which consists of successful women entrepreneurs and outstanding senior managers. Thus, Shi rose to the top of a profession she did not want, but she used her drive and intelligence to become one of the best in a field she fought to avoid.

Feng Lida, Deputy Director at the rank of a General at the Navy Hospital in Beijing, came from a distinguished family background. Her father was an influential general/war lord who switched his allegiance from the Kuomintang regime which was aligned with Chiang Kai Shek to the opposing Chinese Communist Party. Her mother attended a missionary school and university with a loan from the church. So unlike other middle-class women of her time, her mother did not have her feet bound. Feng Lida's mother later became the General Secretary of the YWCA in China, and inspired Lida to study medicine:

"My mother never hit us. She educated us to be hard-working since we were young. To teach me mathematics, she used various objects (cutting the apples into four pieces) to teach me fractions (but at first, I just ate up the pieces all the time). . . . My mother's family was poor, and the economic conditions did not allow her to study medicine, which is what she had wanted to do. Thus she hoped her children would study medicine. At that time, when we were fighting wars, my mother thought of setting up a small hospital when all the children graduated. She thought we could be independent if we studied medicine."

For a generation that grew up with war, her mother, like others at that time, believed that a career in medicine would provide financial security during hard times.

Feng Lida studied medicine in Chongqing during the war, where she met her future husband. They joined her father in his self-imposed exile in the United States, where he fled to avoid persecution by the Kuomintang government after the Second World War. One day, when they were driving on a road trip, her parents asked if the young couple would consider marrying. In the traditional way, they said they did not have any opinion but would follow their parents' wishes. So Feng's father asked them to stop the car and asked a passerby to take a photo for them. Then they were so-called married, a change in status marked by their mutual agreement to abide by their parents' wishes and a roadside photo taken by a stranger. Later that night, her father wrote them a couplet as their wedding gift in which he described them as: "New partners of democracy; two forerunners of liberty." Feng Lida has kept the hand-written couplet in her home all of these years.

But the political turmoil of their time caught up with them. During a boat trip returning to China, Feng's father was killed in a fire on board, which was believed to be an assassination attempt. Despite this cruel event, Feng continued her medical studies in the Soviet Union. She returned to China in 1957, and eventually became a world-renowned immunologist and rose to the rank of general at the Navy Hospital. Though she suffered persecution during the Cultural Revolution, like other educated people of her time, she has since been recognized as a national treasure by the central government. She continues to be active in clinical and research work at the hospital even now that she is in her eighties.

Peggy Lam Pei Yu-dja is a leader of a key women's group in Hong Kong. She is a former Member of the Legislative Council, and was appointed by the Chinese government to the Chinese People's Political Consultative Conference. She was the first Executive Director of the Family Planning Association of Hong Kong from the 1960s until the 1980s, and successfully reduced the birth rate of Hong Kong families to fewer than two children. She was among the few Chinese women in her generation who had a university education. Her Bachelor of Arts degree is from the University of Shanghai. She said that her college degree would not have been possible without her mother's encouragement:

"My mother had a great influence on me. She had a modern mind because my grandfather was a Chinese doctor; therefore, she had the opportunity to study at home. For example, my mother encouraged me to go swimming with my brothers, which was a rare activity for girls at that time. Also, she bought me a bicycle, although many people thought that it was not proper for girls to ride a bicycle. After graduating from secondary school, many classmates did not go further, but my mother sold her jewelry to support me so that I could attend the university. My mother influenced my participation in women's services because she was open-minded and had advanced ideas about gender equality."

Peggy Lam came to Hong Kong before the Communist regime took over in Mainland China. She started work in a trading company because her degree was not recognized by the British colonial government. Her business experience and her social work training landed her the post of Executive Director at the Family Planning Association. After her retirement from this position, she started an active career as a politician. She was elected as a District Board member and Chairperson as well as a Legislative Councilor. In 1993, she formed the Hong Kong Federation of Women, the largest women's organization in Hong Kong, and has served as its Chairperson since that time. In her seventies now, Peggy Lam continues to try out new ventures and does not plan to retire from her active life.

Many of the women leaders recalled the values and expectations their mothers instilled in them. Although their mothers may not have been well educated themselves, they were open-minded and emphasized the importance of education for their daughters. Audrey Eu, former Chair of the Bar Association, Legislative Councilor, and leader of the Civic Party in Hong Kong, describes her mother:

"My mother is a housewife. She is very strict. She demanded that I perform extremely well in school and that I achieve first place in class. She always asked me that if everyone else could do it, why couldn't I? She made me believe that if I work hard, nothing is impossible. She gave me a strong sense that girls could be just as good as boys. She did not come from a family that treated girls and boys in the same way, and she was aggrieved about that."

Audrey Eu completed her secondary education in a prestigious school in Hong Kong, and her legal education in England. She is one of the few female barristers who have risen to the rank of a Queen's

(Senior) Counsel. She is a strong advocate for democracy in Hong Kong and won a popular election for a seat in the Legislative Council, setting the trend of more professional elites' entry into politics.

Sandra Lee belongs to a growing group of senior female civil servants who are rising to the top of their ranks. She has been the Permanent Secretary of a number of policy bureaus, including the Economic Development and Labour Bureau and the Health, Welfare, and Food Bureau, and is now in charge of health policies in the Food and Health Bureau of the Hong Kong SAR government. She traces her own character formation to her mother:

> "My mother was very fair, and we had to take responsibility for our actions. We learned that cohesion is power [which served as the basis for teamwork]. I appreciate my mother very much, as she gave us a lot of space; she trained all of her children to be honest and open. My mother encouraged us to bring our boyfriends home and offered to give her opinion about them. It reduced a lot of potential conflict between parents and children. My mother let us learn about drinking; she thought after we tried it at home under her supervision, it would not become a temptation. She did not want us to misbehave if we had to drink socially. Even though my mother had little education, she was very open-minded."

Anson Chan was the Chief Secretary who headed the Hong Kong civil service before and after the territory's handover to the People's Republic of China from British colonial rule, before retiring in 2001. She was the first woman and the first Chinese to hold the second highest governmental position, second only to the Governor before the handover of governmental power from the British to the Chinese (and second to the Chief Executive after the handover) in Hong Kong. She explained what her mother taught her: "My mother always taught me 'take a step backward, and you will find the sea is wide and the sky is without boundary'; and from her teachings, I learned how to tolerate others."

Anson's father died when she was 10. Her mother raised her with the help of her uncle and grandmother. They have a big family: she has a twin sister, six brothers, and many cousins. Like many twins, she is especially close to her sister. She regards her close family ties as a valuable asset. Family members provide mutual support and help to each other. However, Anson also conceded: "There are also strains and concerns, because you don't pick your family members. We may not always agree with something they do. In such a big family, there are always different people. But blood is thicker than water, so we can be forgiving."

The tolerance Anson learned from her mother shaped her leadership style in the bigger family of the civil service. She prefers to be inclusive and give people the opportunity to express their point of view. She does not feel threatened by opposing views. She believes in the benefits of canvassing diverse opinions and encourages others to speak up, even if their views may sound offensive or unpleasant. She understands she should not have everyone just follow what she says all the time, especially when she is in a senior position that may intimidate others.

Fewer of the American women leaders talked explicitly about their mothers in the interviews compared with those from Mainland China or Hong Kong. One exception was Helena Ashby, who rose to the rank of Chief in 1995 and became the highest-ranking woman in the history of the Los Angeles Sheriff's Department at that time. Helena came from a tight-knit African-American family. She remembered her mother's encouragement:

> "My mother always taught us that a woman is a very strong person, and the hand that rocks the cradle rules the world. And that it was our responsibility to order a family, to run a family, so that everybody gets the most from it. When people said to me, 'Oh, I don't know why you're doing that. A woman shouldn't have that job,' it was always my mother who would say, 'Go for it!' It was always my mother who was pushing me to succeed, even during set-backs: 'Well, so you didn't get promoted that way. Is that what you want to do? Figure out another way of doing it.'"

Helena Ashby grew up in a very poor family in Los Angeles. Her mother worked in three jobs to raise her and her brother and sister. She always knew that they would go to college and that, as women, she and her sister had to be able to take care of themselves. As she knew she had to work to go to college, Helena Ashby wanted to find something that would allow the flexibility of going to college but which paid more than a standard clerical job. The job she landed at the sheriff's department was purely by accident. She started looking for jobs that would pay her enough to take care of her family and pay for her education. In 1964 there were not a lot of jobs held by women that were not clerical jobs. Helena said she would die in a clerical job. The county had an opening for a deputy sheriff. The job paid the same salary for men and women, and all it required was a high school education. She passed the written, oral, and physical examinations and became a deputy. That job opened up opportunities that very few women, particularly women of color, would ever get. Helena eventually rose to the rank of Chief of the Los Angeles Sheriff's Department before she retired in 2000.

## The Mother–Daughter Bond and Filial Piety

Social scientists have studied the special closeness between mother and daughter throughout the life course. In in-depth interviews with adult women, mothers often "starred" in their recounted stories of past incidents (Baruch & Barnett, 1983). In her book, *Linked Lives: Adult Daughters and Their Mothers*, Lucy Fischer (1986) referred to the mothering role and mutual nurturance as the basis of the mother–daughter bond, which is the closest among kin: "The family roles of women provide a meeting ground for the interweaving of generations. The caring orientation of adult daughters and their mothers – the centrality of mothering in both of their lives – means that their lives are linked from generation to generation" (p. 201).

The roles that the women leaders we interviewed have adopted extend beyond motherhood, and are quite distinct from their mothers' experience. Yet, our interviewees did not reject mothering as a restriction on their empowerment as some feminist scholars may suggest (Fischer, 1991). Their mothers continued to support them emotionally and instrumentally throughout life, as can be seen from the later chapters on home economics and childcare. This affective bond is clearly apparent especially among the Chinese women.

We also see another important psychological principle at work. Several contemporary psychologists have found that our own epistemologies, that is, our own beliefs about intelligence and success, have a powerful influence on how and how hard we work toward success. For example, Carol Dweck (1999) found that students who believe that intelligence is a fixed entity are less likely to attempt challenging tasks than those who believe that intelligence can be enhanced in incremental steps. Students and others with "incremental beliefs" about intelligence persisted at learning difficult material, and, not surprisingly, were more successful than those who simply gave up because the task was too hard. Although the mothers in these stories could not have known about this important area of research, they realized that their daughters were smart enough to do almost anything and would succeed if they worked hard. Thus, these mothers went beyond paying for school and supporting their daughters. They gave their daughters a belief system that is essential for success; they instilled in them the belief that they "could do anything."

Women who want to move higher in their profession need to incorporate the belief that they have the ability to learn and do whatever is needed to succeed. Whether it is accounting principles for business, organizational skills, or the ability to work with diverse people, these are learnable concepts and skills and successful people believe that they can succeed at difficult tasks. We can also pass this belief system on to others for their own success, including our own children, partners, and even our parents.

A striking feature of these stories is the differences in responses between the Chinese (Mainland and Hong Kong) and American women. We cannot know if the relatively few women who attributed their success to their parents reflect genuine differences in how these women think about their mothers and fathers, or whether they reflect cultural difference in how they talk about their parents. The concept of filial piety is deeply embedded in the Chinese culture as a basic principle in the teachings of Confucius. Filial piety, which includes love and respect for one's parents, was eloquently expressed in ancient writings:

While parents are alive, one must not travel afar.
    If one must, one's whereabouts should always be made known.
(Analects, Book II Li Ren 19; Jones, 2000)

As seen in this classic writing which is a digest of the works of Confucius, there is a strong admonition to remain close to one's parents, both physically and emotionally. Although modern Chinese, like their Western counterparts, often do move away from their family home, they must always remember and revere their parents. The tales from our highly successful women show that they do.

### With My Mother's Permission

For many of the women leaders, the most important gift from their mothers was the space or the permission to develop their self-efficacy and autonomy. Rosanna Wong, Executive Director of the Hong Kong Federation of Youth Groups, expressed her gratitude to her mother: "Maybe it was because my mother has given me very strong confidence from childhood. She trusted me and gave me responsibility. I don't want to let her down."

Rosanna is a high achiever. She has headed one of the largest non-profit multifaceted youth work agencies in Hong Kong since 1980. For decades, she has been committed to, and made outstanding achievements in, the social, cultural, educational and physical development of young people in Hong Kong. She has also been the Chairman of the Education Commission. Heading the Commission since 2001, she was charged with guiding the implementation of substantial educational reform premised on all-round development of students. She provided leadership and demonstrated her abilities in working closely with the education sector in the challenging times of moving Hong Kong's education system into the twenty-first century. She served as a former Chairperson of the Hong Kong Housing Authority, as well as a former Member of the Legislative Council and the Executive Council of Hong Kong, before and after the handover.

Kim Campbell, who became Canada's first female prime minister in 1993, remembers the way her mother encouraged her sister and her to do whatever they could do and whatever they wanted to do. "I grew up in a family where women did unusual things; they tended to be autonomous and believed that girls should not be afraid to be different from the norms at that time. All that fancied my mind."

Kim went on to take up many firsts in leadership positions as a woman, from high school and college to local and national government posts. She emerged as a leader early in life when she became the first girl to be the student council president in her high school. Her ambition as a teenager was to be the first woman secretary general of the UN and to do something that would make the world a better place. When she was a university student, many people saw her as a leader because she liked to organize things, provide directions and receive input. She did not accept the view that girls are limited in what they can do.

Kim ran for the Canadian Parliament in 1988. Shortly after, she was nominated as the Minister of State of Indian Affairs. Thirteen months later, she was the Minister of Justice and Attorney General of Canada. She has also been Minister of National Defence and Veterans' Affairs. She was the first woman to hold the Justice and Defence portfolios, and the first woman to be a Defence Minister in a NATO country. As Canada's Prime Minister in 1993, Kim Campbell represented her country at major international meetings, including the Commonwealth, NATO, the G7 Summit and the United Nations General Assembly.

Kim has continued to promote women's leadership. After moving to the US, Kim served as President of the International Women's Forum from 2003 to 2005. She also chaired the Council of Women World Leaders (CWWL) from 1999 to 2003. The Council's membership consists of women who hold or have held the office of president or prime minister in their own country. In 2004, Kim Campbell assumed the position of Secretary General of the Club of Madrid, an organization of former heads of government and state who work to promote democratization through peer relations with leaders of transitional democracies. This long list of international achievements shows that Kim achieved her childhood dream of doing something that makes a difference.

## Mothers as Mentors

The important roles that parents played in influencing the future leadership positions of our group of women leaders may be conceptualized in the larger theoretical framework of mentoring and coaching in leadership development. In contemporary models of mentoring, family members may also be regarded as "natural" mentors and part of what Ellen Ensher and Susan Murphy (2005) referred to as the "power mentoring" network. Especially for women and people of color in the US, there are greater barriers to obtaining traditional mentors within an organization's boundary, compared to the barriers for white men. Family-member mentors can foster the future leaders' self-esteem from an early age. In particular, the mothers offered these women leaders the ultimate in love and loyalty. The mothers of our Chinese women leaders also socialized their daughters with the basic virtues and values of humanity.

Although mothers were highly influential in the lives of many of the leaders, other family members were also mentioned as important, especially fathers.

## Atypical Fathers, Distinguished Daughters

In the biographies of some of the world's women heads of state, fathers are often mentioned as role models and mentors. Looking beyond our own sample for corresponding case studies, we use the examples of two women prime ministers in Europe. Norway's Gro Harlem Brundtland, who was prime minister in 1981 and then 1986–1996, was influenced by her father early in her life. Brundtland's father was a medical doctor, and a prominent member of the nation's Labour Party and Defense Minister of the Norwegian cabinet. When Brundtland was 7 years old, her father had already persuaded her to join the Party's children's organization. Brundtland recalled that she was fascinated by the political debate that was always ongoing in her home. At dinner time, she often asked her father about the political issues he faced. Brundtland's parents encouraged their daughter to believe that women can achieve the same things in the world as men.

British "Iron Lady" prime minister from 1975 to 1990, Margaret Thatcher also regarded her father, a shopkeeper and mayor of Grantham, as a major formative influence. The early life of the Thatcher family was lived largely within the close community of the local Methodist congregation, and was bounded by strong traditions of self-help, charitable work, and personal truthfulness. Margaret Thatcher's family played a large part in forming her later political convictions.

These fathers are atypical, and perhaps that is why their daughters became distinguished leaders. Generally, the bond between fathers and daughters is more disjunctive as there are fewer intergenerational links in their roles. In general, fathers are less involved in their daughters' development.

Fathers featured less prominently in our women leaders' narratives. When many of our women leaders were growing up in China, their fathers were absent from home. Many of the fathers were fighting in the Second World War or an earlier war (e.g. the revolution in China). Generally, the fathers were less involved than the mothers in their daughters' development. There are a few exceptions.

Lorna Edmundson, President of Wilson College in Pennsylvania, described her father's encouragement: "My father always admired everything I did. And I enjoyed doing well and always did well in school so that kind of builds on itself. You know you do well, and you get the prize and the admiration. You sort of continue along. And for whatever reason, my parents thought, always thought I could do anything." At that time, Lorna Edmundson found these expectations to also be a burden:

> "On the one hand I loved the fact that they thought I could do anything. On the other hand there were times when I thought it was quite a burden. . . . When we were young, we had financial difficulties. And so, they expected us to be there and hand over my salary check. So I was very responsible at a very young age. I was determined that I would be independent, and I would have my own work, that I wouldn't submit in the way my mother had. I remember that from a very young age, I did not want to be stuck at home like my mother because she clearly wasn't happy about it."

After Lorna finished her doctoral studies at Columbia University, she followed her husband whose law firm posted him to work in Algeria and Paris. In Algeria, Lorna found herself for the first time in an environment that was overtly sexist: "The privileges and liberties I had in the United States were shockingly absent there." Upon her return to the US in 1978, Lorna became the founding director of Columbia University's first Women's Center. That job led to her being hired as the Assistant Dean of Co-Education when Columbia College decided to admit women in the early 1980s. She took on a few other university administrative jobs before becoming the eighteenth president of Wilson College in Pennsylvania, while her husband commutes between New York and Pennsylvania every week to continue his law practice. After Lorna followed her husband's career early in their marriage, he now commutes long distances later in their marriage so that she could move into a position that would advance her career.

Barbara Fei is a world-renowned choral master based in Hong Kong and an active promoter of musical exchange among Hong Kong, Mainland China and the international arena. She was the first Hong Kong choral master to be invited to a solo performance in Mainland China. She attributed her career development to her father's inspiration:

"I lived with my grandparents who governed me in a traditional way. But my father inspired me in ways that allowed me to breakdown traditional roles. As he was in the film industry, he gave me a great push into music. I can say due to him, I started to learn music and regard this as my goal throughout my life. Compared with my counterparts, I got much support, especially in education, from my family, which had a great effect on me."

Barbara Fei continued to describe her father:

"My father was an avant garde artist . . . but he was also a filial son. Although he insisted on his career, on the other hand, he listened to his parents and married a girl whom he had not met before. Despite his high educational background, it is amazing that he could have a happy marriage with an illiterate girl (i.e. my mother). My parents started loving each other after marriage, but they could still keep an equitable relationship; therefore, I think my family is an open family. I adore my father because despite the breakthroughs in his thoughts and experiences (in terms of ideas and living styles) from his previous generation, he still kept traditional filial virtues."

Musical performance was not a common profession that parents would encourage their daughters to take up in post-war China. Barbara Fei's father supported her desire to study piano at the Central Conservatory of Music in China. She later went to Schola Cantorum in Paris, France, for training in vocal music.

## Formal and Informal Mentors

The American women leaders, more so than those from Hong Kong or Mainland China, recalled the importance of mentors in their career development. They referred to traditional mentors who offered career guidance in terms of which assignments to take or how to find the right career path. They also provided emotional support, as well as being effective role models (Ensher & Murphy, 2005).

The term "mentor" typically describes a "relationship between a younger adult and an older, more experienced adult [who] helps the younger individual learn to navigate the adult world and the world of work" (Kram, 1985, p. 2). Kathy Kram referred to two types of mentor functions: "career-related support" which enhances the younger adult's advancement in the organization through sponsorship, exposure, coaching, protection and challenging assignments; and "psychological support" which enhances the "individual's sense of competence, identity, and effectiveness in a professional role through role modeling, confirmation and friendship" (Kram, 1985, p. 32). Mentoring and contextual learning experiences provide important training for "practical intelligence" and leadership skills (Cianciolo, Antonakis, & Sternberg, 2004).

Mentoring can work without a formal program or assignment of mentoring pairs. Sarah Weddington, adviser to President Carter, and the lawyer who won the historic Supreme Court case, Roe v. Wade, teaches students about the use of the "critical eye": "You watch other leaders, what they do right, and what they do wrong. Try to model yourself from the best qualities." That was how she learned many of her human relations skills. "When I'm watching speakers, part of me is listening to what they say, but part of me is listening to how they say it. You know, what their style was, how they organized the speech, and what they did to keep my attention."

Sarah was the first woman from Austin elected to the Texas House of Representatives where she served three terms before becoming the US Department of Agriculture's General Counsel, the first woman ever to hold that position. She later served as the Assistant to President Carter who designated her to direct the Administration's work on women's issues and leadership outreach. The *Texas Lawyer* named Weddington as "One of the most influential lawyers of the 20th century," and the *Houston Chronicle* named her as one of "The tallest Texans – those who left their mark on Texas and the rest of the world in the 20th century." After returning to Texas from Washington DC, Sarah founded the Weddington Center to promote leadership training. She is a sought after national spokesperson on leadership and public issues.

Sharon Allen, the first woman to serve as chairman of a Big Four accounting firm, emphasized the importance of mentors throughout her career:

> "I have had the good fortune to have mentors throughout my thirty-year career. I feel very fortunate to be able to say that. Mentors have made a huge difference to my success. They've helped me achieve my goals. They have guided me; they have coached me. They have provided a lot of reinforcement."

Sharon Allen is Chairman of the Board of Deloitte LLP, leading the firm's governance process, and she is also a member of Deloitte Touche Tohmatsu global board of directors. Allen is the first woman elected as Chairman of the Board and the highest-ranking woman in the organization's history as well as in her profession. While she received her mentoring through informal relationships, she considers it paramount to foster an environment where mentoring is both accepted and encouraged:

"It pushes people towards the notion of seeking out mentors and actually seeking out mentoring relationships that they can help others with. I contend that it's not optional. You actually have to, in some cases, be a lot more formal about it, in particular, in order to allow for your diverse population to get a good form of mentoring."

The barriers women face in mentoring are well documented in the research literature. Women often fail to recognize the importance of gaining a mentor and assume that competence is the only consideration in one's advancement in the organization. Male bosses often avoid selecting women as their protégés to avoid sexual innuendoes and problems. Female bosses, on the other hand, generally have less time for mentoring, and want to avoid the perception of building coalitions along gender lines if they select female protégés (Ragins, 1989). The benefits of mentoring received by male and female protégés also vary (Ragins & Cotton, 1999), with male protégés benefiting more in terms of compensation as well as counseling received from their formal mentors. Female protégés gain less benefit from formal mentoring. Belle Rose Ragins and John Cotton also found that female managers with a history of male mentors received more promotions but less compensation compared to their male counterparts. (The female earnings gap is difficult to bridge.) The authors suggested that, while the mentors were able to sponsor their female protégés' advancement in the organizations, the corporate bias against women still barred them from the compensation associated with their advancement.

In large American corporations, formal and informal mentoring by bosses and senior colleagues has become more common. Doreen Woo Ho, President of Wells Fargo Consumer Credit Group, the highest-ranking Asian-American woman among the top five banks in the United States, recalled different functions of mentoring through the stages of her career development:

"For the early parts and the mid-level of your career, it is extremely important. What mentors do at that stage and later on in your career is different. When you're very senior, it is a question of sponsors and chemistry because that's the way senior executives work together. But I would say in the early part of the career, a mentor can help provide a safe place for someone to say, 'Should I do this or that? How should I handle this situation?' That's one side of mentoring – just trying to figure out how do I interpret things. . . . So if somebody can mentor them and say that's probably not the way you want to go about achieving your objectives, that is very useful. But in my career the mentors that I've had have been people that were also my bosses. However, they've taught me things that I probably didn't know, and that I got much better at."

Doreen gave three examples of what she learned from her bosses. From one boss, she learned about communications:

"I was his chief of staff and so one of my tasks was to write a monthly letter to his boss in New York. Through the process of writing that monthly letter and the many interactions that went back and forth between me and that boss, I began to realize how critical communications is in terms of positioning. It's not just what you say but how you say it. And how you prioritize the order of the subjects that are very, very critical. So I learned a lot about the importance of communications in content and style. It wasn't just listing information. Also I learned the importance of chemistry and relationship. When this boss interviewed me he said, 'We're just going to sit down and talk and see if you and I can get along.' . . . So that's another lesson that I learned from him. I've realized that the more senior you are, chemistry and personal relationship are critical ingredients. It's an intangible that you can't put your finger on, but it's very important."

From another boss, Doreen learned about strategic planning:

"He really had a very strategic focus. He used the same approach in every business he managed, and I saw him do it more than once. He really sat down to understand the business, where the business is at and where he thought it needed to go. He always put the strategy down on paper, didn't just talk about it, and once it was articulated clearly on paper he would put a stick in the ground and start executing against it to achieve the goals he aspired to. So I learned a lot about strategic planning from him."

A third boss saw potential in Doreen and stretched her even before she thought she was ready to be stretched to a new and more challenging assignment: "He could see where I could end up ahead of me. He had the vision and confidence of where I could go and what I could achieve that I didn't yet have in my own head."

Doreen has since led Wells Fargo to become America's leading provider in consumer finance. She was selected as the "Financial Woman of the Year" in San Francisco in 2004. *Money* magazine named her as one of "America's Most Powerful Women Executives," and she has been named on *US Banker*'s list of the "25 Most Powerful Women in Banking" for the past five years consecutively and was ranked number five in 2007.

The mentor's psychosocial function of boosting self-confidence and providing a sense of purpose is particularly important for women who lack assertiveness and confidence. Ann Kern, who is a top executive in Korn/Ferry International, described how she was mentored:

"When I first came into the workforce following my divorce, I was petrified. And then over time I had a wonderful mentor who was a trustee at the university where I first worked. And I would meet him every morning at 7:30 a.m. in the morning at his business office. And much to my surprise, he wanted me at every meeting he had, whether it was entertaining potential donors from Japan, Asia, or here in New York. I realized that he had a lot of respect for me. And his respect for me caused me to have more respect for myself and more confidence. I think having someone like him in my life really mattered enormously to me. So I think a mentor early on is terribly, terribly important. And then, I don't know when I began to see when I moved into the business, I was very good at it."

Ann has since become a Managing Director of the New York office of Korn/Ferry International, which provides executive human capital solutions. Their services range from corporate governance and CEO recruitment to executive search, middle-management recruitment and leadership development solutions. Ann specializes in executive searches in the not-for-profit and education fields.

Another anonymous American interviewee who was a former Commissioner of Social Securities ended our interview with this note:

"I would just add that mentors were very important to me, and I had several people, both men and women, whom I consider my mentors.

They were wonderful people who not only mentored me by introducing me to an array of professionals who were helpful to me, but mentors who were generally pleased for themselves to have been able to follow my own career. So that was nice for me in the way that they mentored me, but it was also good for me in the way that I learned how to be a mentor. . . . I think women are less eager to seek out a mentor. Maybe it has again something to do with one's self-confidence and one's self-esteem and this attitude of, 'Oh, I couldn't do that; I couldn't ask that person.' "

Few of the women leaders from China and Hong Kong mentioned having mentors in their interviews. The boss–subordinate system in most Chinese organizations is focused on management and supervision. Only a couple of our interviewees in the civil service of the Hong Kong government talked about learning from their bosses. Shelley Lee, who retired as the Permanent Secretary of Home Affairs shortly after our interview recalled a couple of her former bosses as her mentors: "I always identify mentors and role models and learn from them. [Former Governor] McLehose and Anson Chan have been my mentors in the government." Shelley described how she selected her mentors:

"Everyone has to learn by himself or herself, but it is important to have good mentors. Don't take short cuts. Those who take short cuts and try to get as much benefits out of the system lead one down the wrong path. There are people who try to show the short cuts, but they are not good mentors. Be wise enough to know whom you should have as a mentor, and you will benefit for life."

## School and Idols

Schools also provided moral values and discipline for some of our Chinese women leaders. For example, Sandra Lee attributed her character formation to her schooling in addition to her open-minded mother:

"I was strongly influenced by my school's values. When I was young, I studied in a Catholic school and then an Anglican school. Both schools emphasized students' character development and mental discipline. For example, in Form 6, there was no teacher proctoring when we took exams. We needed to be personally responsible and self-disciplined.

In a project preparation, I learned that I had to take on the responsibility and could not complain about others or the circumstances."

Sandra extended these moral values to her responsibility as a civil servant: "I observed that civil servants had a heavy burden to maintain continuity and stability. Civil servants need permanence and quality. The society has increasing expectations of us. We have to ask ourselves 'How can we explain our existing values to the public?', 'How to help the civil servants earn the respect of the public?'"

During the revolutionary periods in Mainland China, children often lived apart from their parents. Their schools and the Communist Party inculcated collectivistic values and provided role models that inspired our future women leaders to serve the society. Feng Cui, former Director General of the International Division of the All-China Women's Federation, has served as a member of the United Nations CEDAW Committee. During her childhood, she lived in her primary and secondary school while her parents served in the People's Liberation Army in the northeast part of the country, Beijing and Guangzhou. She traced her courage, philanthropic spirit and initiative to her childhood:

"Because I had been living in a boarding school since I was young, I acquired a sense of independence and the ability to work for the public good. At school, my classmates and the teachers and I were like a big family. When I attended an all-girl secondary school in Beijing, I joined the Young Pioneers which was similar to the Girl Scouts. I had a very passionate, active and motivated character. When I was a team leader in the Young Pioneers, I encouraged from time to time the pioneers to help the community residents in need to clean their homes at weekends. I joined the school chorus and piano troupe and highly enjoyed these extra-curricular activities. I was recommended by my school, on behalf of the students of China, to reply to the letter from a Soviet female student who had sent her birthday greetings to Chairman Mao. I really admired the heroines of the former Soviet Union for their spirit of sacrifice and regarded them as my idols who were patriotic and did not have materialistic demands. Back in school, we had 'red collars' for students who were role models; they were patriotic and did not have materialistic demands. When I was in secondary school in around 1957, I once spent a weekend with a few classmates riding our bicycles for two hours to join the night shift of labor corps constructing the reservoir as volunteers. I was appraised as the student with 'three virtues' (Keep fit, Study hard and Work well) of Beijing. The experience of my teenage period has played a very important role in building up my character and capabilities and developing views which have strongly influenced me in my life."

Feng Cui worked in the Ministry of Foreign Affairs for over 33 years. In the late 1980s, she was working at the United Nations head office in Geneva and was involved in helping China join the UN. In the 1990s, as the counselor of the Permanent Mission of China to the UN, she participated in the preparation of the Fourth World Conference on Women in Beijing and addressed global issues as well as international queries on China. The Conference made her aware of the importance of women's work which she found fascinating. She later joined the All-China Women's Federation and worked there for more than six years. Now in her retirement, Feng Cui is still actively serving her country, and other women and social service organizations.

The personal stories about the importance of mentors, role models, and early childhood experiences with admired others are borne out in research. Mentors provide role models to help us to conceptualize solutions to seemingly intractable problems. Mentors push their protégés at crucial junctures in their careers, providing them with the confidence to apply for a job opening or to attend a graduate or professional school. Later in their careers, as achieving professionals, mentors provide contacts and networks. Another critical area that is often overlooked is that mentors help their protégés on their way up decide which problems to work on – a decision that is sometimes more important than knowing how to solve the wrong problem.

## What Research Says About the Effectiveness of Mentoring

In a meta-analytic review of 43 independent studies of mentoring in an organizational setting, Tammy Allen and her colleagues (Allen, Eby, Poteet, Lentz, & Lima, 2004) confirmed that individuals who were mentored generally reported more positive career outcomes than those who were not mentored. The mentored individuals were more satisfied with their jobs and career than their colleagues who did not have a mentor. They were also more likely to believe that they would advance in and be committed to their career. In terms of objective career outcomes, the mentored individuals were also more likely to have a high number of promotions and receive higher compensation than non-mentored individuals.

Allen et al.'s study also found that objective career success such as compensation and promotion was more related to career-related mentoring, such as through sponsorship, exposure, coaching, and protection, than to psychosocial mentoring. On the other hand, the mentor's psychosocial mentoring functions, through role modeling, confirmation, counseling, and friendship, established a deeper mentoring relationship, and were more highly related with the protégé's satisfaction with the mentor than career mentoring alone. Both types of mentoring were related to job and career satisfaction. We note here that these studies did not use random assignment of women to mentored or unmentored positions, so we cannot conclude that mentoring *caused* the positive results associated with it. It is of course possible that those women who sought out mentors and used them were more committed to success from the time before the relationships began. Future research will have to tease apart the various possible causal routes between mentoring and career success.

The benefits of mentoring have been recognized by many American corporations, which may encourage corporate entities to develop mentoring relationships and establish formal structures that support mentoring. Recent approaches to mentoring expand the concept beyond the dyadic relationship to include access to groups and networks of relationships which an individual takes the initiative to seek out (Higgins & Kram, 2001). In this broader concept of "power mentoring" (Ensher & Murphy, 2005), the relationships are open and "polygamous," and include dissimilar people with complementary needs and skills matched on the basis of a commitment to the protégé's success. These relationships are not tied to one organization's boundary and thus can cut across a variety of settings.

This contemporary approach to mentoring views the entire set of relationships a person has with people who assist his or her personal and career development as a developmental constellation (Higgins & Thomas, 2001). This mentoring constellation ties together the variety of functions that our women leaders learn from their group of significant others. These functions transmit knowledge ranging from knowledge specifically related to an organization to general people skills and basic values. These functions also booster confidence and self-esteem.

A former Commissioner of Social Securities who asked that we not mention her name offered this advice to future women leaders at the end of her interview:

> "I would say to them, put together a personal advisory committee for yourself. Take five or so people that you would like to be able to contact when you need advice, advice about solving a problem or advice about your own career. And ask those people if they would serve on your personal advisory committee and if you have their permission to contact them when you need them. And then I say to them, they'll say yes. I'm sure they will because people like to be invited to do that. After the mentors agree to establish the relationship, you have an obligation of keeping in touch with them. For example, don't let three years go by, and then you phone one of them. You have to maintain close communications, send them Christmas cards, and call them periodically and just say I'm just checking in and I want to know how you are. This is a simple plan that keeps a small group of people interested in you; you, in turn, have the obligation to maintain that process. And I think it works. I mean, I still have older people that I keep in touch with, not so much any more because I want them to help me do something but because I feel so grateful to them for guiding me along the way that I want to give something back to them. So I keep in touch and send them letters periodically or call them with some news that I think they would be interested in or clipping an article and sending it to them. So they've become some of my very best professional friends."

We have learned from our group of women leaders about the parental and mentor influence on their careers – how they build up their self-efficacy, develop an incremental epistemology, and take off on a life course of achievement. They are active learners from their parents, mentors, and early experience. They in turn provide us with inspirational role models: they show us how we can discover the treasure of parents' wisdom; and if we don't have a parent who encourages our success, how to find someone else to fill that role; how to seek out a variety of mentors; and how to develop mentoring programs for others.

# Chapter 3

# Saving and Spending Time

A man may work from sun-to-sun,
But a woman's work is never done.
(Old proverb)

It's about time. Working mothers everywhere are short on time, and they are not alone. Compared with only a generation ago, women and men from all demographic groups are working more hours and living more hectic and stressed lives. When working mothers finish a day at their increasingly hectic jobs, they then begin a "second shift" (Hochschild, 1989). For working mothers, "Honey, I'm home" means that it is now time to care for children and often other family members, make dinner, check homework, read bedtime stories, and throw in a load of laundry for good measure. Of course, working fathers also face the work (and joys) of children and a home, and need to complete a list of chores when they return from their paid employment, but, overwhelmingly, fathers spend less time on parenting and homemaking than working mothers. On average, working mothers spend 25 hours a week on child- and home-care compared to 15 hours spent by fathers working at comparable jobs (Barnett, 2005; Galinsky, 2005). In Hong Kong, a recent Time Use Survey conducted by the government shows that, on average, women in paid employment spend 3 hours per day on household duties, compared to only 1 hour per day spent by their male counterparts (Census and Statistics Department, 2003). In China, women on average spend 4 hours per day on housework compared to 1.3 hours for men (Department of Population, Social, Science, and Technology, 2004).

Workers in the United States now enjoy the dubious distinction of working more hours than workers in any other country in the world, having passed Japan, the previous winner of the longest-workday contest, over a decade ago (International Labour Organization, 1999). Like their US counterparts, workers in China and Hong Kong are also spending more time at work. The hectic pace of life in modern China was captured by the political scientist Anne-Marie Slaughter (2007) in a piece she wrote for the *New York Times* in which she described life in modern Shanghai. She wrote about the commonly held belief that "urban Chinese are catching 'Western disease,' working ever longer hours and chasing an ever more expensive standard of living." These everyday observations are borne out in data from the Key Indicators of the Labour Market (International Labour Organization, 2007), which show that the annual hours worked per person surpassed 2,200 in China and Hong Kong. These are *average* hours worked; anyone at the top of her profession is putting in a substantially longer workday than the average person. Similar conclusions apply to much, but not all, of the developed world. A comparative study of the work hours around the world found that "an estimated 22 percent of the global workforce, or 614.2 million workers, are working 'excessively' long hours" (International Labour Organization, 2007).

At the same time that longer work hours are becoming the norm in the US, China, and most industrialized countries, some countries in the European Union have reduced their work hours. The UK has passed a new law which requires employers to either eliminate work weeks over 48 hours or allow employees to opt out of them. By contrast, the Fair Labor Standards Act (1938; revised multiple times) in the US, which is the principal law governing employment, makes it clear that it is legal to fire an employee for refusing to work overtime, even if the employee needs to care for a family member and there is no one else available to provide that care. Combined with longer vacations, Europeans work fewer hours than their Chinese and US counterparts. Overall, the annual average is less than 1,600 hours a year in most EU countries (International Labour Organization, 2007). Despite the good news about reductions in average work hours for the EU, it is unlikely that there has been much change at the very highest levels, where overwork is the norm. Thus, the message is still the same: achievement at the highest levels requires long work hours, even when other workers in your country are reducing the number of hours they work.

Data from countries where work hours are increasing show that it is not just employed mothers who are feeling the pinch of time shortages. The complaint of "just not enough time" is becoming universal as more people feel squeezed for time. All mothers are working mothers, as anyone who has ever cared for children knows, and even mothers who are not employed outside the home often complain about not having enough time in their busy days with caring full-time for children and managing their homes. So although there may be some obvious qualitative differences between the time shortages experienced by mothers who work outside the home and those who do not, the experience of "not having enough time" seems to be a common complaint of contemporary life.

With the exception of recent changes in the EU, data on the amount of time people spend working support the perception that most people are spending more time at work, with the biggest changes for working women. The National Study of the Changing Workforce (Bond, 2002), which is based on a random sample of working adults in the US, found that although work hours have increased by 2 hours a week since 1977 for men, the increase over the same time period has been 4.5 hours a week for women. When families are considered as a whole, the largest increase in work hours was found for dual-earner families. When the work hours for working couples are combined, the average number of paid hours per week went up from 81 in 1977 to 91 hours a week in 2002. The problem is not just that we are working longer hours, but that work itself has become more hectic, with 52 percent of employees complaining that they "never had enough time to get everything done on the job," compared to 40 percent in 1977. The same study found that one-third of all employees in the US are "chronically overworked." It is a widespread problem which is affecting workers at all points on the long ladder of employment gradients, and not just a problem for those who are working at the upper rungs.

## How We Think About Time

Given that most employed adults are spending more time at work (or, as we will see in later chapters, working at more places more of the time), it is a useful exercise to take the time to think about our time choices and "nonchoices." We all have exactly the same amount of time – every day is exactly 24 hours long and, regardless of our status in the social hierarchy or how hard we try, this is a universal and unalterable fact. Some of us will live more days and years than others, but every day is the same length. We have some choices about how we spend those precious hours.

It is interesting to reflect on the use of the word "spend" when we talk about time. Like money, time is a valuable and limited commodity and we sometimes "buy" time with money, such as when we decide to pay someone to do something we would otherwise have to do ourselves. The aphorism, "Time is Money," which is often attributed to Benjamin Franklin, a famous American inventor and statesman in the eighteenth century, actually dates back to the Ancient Greeks. It seems that time shortages and pressure to do more have a long history. We also talk about "wasting time," which means that we are spending time on activities that we do not value or enjoy. Almost everyone wants to know how to make or find more time for those activities and people that are important to us.

Some portion of our 24-hour allocation each day is spent on mandatory activities over which we have little control or choice. People living at or near the poverty level have far fewer choices about how to spend their hours because a substantial number must be devoted to paid work and they have fewer time-saving conveniences. It is at the lower end of the wage spectrum, where there is much less money to exchange for time, that the difference between the numbers of hours worked by men and women is the greatest. A study conducted in Central Africa and Nepal found that women in these poor countries worked almost 21 more hours a week than men, when paid employment and work at home were combined (Levine, Weisell, Chevassus, Martinez, Burlingame, & Coward, 2001), which is substantially more than the 10-hour difference between women and men in the US. Those of us living in the middle class and above have more options than the poor in how we spend our time, but the options seem more illusory than real when we live in a culture that values, even demands, overwork.

Morgenstern (2000) suggested that we visualize time as space. With this metaphor, a day is like a closet that can hold a limited number of boxes. If we think of the various tasks we do all day as boxes of different shapes and sizes, then the challenge is to fit all of the boxes into the closet. The problem for most of us, and most particularly mothers at the top of their profession, is that there are too many boxes to fit. Some of the boxes will have to be discarded because there is not enough space for them, and others may need to be repackaged into smaller boxes. High-achieving women with family responsibilities need to pack their lives into "time boxes" with great care, allocating less time to some activities and completely giving up others.

## Time Management

The mantra for busy executives who are short on time is "time management." Many of the women we interviewed talked about the need to carefully manage their time. Laura Cha, a Member of the Executive Council of the Hong Kong SAR government and former Vice-Chairman of the China Securities Regulatory Commission, mused on how she managed these high-level demanding positions and also cared for her children and home: "If one wants to have everything, then time management is very important."

When working at the China Securities Regulatory Commission in Mainland China during the 1990s, Laura Cha needed to travel back and forth between Beijing and Hong Kong. She described how she worked during those three years:

> "I feel more at home in Hong Kong. In the Mainland, I live a disciplined life, going to work and going home after work. I face a lot of challenges at work, so I had no time to think of other things. In the first year, I came back to Hong Kong twice a month; and my husband visited me in Beijing twice a month as well. In the second year, I came back to Hong Kong more frequently as my son came back [from overseas studies] to Hong Kong. Then I could see all my family members at once, my husband, son and daughter. In the third year, I felt very homesick, so I came back almost every week. It was very hectic, as I left on Friday late afternoons, and returned to the Mainland on Sunday evenings. Occasionally, I would go back on Monday mornings."

But for people struggling to fit everything in their life, the call for better time management sounds hollow because no matter how much they repackage portions of their life, the 24-hour day is too short to get it all done. A common theme among the women leaders is what Laura Cha called living in a "disciplined way." They carefully determined how much time they would spend on various tasks, and left work at a predetermined time so they would have time with their family. Consider these staggering work hours: *Fortune* magazine found that "62% of high-earning individuals work more than 50 hours a week, 35% work more than 60 hours a week, and 10% work more than 80 hours a week" (Hewlett & Luce, 2006). Given these work-hour norms, is it any wonder that even among the relatively few women who make it to the top, approximately half do not have children? It is hard to see how anyone can fit children and a family life into such a punishing work schedule.

Hewlett and Luce (2006) studied the choices made by women and men who work in "extreme jobs," those jobs that require close to a "24/7" commitment. Extreme jobs are defined by "an inordinate amount of responsibility," heavy demands for travel, a large number of direct reports, tight deadlines, unpredictable work demands, and work-related events to attend in the evenings and at weekends. Extreme jobs are like "extreme sports" – they engender awe and fear and probably should come with the warning, "Don't try this at home." Readers may be wondering, why would anyone choose these jobs? The most obvious answer is the high pay, but that is not what the people who work in these jobs report. Although all of these jobs are high-paying (among the top 6 percent in income), men in extreme jobs rated compensation as the third most important reason for working at them, compared with women who rated compensation as the least important of five alternatives. If the respondents are taken at their word, then money is not a primary reason for working excessively long hours. The most frequent response for women and men was that they love their work; they find it stimulating and exciting. Their colleagues came in second. With so much time spent at work, it is not surprising that extreme workers create their closest social networks at work. People working in extreme jobs rated the recognition they receive for their work and power and status as fourth and fifth for the men, and third and fourth for the women.

For the most part, workers in extreme jobs do not believe they are overworked even when they are working more than 80 hours a week. Thus, while these extreme jobs may look like an extremely bad choice to outsiders, those who put in the long hours at the top of their profession have a different perspective. Despite the mostly positive evaluations of their career choice, it is also true that these high achievers must experience *The Time Bind* (Hochschild, 1997), with little time left for nurturing family ties or for meeting caregiving responsibilities.

It is a simple mathematical calculation to deduce that there is little time left over for anything except work once all of the hours spent at work are added up. Yet, we also know that the mothers who are in these lofty positions do manage to combine work and family, so it must be possible, at least for some people. These extraordinary women must have found ways to "make" or "find" more time. More than any other single factor, the sheer time commitment required by jobs at the top of most professions is a deterrent for women who also want and need to have a high-quality family life.

## How Women Leaders Find the Time

What are the secrets that dually successful women know which allow them to find more time? How are they able to combine work and family when each one alone is like a hungry thief always ready to consume every bit of our time?

The way this question is phrased assumes a scarcity perspective (Greenhaus & Beutell, 1985), which is a common assumption whenever researchers study work and family issues. It assumes that the demands (and pleasures) of family and work are always at war, each fighting for a larger piece of a finite amount of time. The greatest casualties in this war are the women who are in the middle. The conflict over time has been described as a "time famine," with working mothers starved for time. Like the workers in the study of extreme jobs (Hewlett & Luce, 2006), the 62 women we interviewed did not see themselves as needing to be rescued from a frantic lifestyle that was threatening their health and well-being. The good news is that they are all managing quite well. The bad news is that they all work long hours. They have no magic for increasing the number of hours in a day; instead, they have devised strategies that allow them to combine their work and family in ways that protect their own mental and physical health. Like successful people in every demographic category, they work very hard. They enjoy their successes at home and at work, so we may want to question the use of the word "work," when there are so many positive attributes associated with it. Work is a very important and positive component of their lives, yet they are also dedicated to being good mothers, wives, and caregivers.

Here is how dually successful women "make" time.

### *Basics of Time Management: Scheduling and Planning*

An essential first step in taking control of your time is to keep a schedule that includes everything you plan to do. It is an essential memory aid and a way of keeping track of how you are spending your time. It doesn't matter if the schedule is in a "date book" or your PDA (personal digital assistant – an anthropomorphic name for a small electronic device that is used as an easily portable computer). PDAs usually include calendar programs so you can keep track of everything that you have planned. Whether you use a PDA or an old-fashioned "date book," it is critical to write down every commitment to avoid double-booking and to ensure that you block out enough time for each task. This strategy is essential. It is unlikely that anyone would make it into middle management without keeping a calendar of all their activities.

Jenny Ming, President of Old Navy/Gap, explains how to make it work: "Having a great assistant and making sure that all of my schedule and calendars are working are really important. (And that really makes a difference). Yes! My assistant does not just keep charge of my professional calendar; she also keeps track of my personal calendar as well, which includes all of my personal travel, my family travel, everything."

Barbara Franklin, former US Secretary of Commerce under the senior George Bush administration, illustrates how she synchronizes her schedule with that of an equally busy husband:

"First, you have to recognize what your needs are – what is personal and what is professional. I have to be a good juggler of various personal and professional things. My husband is busy too and we have a complicated lifestyle. We have an apartment in Washington, where my business is headquartered, and we have a home in Connecticut, which is his base. We go back and forth between the two places. There's no particular pattern to it, just what works best, juggling personal and business commitments. My husband flies a plane, so that helps our going back and forth. We spend time at least once a week working on our calendars. It's like putting pieces of a jigsaw puzzle together and we make it fun. We are always asking ourselves, 'How are we going to do this? Where are we going to do that? How are we going to make sure that we have enough time together?' And it works out very well when you keep calendars up-to-date. We carve out time for different things and put our plans on the calendar. It's more than time management. It means setting priorities and then being flexible as things evolve and change, as they always seem to do. If personal needs come first at a given time, then we have to fit work activities around them. It is harder when you are in a public position or in a highly demanding job, as we are, to work in the personal needs. But we work on it as a couple. It takes patience on both his part and mine, but the time and energy we put into making our joint calendars work is well worth it, and we are able to spend a great deal of time together. We have to be really organized to get everything accomplished."

Marjorie Yang is an extraordinary business leader, named in the Fortune top 50 most powerful women in business for 2004. She is Chairman of the Esquel Group, where she succeeded in transforming a small company in Hong Kong into one of the world's leading high-quality cotton shirt manufacturers, supplying such household-name brands as Polo Ralph Lauren, Hugo Boss, Tommy Hilfiger, Nordstrom, and Abercrombie and Fitch. Her company now produces over 60 million cotton shirts a year, which is more than any other company in the world. This is how she was able to care for her daughter and other family members while building a high-powered company:

"In order to balance time, I have to work efficiently and be able to simplify and distribute my job to others. I am like my mother; I know how to delegate and arrange helpers. I have an infrastructure to organize the helpers. For example, for social entertainment arrangements, I have a checklist for my assistant and there is a feedback cycle. I am very clear-headed and do not muddle with things; so I can have time to do many things and still keep my personal time. Also, I have good planning and I will prioritize the tasks and consciously manage my time. I use a planning tool: for example, I use a graphical method every year to do an annual plan, prioritize and plan time, and balance my needs. I think the most important strategy is to consciously plan and balance our own time. I understand my needs and so I will set guidelines for planning my time."

Yang's no-nonsense approach to finding time for her family and her work has paid off handsomely in her incredible success.

## Know What Your Priorities Are and Plan Around Them

Powerful women leaders with families are skillful in setting priorities, and they are clear about their ground rules. Jenny Ming understands that keeping a calendar is, in large part, emotional because it forces you to make a written commitment to do some things and not to do others. It is a statement of your values and goals because it represents a decision about what you will spend time doing. Every time management program starts by asking people to establish their priorities so that they can plan time for those activities that are most important to them.

The women leaders we interviewed were clear about their priorities. Consider this typical response from Sarah Weddington, who was divorced and caring for her aging and ailing father at the time of the interview. Sarah, who served in many public roles including Special Assistant to US President Carter, is probably best known as the attorney in the landmark trial of Roe v. Wade, which legalized abortion in the US. She told us: "I have never claimed to have a balanced life because I've always emphasized more the professional. But I have enjoyed it so much that I don't regret it at all."

Now that she is the primary caregiver for her ailing father, Sarah has to divide her time between her busy work and his needs.

> "Well, his needs have to come first. He's the only person I'm really responsible for. I think a lot of women are now caring for their parents, and they know that there are certain basics that you have to do. But a lot of stuff comes up on a weekly basis. I guess three or four months ago, Daddy called me and he said, 'I need to go to the hospital.' So I took him to the doctor, and the doctor said he's going to have to go to the emergency room and so forth. I took him to the emergency room, and they said he's going to have to be admitted to the hospital. So you just call the office and say, 'Cancel anything I've got going. I'm just going to need to go to the hospital and help Daddy right now.' I think there are times the people you are providing care for just have to be a priority. And you just have to rearrange your professional life; there's nothing else you can do."

As we see in this interview, Sarah Weddington's priorities changed as her situation changed. Earlier in her career she was totally focused on her professional work, but later, as her father became ill and she needed to care for him, his care became her highest priority. Women's responsibilities change over their lifespan; some start families at young ages, while others wait until they are established professionally to begin their family. But, a parent or other loved one can become ill at any time, so our needs and priorities need to change with each life event. We note here that Sarah also fought a valiant battle with breast cancer herself, which she chronicles in her newsletters, which are written for women. This life-threatening disease may also have caused her to alter her priorities. Regardless of the reasons for the choices she made for her life, it is clear that Sarah maintains a high sense of what is most important to her and spends her time accordingly. This is an exercise that would work well for anyone who is having trouble "finding enough time" for all that they have to do. A list of personal priorities may cause readers to reallocate their own time so that those people and activities that are most important to you are given more time than people and activities that are ranked lower in priority.

Jenny Ming, President of Old Navy/Gap, has clearly thought through her priorities. When she was asked, "At times when you have conflict between what your family events are and what your work demands are, how would you negotiate the two roles?" Jenny Ming had a ready reply:

> "I was there [physically present] for every one of my children's events, such as soccer games or ballet rehearsals. I made sure I was there for the most important things. I make sure that my calendar has all of these events clearly marked. I know when I have to travel, so I put my travel schedule and all the important events on the same calendar with my family events. And after you put your calendar together, you find that there will always be conflicts. That's when you have to make decisions. My kids were very comfortable with the fact that sometimes if Mommy is not there, then Daddy will be there. It might not be both of us, which we prefer, but one of us is always there. My kids really understood these arrangements because they know . . . if you talk to them today, they would tell you, 'My mom loves what she does.' And so they were very understanding. Something else I also do is whenever they call me, at any time of day, even if I have the most important meeting, I will step out to answer their call. So it works both ways. They know that I am accessible if they ever want to talk."

### Setting Priorities Also Means Just Saying "No" to Some Requests

If we return to the metaphor suggested at the start of this chapter and envision all of the things we need to do as boxes that we cannot squeeze into a closet, then some of the boxes will need to be made smaller and others will need to be discarded. Given that time is limited, busy people need to cross out some of the activities that are not their highest priorities. In other words, they need to get good at saying "no" to the unending demands on their time.

Carrie Yau was the Permanent Secretary of the Health, Welfare and Food Bureau in Hong Kong at the time of the interview. In her earlier post in the government, she had to interact closely with foreign diplomats and consulates. As a mother with family responsibilities, she told us that she "usually declined invitations for evening functions. My predecessor was single so he could go to these dinners all the time; I could not due to my family. My strategy to handle this was to decline all invitations, rather than attend some and not others. This way, my boss will also not blame me [for showing favoritism to some government officials or offending some diplomats]."

Anson Chan was the Chief Secretary and head of Hong Kong's civil service. At the time we are writing this book, she is in the middle of a hotly-contested political run-off for a key position on Hong Kong's Legislative Council after she retired from the civil service. She told us: "My strategy was learning how to organize time. People create problems for themselves because they don't organize their own time. Also, I had to learn to say no, as I cannot do everything." This is good advice that is essential for anyone who has to cut back on their time commitments, regardless of whether they are heading to the top of their profession or happily working elsewhere in the work hierarchy.

## Outsource Low Priority Commitments

Once priorities are clearly listed and time planners are filled in so that busy people can clearly see if there is a match between what is important to them and how they spend their time, the main problem looms even larger – like a fire-breathing dragon that can kill careers and wreck havoc in families – there is more to do than there is time to do it in. Everything that is important to do and everything we must do at work and at home will not fit into the time blocks that mark out our days, weeks, and years. Women with multiple responsibilities know they will have to spend some money to save time.

For some women, the decision to pay others to do things they believe they should be doing themselves is very difficult. Many women are socialized to believe that it is an important part of the role of women to prepare meals, bake for family events, clean their own home, mend clothes, and so on. Women socialized this way may be embarrassed to pay someone else to do things that they believe *they* should be doing. Some women, especially if it is early in their career, find it difficult to pay someone to clean their house or do some work-related job, such as secretarial work. If money is tight, which it often is at early stages in one's career, it may be hard for women to justify paying someone else for something they could do themselves. In the US and other places in the world, family members who are not used to the idea of paying someone else to do household tasks may react with scorn or ridicule, asking questions like, "Are you so high-and-mighty that you need to have a maid?" It is unlikely that women working in Hong Kong would get the same negative reaction from family members and friends if they hired help for household work and childcare, because it is a much more accepted practice in Hong Kong, with its large supply of affordable foreign domestic workers. One-third of the women in Hong Kong who have dual roles have hired domestic helpers (Census and Statistics Department, 2003).

It is constructive to think about the issue of hiring help for the home and office from the perspective of South African society, where the unwillingness to hire household or office help is a sign that the person is stingy and not willing to share her resources with other people who need employment. Whatever your cultural background, you may need permission to pay for assistance. We don't mean "permission" in its more usual sense, but support in this decision. You may need support from someone who can help with your decision by agreeing that it is a good practice for working mothers to hire help for tasks they do not want or need to do themselves. The traditional customs around women's work do not take into account the fact that many women are now doing what was traditionally thought of as men's work, and unless overworked professionals hire additional help, they will end up exhausted and failing at both of their cherished roles. Many demands in life can be outsourced. Outsourcing everything that is not "value added" to the family gives women more time to actually spend with their family and means they have less pressure. Sharon Allen, the first woman to be elected Chairman of the giant accounting firm Deloitte, explained her thinking about priorities and hiring help this way:

> "There is only so much time, and there are a number of paths to the top. People have to make each decision personally. At the end of the day, it's still about time, personal relationships, priorities, and making

individual decisions about how to make all those work. And, and in some cases, it's also about others' expectations. Many women are overly influenced by others' expectations, whether it be other family members or people at work who have their own personal guidelines they try to fit into someone else's life. You need to do what you feel is right for yourself."

This is personal advice worth listening to; *Forbes* magazine listed Sharon Allen as number 64 on their list of the "Most Powerful Women in the World" in 2007.

### Keep the Worlds of Family and Work Separate or Integrate Them: Flip Sides of Time-Saving Strategy

The outstanding women leaders we interviewed favored a combination of strategies that keep work and family life as separate spheres for some activities and, at other times, integrate them. Both segmentation and integration of the work and family domains have their costs and their benefits. They are not mutually exclusive. By segmenting the domains, the distinct roles are more salient; by integrating the two domains, the transitions across boundaries are simplified. Our women leaders switch between the two approaches with ease.

For example, consider these ideas when traveling between home and work. Andrea Van de Kamp, former President of the auction house Sotheby's' west coast operation and a philanthropist in Los Angeles who serves on multiple boards, began her discussion about how she finds time by reaffirming the importance of being organized and setting priorities – the two basics we have already discussed. She then provided a useful strategy for "turning off work" when you head home, and for "turning off home" when you head to work:

"You've heard this a lot. Whether you're a homemaker or you're a professional woman, you need to be organized and you've got to learn how to set priorities if you're going to have a successful career. . . . I tend to think when I'm going to work, I'm going to work. When I'm coming home, I'm coming home. In fact I even went so far as to designate a place on the freeway that I would pass. When I passed that building, I would start thinking about home, saying, 'Do I need milk? Do I need to stop by the grocery store? Do I need to pick up the shoe repair? Have I been to the cleaners?' I would do just the opposite when I would pass that building when I was coming into work, I would turn off home."

Andrea Van de Kamp found that making a clear separation between her work life and her home life worked for her because it allowed her to focus her attention, energy, and time on one part of her life at a time. At the same time, she also brought her daughter to her office on Saturdays so her daughter would understand what she would be doing everyday after she left the house.

Many of the other women preferred to integrate these dual aspects of their life. A clear example of the integration strategy is seen in the comments of Jenny Ming, who helped Old Navy make history as the first retailer ever to reach $1 billion in annual sales in less than four years. In her life at work, the demands on her time are unending. In recognition of her business success, Jenny Ming was named in *Fortune* magazine's list of the 50 most powerful women in business for two consecutive years (2003 and 2004), and was also recognized by *Business Week* magazine as one of the nation's top 25 managers in 2000. Here is how she does it:

"I leave my house at 7 o'clock and come into work at 7:30. And I always go home for dinner. So even if dinner is as late as 7:30, I always come home for dinner. I know I'm going to have to do some reading at home, but that's OK. I set up some ground rules for myself. When I'm not traveling, I don't work weekends. The weekends are for my children, except Sunday night after dinner when I would have a few hours of quiet time to pick up my work again. But, when I'm traveling, I work seven days a week, so I can get home as soon as possible. So I integrate my work and family this way. It works for me."

Mary Ma, Chief Financial Officer of Lenovo at the time the Chinese computer company purchased IBM's Personal Computing Division, also reserves her weekends exclusively for her daughter: "I would spend the whole of Saturday and Sunday with her, without going anywhere. You just have to compensate and balance. I believe that there is nothing that is impossible and that it all depends on how you handle things." Thus, it is possible for women at the top of their profession to set priorities and use strategies that allow them to spend substantial blocks of time with their children, even during intense periods of work-related activity such as overseeing a major acquisition. There are people who will say that it is simply not possible, but all of these women show that it is.

Chen Naifang was President of Beijing Foreign Studies University at the time of the interview. Like working mothers everywhere, she expresses her sense of guilt for the time she spends away from her family and the strains of a hectic pace of life. She shows her love to her children through her cooking, a time-honored custom of mothers everywhere. To manage it all, Naifang uses a separation strategy:

> "Sometimes when work is extremely hectic, I feel that I don't take good enough care of the children. But on weekends, I completely devote myself to my family. I usually wake up rather early in the morning, and because the food selection was not that great [in China] when my children were young, I would travel long distances to buy live poultry and seafood because it would be fresh. I would have the poultry slaughtered at the store, and then I would bring the fresh food back home to cook for the children. We would all have such a good time feasting that day and I would tell them that because I was usually too busy during the week, I would do my best to cook good food and we could have whatever they wanted to eat."

Sophie Leung is a Member of the Legislative Council of Hong Kong, which is the main governing body, and a Deputy in the National People's Congress of China. She has held a variety of key positions in business, including directorships of a number of large textile conglomerates in Hong Kong with businesses extending to the world market. Like most of the other women with family responsibilities who made it to the top, she talks about time management, but she also provides a personal example of how she manages to keep freshly arranged flowers in her home, which is important to her husband, and how her priorities have changed now that she is older.

> "I had to learn how to juggle many things at the same time, and I am good at it. Time management is important; every minute is prioritized. For example, my husband likes flowers; I had to remember to buy fresh flowers and arrange them myself. Once I prepared two pots of flowers when I was entertaining [in case something went wrong with one of them]. I had to plan ahead to decide what should be bought from the market; who should be instructed to get the flowers; and to make sure that my phone was on in case the type of flowers I wanted weren't available. I studied logic and computer studies, so I am used to thinking in sequences. However, now that I am getting older, I want to take a

break and do more things that interest me. For instance, I like flower arranging and often take note of others' flower arrangements. Now I have many fresh ideas about ways to arrange flowers. I used to assign others to arrange flowers for me, but my husband didn't like the way they were arranged, [so I was happy to do the arranging for him]. I believe that some people are concerned with their own self-interests and this attitude can cause many problems."

Thus, it seems that Sophie Leung decided that she should be doing the flower arranging and should not outsource this task because it was important to her husband. Over time, she got better at arranging flowers and found that she enjoyed it.

## Sequencing as a Method of Time Management: Work, Then Family, Then Work

A few of the women we interviewed employed the strategy known as sequencing, in which women focus on their career during their early adult years, then usually take time off or cut back on their work to care for their family, and then, when the children are older, return to work as their primary focus. Sequencing is usually not a good strategy for women who want to make it to the top of any profession because the time out from work has a disproportionately large negative effect on their advancement. Despite the general findings from the research literature, there are some women who believe that the best way to handle the demands of young children and a high-powered job is to make them sequential.

This plan worked for Laura Cha. Laura has held many important government positions in Hong Kong. At the time of her interview, she was a member of the Executive Council. She was the first person outside Mainland China to join the Chinese government at the rank of Vice-Minister. Prior to that, Laura was Deputy Chairman of the Hong Kong Securities and Futures Commission, and headed the Corporate Finance Division where she played a key role in all the major reforms of the Hong Kong securities market. She described how she does all of this as a mother:

"There is a time for everything. Two of my subordinates were very bright professionals with young families. They were both struggling with young children and the heavy demands of our work. My advice to them was that other people can substitute you at work; but it's harder to find a substitute for you in your role as a mother. You can re-establish your career later; however, the relationship between mother and children is harder to re-establish. I think there is a time for everything. You may be able to have it all, but just not all at the same time. We can experience different things at different times."

Sequencing her career worked well for Laura Cha. She got married right after graduation from college at the age of 22 in the US. She became distressed as a stay-at-home wife and mother while her friends took up professional careers. She waited until her older child was 6 and her younger one was 3 years old before she went back to law school in California. That worked out well. Her studies synchronized with her children's school schedules:

> "I could not have studied when my children were younger because we had no maids to help out in the US. So I stayed home. When I returned to law school, the timing was better because my academic year coincided with my children's school year. I would have eight months of intensive studies in law school during their school year. We could have summer vacation together . . . I thought it's a matter of timing. You may have children first and then develop your career, that's not interrupted; you may also have your career first then have children."

Laura Cha's career blossomed as her children were growing up, but research shows that the financial and career costs of stepping out of the workforce for even a short period are larger than most people would estimate. Women not only lose wages and promotions while they are away from work, but most find that it is difficult to re-enter at the same level they had attained when they left the workforce. In addition, women who take time out of the workforce find that their wages are significantly reduced when they return, relative to the wages of those who worked continuously. Another unpleasant reality that needs to be considered is the high rate of divorce. The strategy of sequencing assumes that there is a partner who will share his lifetime earnings with you in exchange for the time spent on childcare. Unfortunately, this is not true for close to half of all married women whose marriages end in divorce in the US, or who find themselves as the financial head-of-household for other reasons, including the early death or disability of their spouse.

In a study conducted by Hewlett (2007) at the Center for Work Life Policy, researchers studied what is known as moving "off-ramp" and "on-ramp," which are terms used to describe the sequencing options when women leave the job market (off-ramp) with plans to re-enter when their family responsibilities, usually childcare, are reduced (on-ramp). Among women in professional jobs who took the off-ramp option, 93 percent said that they wanted to return to work, but only 74 percent of these women succeeded in finding jobs (before the study ended) and, among these women, only 40 percent had returned to full-time professional positions. On average, these women took 2 to 3 years off from work, but the reduction in lifetime earnings was substantially greater than the loss of income for these years because of lost promotion opportunities and reduced salaries when they returned.

Other studies show that when women first enter the workforce, they earn about 87 cents to every dollar earned by a man, but when they start having children, wages fall to 71 cents to every dollar earned by a man (Institute for Women's Policy Research, 2005, updated 2006). Approximately 40 to 50 percent of the decline in wages is due to stop-outs from work. The rest of the gender gap in wages remains unexplained and is generally attributed to discrimination.

When we look at the effect of reduced earnings in later life, we find that more women are working into old age because they cannot afford to retire. The overrepresentation of women in poverty has many different causes around the world; the reduction in retirement income caused by periodic stop-outs from work is now being recognized as one important reason for the excess of women in poverty in old age. Anyone who is considering the strategy of sequencing their career as a means of managing the dual demands of family and work should consider the long-term financial implications. Of course, it is not a realistic alternative for most women, who do not have the financial support of a spouse or some other source of reliable income. For Laura Cha, who had a supportive husband, it was the right strategy, but it is not for everyone.

## Work Harder and Smarter

Ophelia Cheung has served as one of the founding members of the Women's Commission under the Hong Kong SAR government. She was the first Executive Director of the Consumer Council of Hong Kong, which has become a major voice in protecting consumers' rights. After leaving the civil service, Cheung joined the international accounting firm Arthur Anderson and then established her own political lobby consultancy. For her contributions to society, Cheung has been named as one of the "Ten Outstanding Young Persons" by the Junior Chamber International in Hong Kong. Her strategies for success are based on the idea that women have to work harder:

> "In 1969, I was the first female Administrative Officer assigned to assist the District Commissioner. I realized that, being a woman, I have to work harder than men in order to be recognized. Men often watched us, tried to catch us making a mistake, and challenged us. There is an extra burden at work for women, so women have to be better pre-pared, exert more effort, and convey more confidence."

On the other side of the globe, Helena Ashby, the first woman to hold the position of Chief in the history of the Sheriff's Department of Los Angeles County, also realized that she would have to work harder to make up for the work activities she missed when she spent time at home with her family. This is how she explained it:

> "When we had to travel, I wouldn't, and I made that very clear on scheduling [that I could not travel]. But what that meant was I was willing to put myself out to work longer, to stay late, things that I could control because I realized that if you asked for special things, you had to make up for it in another way. So I was always the one that would work longer, that would take projects that were not mine, that kind of thing. But what that allowed me to do was to learn other people's business, other skills. So even in that I think it was always beneficial for me."

It is interesting to note that Helena Ashby put a positive spin on the extra work she took on so that she could control her schedule and avoid traveling. Surely her positive attitude toward the need to work extra hard was a factor in her promotion through the ranks of a sheriff department to its highest rank.

## Cut Back on Sleep and Rest

If additional time has to come out of some portion of the day, working mothers everywhere look to their sleep time to steal a few extra hours. Estimates vary among studies, with mothers getting somewhere between 5 and 7 hours less sleep each week than mothers who are not employed outside the home (Bianchi, 2006). Cutting back on sleep is not a preferred strategy because research has supported what we know to be true – there are negative consequences to not getting enough sleep, including poor health and worse performance at work and at home. Even though it is not a good strategy, like all working mothers, the exceptionally successful leaders we interviewed cut back on their sleep to get it all done. Ma Yuan, a former judge of the Chinese Supreme Court, told us:

> "I almost never went to sleep earlier than midnight before I was 60. My own time would usually start after 9 p.m. when everyone else in the family had been put to bed. There is not a case law system in China, but, as a judge, I have to read a huge number of court cases as well as to hear cases. I also participate in legislative work and judicial interpretation work. Making judicial interpretations and providing legislative suggestions requires massive court case reading. After all, you cannot base your judgment on imagination."

Life circumstances could not be more different for Margaret York, a Los Angeles police officer who rose to the rank of Chief of Police in the Los Angeles Police Department, one of the largest police departments in the US. Yet, despite the obvious differences in most aspects of their lives, they both gave up their precious sleep to make it to the top of their profession. Margaret York described how she found time:

> "In the early part of my career, I wasn't a supervisor. I was just a basic police officer. During this time, I always worked through the night; during the early morning hours, I would hire a babysitter to come in and sleep at my house when my children were sleeping. Then I could adjust my sleep in the daytime around their schedule. If they had a meeting at school where I needed to go in and meet with their teacher or something to that effect, I could adjust my schedule. When I was at the police academy it was very, very intense. Most of the women who went through the academy at the same time were not married, and if they were married, they did not have children. So they would just go home and study, and, their life revolved around the police academy. I would go home and make sure my children had done their homework, make sure everybody had a bath, make sure they had dinner. And then when they went to bed, I would try to study. It was

very difficult. [*What would be the hours you would do this?*] Well, the police academy was mostly daytime hours from about six in the morning until about three or four in the afternoon. The police academy was very strict because you had to show that you really wanted this job. If you were late to work or to class, for example, it appeared that maybe you didn't really want to be a police officer. Maybe you wanted to be a mommy instead. Those were the kinds of pressures that were put on me and that I put on myself because I was very determined to be successful in the police academy because I needed to have a job where I could make as much money as a man in order to support my children. I was very determined to be successful."

Feng Cui was Director General of the International Department of the All-China Women's Federation and a UN CEDAW Committee Member before her retirement, and is currently Vice-President of the China Association of Women Entrepreneurs. Although her response takes a different tone, the underlying strategy is the same:

"I believe that a successful career and a harmonious family are important elements of a fulfilling and complete life. As a woman, these two things are what I strive for in life. Therefore, I feel the time I spend with my family cannot be lessened and sacrificed. So, if I do not have enough time, I would rather reduce my resting time."

Feng Cui recalled a time when her children were young, and she had just got home from a long day at work. Her children said they were yearning for dumplings. So she ran off to the market and bought the ingredients. Her husband chopped up the meat and vegetables while she rolled out the pastry. She proudly recounted that they were able to serve a fulfilling meal of dumplings to the children in 45 minutes.

Ginny Gong, who is the Director responsible for multi-million-dollar county facilities in Montgomery County around Washington DC and is President of the Organization of Chinese-Americans, expressed sentiments similar to those of Feng Cui: "My children and my work enrich me as a person. I hope to make this world a better place for my children. But I won't do it if it takes me away from being with my children. So I take away sleep, not my time from my children. I am very efficient; I get a lot done." When her children were young, she got up at 5 a.m. to drive them to her mother's home before she commuted back to work.

Mary Ma, Chief Financial Officer at Lenovo, described a typical evening at home where after dinner she would chat and exercise with her family.

"After 10 p.m., I go back to work. I usually work from 10 p.m. or 11 p.m. to 2 a.m. [*Comment: So you give up your own sleep.*] You have to give it up. I give up my own leisure time. Also you have to organize. I have a home-helper and a driver so I don't have to worry about this. I try to encourage my daughter to be more independent. If you want to balance, you can do it. There are many people who complain how they cannot balance time between family and career, and I don't believe that. For instance, many businessmen spend all their dinner time outside, and even go drinking after that. I don't do that."

These women leaders scrutinize their schedules to look for slots where they can squeeze out more time. Typically, they sacrifice their own personal time. Some of the women leaders talked about how they cut their lunch times so that they can work on tasks for their children. Their family and work always come before their own rest and personal enjoyment.

### Practice Multitasking

There are severe limits to how much time can be taken from sleep before serious consequences occur to one's health, and performance at home and at work decline. Sleep is a necessary function, and active people cannot afford to shortchange their sleep. Another way to make more time is to do multiple activities at the same time. This practice is known as multitasking, and the professional, high-powered mothers in our sample know it well. Time use surveys have not adequately measured how several tasks could be accomplished within the same amount of time. It is generally assumed that we do one thing at a time.

Research from cognitive psychology has shown that when tasks are routine or well-learned, they require less attention and cognitive effort than when they are difficult or novel. Thus, multitasking is a good strategy for routine activities like washing dishes, but it is not a time-saver when the demands of the tasks combine and exceed what you are capable of attending to. Highly successful women seem to know intuitively when to use multitasking and when to devote all of their attention to a single task.

Mary Ma uses multitasking to her advantage:

"When I was in Beijing, I was very busy and I had to entertain business people at dinners. If I had to entertain clients at dinner, I would arrange the dinner to be held at a restaurant close to where I lived. I would normally go home first to prepare dinner for my family, and later I would bring back something from the restaurant to share with my daughter and husband. I purposely arranged all of my dinner entertaining this way. Although I was tired, I had to do that. My husband and I tried to make sure that one of us would be at home every night to look after our daughter. It is very tough, but we made the schedule work. You can do it if you want to make things good for your family and your employer. I don't have much leisure time, but I can spend time with my team members chatting and socializing. The way people put together their work and home life is very subjective in terms of how to view it. For example, on Saturday afternoons, you can certainly have tea with your family, but you can also have afternoon tea with one or two of your colleagues, and spend some time chatting about life and work. Colleagues do not feel too stressful when you are talking about work with them in that kind of environment. It is not a bad strategy because you can enjoy spending time in this way. If you want to balance it, then you can do it. I believe there is nothing impossible."

This last sentence from Mary Ma sums up the comments from all of the women. It is a very positive statement for anyone who is wondering if it is possible to be at the top of your profession and be a dedicated mother and wife. These women leave no doubt that it can be done.

Figure 3.1 depicts a time-saving model for mothers and high-achievers who need to reduce the amount of work that they do. The top half shows work and family as two separate domains. The total amount of work in the two domains is too much for any one person to complete, but when the two domains are overlapped and portions of the work in each domain are given away to coworkers and home- and childcare assistants, then the work that needs to be done is reduced to a heavy, but manageable, amount.

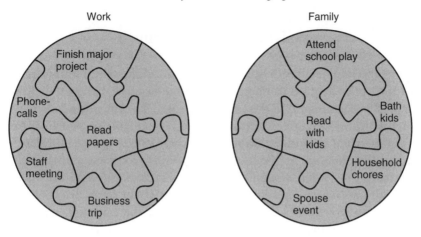

Distinct Work and Family Domains in a Segregated Model

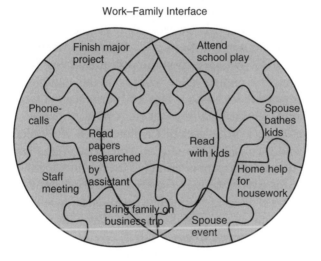

Overlapping Work–Family Domains in an Integrated Model

**Figure 3.1** A time-savings model for mothers and high-achievers who need to reduce the number of activities in which they are engaged. The top half shows work and family as two separate domains. The total area represented by these two circles is too large for any one person to complete all of the work/activities represented, but when the circles are overlapped to represent integrations of work and family, such as when selected activities are given away to coworkers and home and childcare assistants, then the number of activities that remain is reduced to a heavy but manageable amount

## Solving the Time Crunch

The successful leaders in our study recognized the critical importance of time and the need to manage their time in ways that would allow them to be successful in their multiple roles. The time demands seem almost insurmountable, yet these women were able to find time for the important activities and people in their lives. No one said that it was easy, but all of the women expressed confidence that high-pressure jobs could be combined with a satisfying family life. They are not harried people suffering from a variety of stress disorders. In fact, the picture we see of their lives is just the opposite, with the women projecting images of professionals who took control of their lives by making good decisions and refusing to give up their two most important roles. Their confidence in their own abilities and self-worth made it easier for them to make time arrangements that fitted with their needs. Earlier in their careers, some of them "flew below the radar" and just left work to be at after-school events, or to take kids to music lessons or whatever was important to them, working later in the evening to complete their work. For their employers, it was their performance that counted. This attitude is seen in the comments of Nellie Fong, who is Chairman of the Chinese operation of Price-waterhouseCoopers. She described a time when she called into her office and told them she was going to "take two weeks leave, which coincided with the Christmas holidays [to go on vacation with her family]. This is my priority, and if the company cannot accept this, then I would feel very unhappy if I continued to work there. The company views me as an asset, so they are left with no choice. They should be willing to cater to my needs."

These are appropriate sentiments for closing this chapter. Smart employers will recognize the value of key employees and will support their efforts to find the time for all of the important events and people in their lives. It is good business to retain such superstars.

# Chapter 4

# Happy Homemaker, Happy Marriage: The Female Executive Edition

## New Home Economics

High-achieving women do not conform to the "Happy Homemaker" or "working male with a wife at home" model of how housekeeping should be done. Because they still shoulder the second shift when they get home from work, powerful women leaders with caregiving responsibilities at home become experts at multitasking. They call themselves great jugglers. With all of the demands on their time, how do they juggle the work of running a house – the cleaning, cooking, laundry, shopping, and general arranging of the myriad tasks that need to be done to "run" a home?

Several studies have examined how much time women and men spend on housework. There are wide variations in the estimates of the time spent on housework, which seem to depend on the method used to collect the data. Regardless of the way data are collected, working women are doing less housework than their mothers did a generation ago, and their husbands are doing more than their fathers did, but we hasten to add that working women spend much more time on housework than their husbands (Bianci, Milkie, Sayer, & Robinson, 2000). In this study based on time diary data, which are collected from daily diaries that chronicle how much time people spend on different activities, married women who work full-time reported an average of 19.4 hours a week compared to 10.4 hours a week for married men. It is noted that time use diaries yield lower estimates than other measures, but the gender gap is consistently found.

It is interesting to look at the variables that influence the decision to hire help to take care of household tasks (Gupta, 2005). Researchers found that the decision did not vary with how much the husband earned, so the decision did not depend on how much money the couple had available. The decision depended solely on how much money the wife earned, with wives who earned high incomes more likely to hire household help than lower-income wives. It seems that women use their own money to pay for household help. It is as though the wives fulfill their gendered roles by buying themselves out of housework. Some psychologists call the fact that women do the majority of household work "doing gender" because housework is part of women's gender role. Even women (and men) who deny that they are constrained by sex-role stereotypes report that the woman does most of the housework.

Comparable data from China on time spent on household tasks show a similar pattern of gender gap. Data from the 2000 China Health and Nutrition Survey, which is based on a random sample of 2,400 married couples, show that women spend an average of 17 hours a week on cooking, cleaning, shopping, and washing, compared to an average of 3 hours a week for their husbands (Yang & Short, 2007). Unfortunately, the methods used to collect these data in various Chinese studies differed, and they also differed from those used for the US samples, so we cannot compare the number of hours across these two cultures and across some of the studies. Nevertheless, the disparities found within each study between working wives and husbands in terms of housework send a clear message: for working wives to get even close to "having it all," they need to reduce the time spent on housework. These data also suggest that we may be closer to achieving gender equity in the workplace than in the home. As long as women are doing a disproportionate share of the housework, they will be handicapped in the workplace.

There are several possible solutions to the problem of spending a disproportionate amount of time on housework. Women can reduce their hours by sharing the work more equally with their husbands, they can lower their housekeeping standards, learn new housekeeping efficiencies, or enlist home help, including help from other family members.

A reduction in the number of hours spent on housework does not necessarily mean that women would be less responsible for the housework. The normative roles of wife and mother are still strongly ingrained and they include the multiple tasks that constitute running a home. Some of the women leaders have integrated these roles into their identity.

Ma Yuan, former Deputy Chief Justice of the Chinese Supreme Court, described the family responsibilities that women implicitly assume:

"Women professionals have to travel often on business trips. When our husbands have business trips, we are ready to help them pack. But when we travel, we pack for ourselves. When our husbands return from their trips, we immediately help them relax. But when we are back, we feel that we owe the family. So we change our clothes and immediately go to the kitchen. Although I have my mother helping me then, I still need to do lots of household chores by myself. Every day I finish the household chores before 9 p.m. so I can get to my own work after that. I work until midnight or even later, studying newly promulgated law and judicial interpretation."

Sun Yuehuan, who heads the top enterprise appraisal firm in China, works a second shift after work. While she can more than afford it, she does not hire a domestic helper at her Beijing home because her husband is not comfortable with a non-family member living with them. This is how she manages:

"I work 12 hours a day. I spend less time at home, but I will bring food from the dinner party to my husband (because he cannot cook), regardless of others' opinion. I phone him every day after work because he is always on my mind, although I will not let my family affect my work. I will not dine out unless it is absolutely necessary so I can have dinner with him at home. When my husband goes to foreign countries, I help him to pack if I am at home. If I am away on a trip, I will phone back to remind him to take care of himself. I will call my family as soon as I step off the plane. But as he does not know how to cook, I feel guilty every time I go on a trip. So after I come home, I will do housework immediately to show my concern in action."

## Overthrowing the Tyranny of the SuperMom Syndrome

Increasingly, many of the women leaders we interviewed have overthrown the tyranny of the SuperMom Syndrome as it applies to housework. Having it all does not include doing *all* of the housework. The new home economics practiced by executive women takes a more relaxed and creative approach to running a home. They have learned to let go. They devised strategies for a new "home economics," where homes are important, but homemaking is not. Since high-level executives are often perfectionists, they needed to learn how to maintain their requirements for the highest standards at work, and then relax these standards when applied to their own housekeeping. It is time for women to give themselves and each other the permission to do so.

Jenny Ming, President of Old Navy/Gap, learned early on that it is OK to have household help. When she first became a mother, she was overwhelmed with her multiple roles. Her husband persuaded her that she did not have to do it all herself. Apart from getting part-time help, she adopted a rational approach in negotiating with her husband about the night feeding of her infant at that time:

> "When we had twins, my oldest daughter was only 17 months old. We had three kids under the age of 2 at one time, so he [my husband] had to help. I found that once I get up to do the night feeding, I can't go back to sleep. My husband could do night feeding; he'd go back to sleep just like that. I said, 'Why don't you do the night feeding? It's just so easy for you.' He says, 'OK.' So he does the night feeding."

Emily Lau, the first woman to be elected to the Legislative Council in Hong Kong in the early 1990s, is well known for her outspoken criticism of the government. She is a former President of the Journalist Association who quit her job as a journalist to become a full-time politician. She said that before the handover she was considered by the colonial Hong Kong government to be "radical," "outside mainstream public opinion," and a "solitary exception." She defined the objective of her work as making government and politicians accountable to their job. Her husband is a barrister by profession. She was just as forthright in her emphasis on equality and economic independence for women:

> "The most important thing for women is to be financially independent; then you can do what you want to do. Many women take all household duties upon themselves; they should change their mentality and give themselves more space. The family should share housework; it's fairer. They are too dumb to do everything themselves. In my household, my husband takes up all household duties, even though we have a maid, because he enjoys cooking. He is artistic. He decides there is only one way to do things, so he can take it over. With choice, I can concentrate on things I am good at and enjoy, even though I can still cook if needed to."

Valari Staab, President and General Manager of the TV station, KGO-TV, ABC-7, works with many women employees in the television industry who are always pressed for time. She understands the importance of letting go:

> "Here a lot of our women are perfectionists. It's a thing with on-air people. They tend to be perfectionists. So they want their child to be perfectly clean and adorable every minute; they want their house to always be clean. They put unrealistic expectations on their life, and then they end up just worn down to a frazzle. So I try to get them to take a step back and say what is really important. Like, some of them will say, 'I don't let my husband load the dishwasher because he breaks the glasses.' I say, 'Here's a website called replacement.com; replace the damn glasses when he breaks them. Let him load the dishwasher.' Women get caught up in wanting things exactly a certain way instead of focusing on what's important. What's important is they don't wake up and realize they don't even remember their children being little because they were too tired the whole time to notice. Or that they're so mad all the time with their kids because they're exhausted by the time they spend time with them. So I try to help them to understand that they have to make choices and trade-offs. And maybe the house isn't as clean as they like it to be, but they hire someone to come in every two weeks and clean the house. You know, try to get them to make good choices that set their life up in more balance because it's just a crazy time."

## Finding and Trusting a Reliable Helper

Even when domestic help is available, the superwomen have to let go by trusting their helpers. Rosanna Wong, who has been a Member of the Executive Council in the Hong Kong government before and after reunification with China, has this advice:

> "When my children were young, there were two maids taking care of them. I had to trust people. I gave maids the responsibility and trusted them. At work, I trust people and give them the freedom and responsibility; same with my maids. This one maid has worked at my house for 16 to 17 years. I don't monitor day-to-day work. I'm ready to take the risk; it is better than constantly checking on them."

Part of the trust comes from having reliable helpers who have stayed with them for a long time. However, it is not only the Chinese women leaders who have benefited from the help of loyal domestic helpers. Some of the American women leaders also relied on such help when their children were growing up. While they were able to afford it at that time, they reminded us that they were not as successful and well-off as they are now. It was a matter of necessity and choice if they wanted to have children and pursue their career. They all counted their blessings in finding a person whom they can trust and who can give them peace of mind.

However, having home help did not mean that the women leaders did not need home management. Many mothers were worried about whether their helpers were bringing up their children in the same way as they would themselves. The women leaders knew how to manage well. As one former American senior government official, who preferred to remain anonymous, illustrated: "Another part of organizing the household to make it work for me was being very clear about what I wanted my live-in help to do; and being very clear with the children about my expectations for them so that they had expectations that they had to meet as well."

Lorna Emundson, President of Wilson College, was all praises about her housekeeper who helped to raise her children: "She was such a loving caregiver. She was firm; she learned how to be firm but gentle with the children. And we always made sure we were of the same mind in terms of discipline."

Often, husbands and extended family members are around to help to supervise the helpers. Doreen Woo Ho, President of Wells Fargo Consumer Credit Group, lives in San Francisco. She had a full-time nanny for her children when they were growing up. She said:

> "The most important thing is I knew my kids were in good hands. If you don't have that peace of mind, then I think it would be a lot of pressure. My husband and I were fortunate enough not to face travel conflicts at the same time. When I traveled, I knew my husband was at home and vice versa, he didn't worry when he traveled. So I knew I had the housekeeper and my husband that I could count on. And then, worse comes to worse, my mother was available if we needed help."

Whether or not they have live-in helpers, the Chinese women leaders in Hong Kong and Mainland China, as well as in the US, are more likely to rely on their extended family. Especially in the earlier days when most families were poor in Mainland China, and couples could be assigned to work in different parts of the country, it was not uncommon for children to be left to the care of their grandparents. The closer family ties and the proximity of their extended family make it possible for the women leaders to call upon reliable help. We note that among our other American women leaders, those with their parents living close by also call upon them for help with childcare, but not as regularly.

If the extended family was not around, some of the women leaders created their own resources. Wilma Chan is the Majority Leader of the California State Assembly representing the cities of Oakland, Alameda, and Piedmont. Her parents were staying on the east coast when her children were young, so they were not around to help. She was active in her children's school and other community services. She had many friends who were also involved in volunteer work, so they did a Co-op. They would take turns different nights or different times on the weekend taking care of a group of children so that they could all do the activities they wanted to do.

## Equal Partnership in the Housework

Our group of women leaders were unanimous in citing the importance of their spouses' support in their success stories. One major source of support for which the women expressed their appreciation was the spouses' willingness to share in the housework and childcare, something that highly achieving men often take for granted. Recent American studies have shown that perceived spouse support is an important requirement for the management of work–family conflict for dual careerists and dual-earners. Equity appeared to be more important than equality. Regardless of whether or not the division was equal, if it was viewed as fair by the partners concerned, tension was low (Gilbert, 1988). The women in these studies often acted in accordance with traditional role expectations with respect to their family caretaking role. At the same time, their own heavy involvement in their career might contradict society's norms on the roles of women. Their expectations would still conform to these norms. While they were getting some spousal help with household work, they would not expect equal sharing of all household duties from their spouse. They would accept household inequities as a social reality and were not affected in terms of marital well-being.

The Chinese women leaders we interviewed were particularly expressive about their appreciation of their spouses' involvement in housework in their narratives, probably because they considered their husbands to be different from the normative expectations of men's roles. There is no doubt that the husbands or partners of the American women leaders are also contributing to housework, as domestic helpers are less common in the US. Many of them also go to the grocery store, cook the meals, clean up the dishes, do the laundry, play with the children, and attend their ball games. However, the discrepancy between the husbands' behaviors and the expected norms would make their housework contributions more prominent in the Chinese context.

Feng Lida, the Navy Hospital immunologist, married her husband during her father's exile in the US during the Chinese civil war. Her father's wedding gift to them was a hand-written couplet wishing them to become new partners in democracy, not only in their country but also in their marriage. After Feng's father's unexpected death, they went to study in the Soviet Union before returning to work in the new China. Feng Lida's husband taught economics at the university. They had only one son, at a time when it was common for most couples to have three or four children. But that was a difficult period because she was studying in the medical school in the Soviet Union. So she did not want more children. Feng Lida recalled:

> "When my child was born, he stayed in the day-care center. Then I went to study in the Soviet Union. When my child was back from the day-care center, my husband took care of him. My mother was busy at that time, but she loved my child very much and would always make time to take care of my child. Basically it's my husband and my mother who took care of the child. This was really hard. Actually my husband wanted to have a daughter. But he said he respected my decision. I think two people should respect each other. However, because I had to study overseas, my child was unfamiliar to me when I came back. Now my son always recalls the times when his father taught him poetry.
>
> When I was back in China, I had to work and I had business travel all the time. My husband always stayed at home [university professors worked from their home in those days as they did not have an office to themselves in the university], so he took care of our child instead. I think my husband came from an open-minded family, so he helped me so much. He does not complain about taking care of the child. He is great to the family, which can be considered as a role model. I put my priority on my family. Because he can work in the family home and I must work in the office, we complement and care for each other."

Chen Naifang, President of the Beijing Foreign Studies University, described how her husband shared the household responsibilities with her:

> "When he is back home [from his outpost assignments], we will usually divide up the responsibilities. He will cook breakfast in the morning before rushing to work while I will prepare dinner after work. After dinner he will do the dishes. In this respect, we are very responsible towards our respective duties. Because he knows I usually work hard at caring for the children, he will do more than his share of work whenever he is home."

Now that Chen Naifang's husband is retired, he spends most of his time at home helping her. She described touchingly how he told her that serving her "means serving the Chinese people" because she is doing important work for the country.

Audrey Eu, Member of the Legislative Council and House Leader of the Civic Party in Hong Kong, admitted that her husband took care of the household chores much more than she did. Her husband has a successful medical practice, and they also have domestic helpers. But he took care of the details in the house:

> "My husband is an incredible partner. He is understanding and sympathetic. He bends over backward taking care of everything in my life. Yesterday I found that he had changed the toothpaste for me. He always attends to small details and little things like that. I appreciate it.
>
> My husband takes up almost everything in the home, almost by habit or default. He enjoys taking up the role, so I've said I am not the typical case. I can't remember when he's like this, it seems that he's increasingly like this. I don't remember a time when he complained. He doesn't have many complaints, but his complaints are a kind of 'pretense of complaining' instead of a serious one. He doesn't really put his foot down. He really enjoys taking care of children's homework and arranging trips. He is like a travel department. I just have to go. He's also a household department. He is responsible in the maintenance of home machines, setting the alarm clocks, instructing the driver to pick up everyone. . . . Maybe he does it increasingly well and takes up more when I become more and more busy."

This is not the typical role that women expect their husbands will take up readily. Audrey attributed it to her husband's personality and sensitivity, and his love and care for her.

Some of the women leaders preferred not to involve their husbands in the household chores at all. Part of the reason is that they had other options, such as domestic helpers. Sophie Leung, Legislative Councilor in Hong Kong, had another important reason: "My husband was not involved in household chores. If he was not aware of details, he would have less complaint."

## Husbands and Intimate Others

Can women at the top have a happy marriage? The conventional belief that they cannot presents a dilemma for many young women embarking on their careers. It is a fact that a high proportion of top women leaders remain unmarried. Most women want to have a husband (or partner) and children, if not immediately after graduation, then at some time in the future. Do the young women of today have to trade intimacy for high-level success?

The most famous first husband in politics is Denis Thatcher, husband of Margaret Thatcher, Prime Minister of the United Kingdom from 1979 to 1990. They were married in 1951, and Denis Thatcher supported his wife's studies for the bar. After she became prime minister, he was often seen as the man walking behind the Iron Lady, but holding his own with a strong business background. Margaret Thatcher said in her autobiography that she could not have been prime minister for as long as she held that post without her husband by her side. When he died in 2003, Margaret Thatcher paid tribute to the man she loved: "Being PM is a lonely job. In a sense, it ought to be – you cannot lead from a crowd. But with Denis there I was never alone. What a man. What a husband. What a friend" (10 Downing Street). This eulogy is most revealing of the emotional intimacy behind the tough persona of the Iron Lady.

All the women leaders in our study have had a marital partner. Some have divorced or are widowed, and a few of them have remarried. Their success stories show that a woman's leadership position and her marriage can be compatible. Why do some marriages work while others do not? This is not an easy question to answer because there is no single answer to such a complex human endeavor as marriage. The answer has to be contextualized to the persons themselves.

## Emotional Support

Studies on marital relationships show that one of the biggest problems for working women is their husband's lack of support for their career (Gilbert, 1988; Vannoy-Hiller & Philliber, 1991). Social support is integral to reducing work–family conflict, and a supportive husband is essential to any woman who aspires to become dually successful. Social support from a spouse or significant other could be in the form of implicit and explicit encouragement received for the pursuit of one's career. This type of support can be characterized as emotional in nature, in contrast to other forms of financial or task-oriented support (Burley, 1995).

The women leaders came to exactly this conclusion based on their own individual experiences. The best marriages were described as mutually supportive, with wives supporting their husbands' careers as well. Egalitarian marriages really are the happiest ones, especially when the wife is in a top leadership position. These women tell about thriving marriages with husbands who have their own interests and successes and can take pride in the success of their wives. They appreciated the good fortune of finding a supportive husband.

Anson Chan, the first Chinese and the first woman to become the Chief Secretary of Hong Kong under both the British colonial government and the government of the Hong Kong Special Administrative Region under China, described her model of a successful family life:

> "A husband's understanding is very important for a woman in high (public) profile. For men whose wives are in high-profile jobs, in order for the marriage to succeed, the husbands need to be very confident. I'm lucky in this way. My husband is very confident and has his own career. He was not worried or jealous. For women in demanding jobs, we need to have a shoulder to cry on when we get home. My husband and I are very supportive of each other."

As we were writing this book, Anson, who was a few years into her retirement from the civil service, decided to represent the pan-democratic camp and run in a by-election to fill a mid-term vacancy seat on the Legislative Council in 2007. Her husband, Archie Chan, initially told the press that he was against her running. But when she eventually decided to enter the race, he turned around and was 100 percent behind her decision. Anson confided that Archie was actually protective of her and was concerned about her getting hurt in the political arena. After she made up her mind, then Archie supported her decision all the way. Archie was a corporate senior executive before he retired. For Anson, Archie was the source of her sanity and balance.

> "My husband's support for me is not due to me, but more due to his personality and his confidence about himself. It is not something that can be forced. We just work out this approach that both of us feel comfortable with. I'm very supportive of his company's functions and attend his functions; he also attends mine. Except that I have so many functions, so he can choose. We have this understanding: if he enjoys the nature of the function and knows the people (he likes more social functions rather than talking shop; the men usually talk about the office at these functions, and he does not enjoy that as much), then he will join me. He can fit in and enjoy the conversation. If he doesn't want to come, I understand too. I think mutual respect and trust is important in any marital relationship."

The emotional support that the women leaders get from their husbands can be implicit. Some of our interviewees expressed relief that their husbands were not complaining about their work involvement, or that their husbands could take care of themselves when they were busy. Fanny Law was Permanent Secretary of Education and Manpower in Hong Kong when she enrolled on a part-time Master's degree course in Education to learn how to do her job better. This is on top of her already heavy work and family roles. She talked about her husband's support:

> "My husband supports me, and he is proud of me; he considers that what I'm doing is meaningful and would counsel me if I complain about work. These two years when I'm so busy with my studies, he goes back to his high school to help out as a member of the Alumni Society so he can keep himself occupied. Also, he can learn more about the education system through his work in the school."

While her husband, a medical doctor, has a busy practice, Fanny wanted to ensure that he kept himself occupied while she carried on with her busy life: "My husband is a quiet man. He likes reading, so I will supply him with many books to encourage him to read."

## Buffer against Pressure from the Extended Family

In traditional Chinese families, pressure may come from the extended family for women to conform to their normative role at home. In Hong Kong, some wealthy families consider it a loss of face if their daughters-in-law have to work for a living. Some of our women leaders have married into these families. They managed to withstand the family pressure with their husbands' support.

Peggy Lam, who was the first Executive Director of the Family Planning Association of Hong Kong, belonged to the generation where rich women typically stayed at home. She was a free spirit and continued to pursue a political career as a District Board chairperson and a Legislative Councilor after her retirement from her employment, and then continued to found and lead the largest women's organization in Hong Kong. Her husband's family was an old-fashioned and large extended family whose members all lived together in the same house. However, she got the support of her husband to do the work she liked:

> "I told my husband that I wanted to work outside before we got married because the family already had a housekeeper, so I would have nothing to do at home. As my husband was the eldest son, every family member listened to him. Therefore, no family member rejected my request of going out to work.
>
> My husband was not a very traditional man and always wanted to be 'care-free.' So he did not insist on having a son. But my father-in-law wanted us to have a son; he would give our daughter a double red packet during Chinese New Year as a symbol for her to 'bring a younger brother.' But for me, I did not care about the gender of the children. I believed that I have to bring up my children anyway, regardless of their gender."

Peggy described how she managed in this traditional family:

> "Although I married into such a big family, I had a good relationship with my father-in-law's concubines [multiple wives, not including the first wife who has a special and higher status in the family]. And as I went out to work, I did not get involved in their gossiping. My husband was very independent. His mother passed away when he was young, and he could take care of himself. . . .

At the same time, I am also very family-oriented, so I would not go home late. I was influenced by my traditional and caring mother. My mother loved her children very much and would sacrifice herself to fulfill our needs. For example, during the war, she would give us as much as possible, although she would give boys a bit more. I was influenced by her traditional values and so I would not dine out late. My husband would not come home late either. And I would always be home by the time he came back, especially when my daughter was young."

Sophie Leung, the Legislative Councilor representing the textile industry in Hong Kong, also received pressure from her husband's family:

"In the late sixties, I got married in the US after college. I stayed there to work for three years in an advanced science lab and then became a research consultant in chemistry. I found the work exciting and challenging. After that I returned to HK, my mother-in-law pressured me not to work. She always had two tables of mahjong game going at home. She would ask me 'why don't you stay home?' It was time-consuming for me preparing dinner after a heavy day at work. So I went out with my daughters while they played.

My husband was supportive generally. He did not side with my mother-in-law. My first job back in Hong Kong was working in a bank. I was overhauling the computer system; sometimes when there was a system error, I needed to go back to work at night to solve the computer problem. My husband drove me to work and took a nap on the desk through the late night."

### Coach and Cheerleader

Some of the women leaders described their husbands as their best coach, fan, cheerleader, and mentor. Their husbands prodded them to aspire to higher ground, to develop their potential, and offered them guidance along the way.

Frances Hesselbein, who is a respected expert in the field of leadership, described her own career development and how her husband cheered her all the way:

"I never intended to take a professional job in my life. I was married to a journalist who was a filmmaker; he made documentary films. I had a little boy. Our family had a communications business. In a small family business everyone helps, I never thought of it as a career, I called it, 'helping John [my husband],' never realizing that years later having this communications background would be so valuable in the work I would do. My first professional job was the CEO of Talus Rock Girl Scout Council, headquartered in Johnstown, Pennsylvania. I had been a volunteer on national and international levels, but never was interested in a professional career. And I was there for four years, and then I had a call to move to the eastern part of Pennsylvania and become the executive director of that very large Girl Scout Council. So I went, and 18 months later, the national organization called: 'We want you to come to New York and speak to us about being a CEO of the National Girl Scouts of the United States of America,' which has over 3 million members, the largest organization for girls and women in the world. I almost didn't go because I didn't think they were serious. But my husband said, 'It's exactly the right job for you. I will drive you to New York.' "

When Frances was offered the job, she moved from Pennsylvania to New York. She remembered her husband's encouragement: "He said, 'I'm a filmmaker so I can live anywhere. And I've always wanted to live in New York.' "

The first two years, when Frances was working to transform the National Girl Scouts of the USA into a diverse and inclusive organization, were the most difficult. She recalled:

"I would come home and say, 'Oh, this is so tough.' But John would say, 'Not for you; you could do this with one hand tied behind your back.' He was my chief cheerleader, and those were marvelous days. And of course he believed as fervently as I did in the concept of the richly diverse, inclusive organization that is totally representative of the country. . . . We had always had a wonderful partnership, and it just intensified. And those last two years were two of the best years of our marriage. Then he died tragically. In eight weeks he was gone; he had a massive malignant brain tumor. And there was no way to save him. But I often think the first two years that were so difficult . . . so demanding, and they were the pivotal two years. . . . So it was providential that in my most difficult and demanding years, John was right by my side, cheering me on. And I always remember him."

Margaret York, Police Chief of Los Angeles County Office of Public Safety, was newly married to her second husband, Lance, when she got promoted to lieutenant at LAPD. At that time Lance was a young lawyer in the district attorney's office. Margaret said:

"He's very supportive; he's always been very supportive. He thinks I have a fun job. He's been with me every step of the way. Every exam I studied for, he encouraged me. Getting my degrees, he encouraged me. Every time I took on a new job or a new assignment, he encouraged me and supported me. And probably more so than maybe a lot of men might have."

On the other side of the globe, Wu Qidi, the Chinese Vice-Minister of Education, also attributed her aspiration to the encouragement of her husband:

"My husband was very supportive of both my study and work. If he had not encouraged me to apply for graduate school, I wouldn't have applied for it because I already had a family and a child. Although we are from scholars' families, I did not regard studying to be important because of the Cultural Revolution. Working in the factory was good; it was fine to live like that. But my husband was more motivated; he thought we should study. He is different from other men who think it's good enough for the wife to do the housework well. He believes I should continue to advance myself. In this respect, he had a great impact on me, including when I came back to China [from graduate studies in Switzerland]; became a lecturer and professor in the university; became senior management; and then became research institute director, assistant president, vice-president and then president of the university. During these stages, my husband gave me a lot of support. If I didn't have his support, I couldn't have done all these jobs so enthusiastically. He is more open-minded. . . . He wasn't like other men who would be looking for someone who looks pretty or can do housework. I thought he was in a disadvantageous situation, because I can't do housework well. . . . Maybe he wants someone who can communicate and exchange ideas with him continuously; he has higher demands in this area. In this respect, he is not chauvinistic. On many occasions, I have said that if he hadn't pushed me to step forward, I wouldn't have done so."

Other women leaders concurred about their husbands' appreciation of their intellectual compatibility and mutual interests. Doreen Woo Ho described the intellectual support she and her husband gave each other:

"I think that he never wanted to have a non-working spouse. He wanted someone who could keep up intellectually with him on what's going on in the world and especially the business world, not to say that one can't do that if you weren't working, but it's a lot harder. Obviously when you're working, the stimulation is greater because you can talk about work content and even get advice from each other. But you have to keep up with what's going on outside the home and equally on an inside focus in terms of the family. He always wanted me to be the best that I could be . . . I would say that he's always looked at my career as something that he has contributed to as well. And he has coached me well. So I think it's been a very symbiotic relationship and he's been very supportive."

The message from the stellar women leaders is consistent and clear. For high-achieving women who are married, it is important to have a husband who is supportive of your career. It is hard to imagine how any woman could create a successful life if her husband was sabotaging her career or even failing to provide the much needed support to successfully combine work and family.

## Wives in the Limelight

Women in top leadership positions are often in the media limelight, a constant focus of public attention. Most often, they will be more famous and more sought-after than their partners. Research on gender differences in the choice of marital partners shows that women usually prefer to marry "up," which usually means men who are taller, heavier, older, better educated, and earn more money than they do; and men prefer to marry "down," which involves all of the variables that women use for mate selection, but in the opposite direction (Schoen & Weinick, 1993). So, what happens when the wives outshine and/or outearn their husbands?

Many of our interviewees have stayed happily married, and their husbands did not find their partner's success to be a problem. Instead, many of the husbands were proud of their wife's achievements. Betty Yuen was initially sensitive to this potential threat:

"I think I am very lucky because I met my husband when we were young. At that time, we did not have anything and were not in high positions. On the other hand, I am afraid if I were to look for a boyfriend now, I would not be able to find one because many men would be afraid of dating me as I am in a high position. Therefore, I think that the foundation between two people is the most important.

In the beginning, I was also worried whether my husband would mind that I was in a higher position and had a higher income than him. But later I found that he was mature in this aspect. He would be proud of me as a capable person. So, he would not compare his position with mine and would not care about others' view. To me, our social status or income is not important. The most important thing is our psychological characteristics like personality."

Rita Fan, President of the Legislative Council in Hong Kong, is much better known in Hong Kong than her husband. However, she remains very humble about her own accomplishments in comparison to her husband's:

"All through my career, he saw me as an ordinary person who was in the right place at the right time. We both knew that he was much better than I was at many things, such as financial matters. He was more sociable and knew more friends; he had smoother social relationships. The fact that I'm well known in political circles is because of fate. I was able to do a good job because I don't have an ambition or desire for getting certain things for myself. I only want to do things properly. He encouraged me to do it the way I did. I did not use my position for personal benefit, because I had no such pressure.

Of course, there were things he did not like, such as when he was addressed as Mr. Hsu [my maiden name] and not Mr. Fan. Then I would step up and introduce him as Mr. Fan, and I'm Mrs. Fan. If they don't have his name on the invitation, then I won't go, even though I know he would go if I wanted him to do so."

Emily Lau's husband, Winston Poon, is a barrister. He took his wife's fame with a sense of humor. Emily recalled an incident:

"Although I am in the limelight, he does not mind. Even when he was called 'Mr. Lau' by some outsiders by mistake, he did not mind. One time when we went to Japan, we were greeted by the airline's manager at the airport. He thought my husband was the legislator and did not even greet me. My husband enjoyed the incident of being mistaken as the legislator in Japan, and we still talk and laugh about it."

Jenny Ming's husband came from a traditional family in Hong Kong. She would have expected him to be less egalitarian than other

American-born Chinese. She was very appreciative of how he differed from the norm:

"Actually he's a big proponent of my success, seriously, and I'm not just saying that. And I say that to a lot of people. I wouldn't be where I am today if it weren't for him. If your husband is jealous, or your husband doesn't encourage you, it would be very difficult.

He's very comfortable with himself. He's not resentful because I got the big title and I'm in the newspaper. He doesn't feel that's strange. He thinks my success is his success, and we share in it. And I'm very comfortable saying that. I don't feel he's proprietary. So I think that we were very fortunate that we are so comfortable with that."

Similarly, the former American top-level government official described how her husband shared a sense of pride in her success:

"He was always so proud of what I was doing. And he was always encouraging me to do more and to take on more responsibility. He had many successes of his own. That was never a problem with us. I'm very sure about that. He would tell my friends, he would say things to my friends about what I was doing. And he would say it with such excitement and pleasure. And then my friends would tell me, 'Your husband is extraordinary; he really feels very good about what you're doing.' And the feedback would come in that way through my friends who had talked to him. And perhaps it had to do with the fact that he had successes of his own. He wasn't at all threatened by what I was doing . . . I think he recognized that what I was doing helped people to do a lot of things that they wouldn't otherwise do. And he vicariously shared in that."

## Power Struggles and Threats

When husbands feel threatened by their wife's success, the power struggles and competition will create strain in any marriage. When there was conflict over these issues, the effect was severe discord or marital breakdown. Research shows that power within marriage relationships often depends on who brings in the money. One of the American women leaders who asked to remain anonymous described the strain with her former husband which led to their divorce: "My accomplishment reflected his frustration; my gain was his loss."

Sarah Weddington was married at the time she argued the landmark Roe v. Wade case before the US Supreme Court in 1973. She talked about the strain in her marital relationship at that time:

> "I think it was really hard for my husband: one, he ran for office before we were married and was not elected. And then I ran after we were married, and I got elected. That's hard on a man's ego now, but it was even harder at that time. We were both lawyers, but I had the US Supreme Court case. He was very helpful to me, but he didn't argue it in the Supreme Court. So I think that was hard. People would say to him, 'Oh your wife is so wonderful.' And he would be thinking, 'Well, ain't I wonderful too?' And then I would say, 'Oh, well you know my wonderful husband?' It got so awkward for everybody."

Barbara Franklin, former US Secretary of Commerce, talked about her unsuccessful first marriage and her happy second marriage:

> "I got married right after business school. For those seven years, it was a 'mistake.' My first husband had an element of male ego and felt threatened by women who were too successful. I considered that was a mismatch, despite his overt 'acceptance' of my success, which was difficult for him to put into practice. I admit that my career advancement was one of the factors that contributed to my first marriage breaking up. He was threatened by my achievement."

Barbara knew how important it was to find the right man:

> "It is important to make the right choice at the beginning – it takes a certain type of man not to feel threatened or upset by a woman's aspirations and success. Men do not see this as a problem. I think finding the right mate for a woman starts at the beginning of any relationship, before any negotiation. In my second marriage, I married someone older than I who was already very successful in his own life. He was a CEO then, now retired, who has also been in elective political office. He is secure in his own accomplishments and very proud of my achievements. We have been happily married now for 21 years."

Dong Jianhua, General Manager of the state-owned enterprise Red Pagoda, who oversaw the development of her company from a small factory to the biggest tobacco firm in China, described similar experiences of her two marriages:

"My first husband and I fell in love with each other and got married when we were working at the [factory] workshop level, before I went on to study. After we got married, we had a child; we had loving relationships in the family. I invested a lot in my work; I worked very earnestly, and studied very hard as well. I thought I treated the family and my child very well. But later my husband and I had conflicts partly because I was getting busier at work and spending less time at home. Moreover, when I became a leader, my husband got upset probably because he thought that he was losing 'face.' When I came home from work, he was unhappy and over-sensitive and we had arguments. I tried to encourage him to pursue further studies, yet he missed the opportunities due to various reasons. Later I discovered my husband was having an extramarital affair. I attempted to save our marriage and negotiated with him calmly – I asked him to choose between divorce or ending the relationship he was having with someone else. But it didn't work out and he continued his relationship with the third party. Finally, we agreed to separate very peacefully. At that time, my child was 8 years old. I was afraid that it would affect him, so we did not tell him about his father's affair. We did not let our colleagues and our parents know either. I was also worried how the company would look at this. If they knew there was a family problem and a third person was involved, they might send someone to counsel us. At that time, few women would divorce, as it would affect one's reputation (face) and the social pressure was very great."

Dong Jianhua continued to describe her second marriage:

"Later, someone introduced to me a male colleague in my company who had recently got divorced. Although his position was lower than mine, I didn't mind as long as he was understanding and had a good personality. I discussed it with my child. At first he did not accept my boyfriend, but after several discussions he was willing to accept him. My son even wanted to check out my boyfriend for me. The personality of my second husband is good; he accepts that I am stronger than him. He did not mind being identified as my husband, neither did he treat it as a source of pressure. (My first husband did not accept that.) He acknowledged and accepted my work and my personality.

Since our marriage, our family is full of happiness. My husband supports me and is good to my child. I think that his status does not matter. As long as he treats me well, I am happy. Family serves as a very important support to one's work and life (especially to women). We are of similar age and we share common interests and similar experiences. He has been good to me and my child. So I decided to re-marry. Soon after we got married, I was in charge of a big project from 1993 to 1997 when my child was attending high school. I was away most of the time. My husband helped me to take my son to school. I called back home every week. As I now think back, I feel grateful to him. I was too busy at work at that time.

Now I can manage well in both work and family. I have a loving family and my husband is good. My child has grown up well. I think one important thing to consider about re-marrying is finding the right person in life, but it's even more essential for women to be independent and self-reliant. After we got married, he had a lot of improvements in his professional life. He has been promoted; he works with the union, and everybody likes him."

Kim Campbell, Prime Minister of Canada, knows how important a supportive husband is for a woman in high political office:

"[When we first got married], my husband was very supportive of my political career. He thought I was doing what I should be doing and that I was the right person to be doing it. When I was in Ottawa as Minister of Justice and Attorney General of Canada, and then as Minister of National Defence and Veterans' Affairs, he began to understand what it would mean to be married to the Prime Minister. It was very clear that I was walking to that direction. I think this brought up his ambivalence. He didn't think I should stop doing what I was doing. But he was uncomfortable being part of it."

After leaving office, Kim Campbell served as Consul General of Los Angeles and then later taught at the Kennedy School of Government at Harvard University. She is now re-married and spends her time between the US and Paris. She has found her current husband to be much more supportive:

"It's very funny that my current husband is very much younger than I am. We have a very good marriage. I travel a great deal. We have interests in different fields. He is an artist. But we understand each other very well. He has been my spouse when I was the public wife and I am happy to be his wife when he is in the spotlight. We don't compete with each other. We are very much alike in the sense that we are both public figures. We both know what it is like to be out there. And we kind of protect each other.

But politics is hard on marriage not just for women. A lot of men get divorced because of traveling back and forth. Politics is hard on family and marriage for both men and women. Women like me either did not marry, or divorce or they had very supportive husbands. Many women politicians are not married for whatever reason, but those who have supportive husbands are very lucky."

With high-powered jobs in which the couple may need to be commuting between cities, or one of the spouses has to relocate, the adjustment is particularly difficult. One American interviewee who was recently divorced considered her job move to be one of the reasons for the breakup:

"I think that we did not adequately communicate what my professional needs were, as I perceived them, and what the implications were for him and at what level professionally and emotionally. But I don't think he was a very good emotional communicator either. I've seen other people in these positions that didn't have these problems.

The other question would be, if a woman has a very strong professional identity, whether you're providing enough emotional support. Whether it's physical presence or just you, a lot of your energy goes into your professional job because these jobs are very demanding. It may be that it's difficult to provide enough emotional support that your partner needs. And that may be that I didn't provide enough emotional support. But if I wasn't providing enough emotional support, and if he was pretty inflexible about moving around . . . then something comes to a head at some point."

## Flipping Normative Roles

One of the most difficult hurdles for professionals is the need to move in order to take the next career step. When one partner in a dual-career couple makes a move, there are many sacrifices that the other partner needs to make. In many marriages, the wife typically accommodates to the husband's move, which is often necessary for a promotion. As more women reach senior positions, more husbands become the trailing spouse. How have our women leaders managed to maintain a strong marriage when they are asking their husbands to sacrifice their own career to further their wife's career?

Valari Staab, President and General Manager of KGO-TV, tried to juggle her career so that her husband could keep his own. They commuted; and they changed jobs to be near each other. When Valari first got the General Manager job at the TV station in Fresno, her husband was not able to find a job that he really cared about, so he went to work in San Jose and lived there Monday through Friday, driving to Fresno on the weekends. She remembered:

"It was a big decision, but he very much looked at it as overall for our family, for the two of us, it was such a huge opportunity for us for our lifestyle for the rest of our lives that it was worth the sacrifice he was going to make on his career. So, for four years, we had a less than ideal lifestyle with the hope that I would be good enough at my job to end us in a major city again."

Eventually, when Valari became President and General Manager of KGO-TV, the couple moved to San Francisco. Her husband decided to work three days a week for a newspaper while helping her with her job, and was quite happy with this role. They shared housework 50–50, but he did more of the other errands during the two days he stayed at home, leaving more time for both of them to enjoy the weekend. Valari explained how they managed:

"We just always maintained a close relationship. I mean, we're best friends as well as partners in marriage, and we were just really honest with each other. He told me what he thought and what he felt. And we tried to look for ways to manage it. We're both very fair-minded people. We try to figure out what's fair for each other, and we try not to create extra burdens for each other. So I got lucky in that I absolutely married the perfect man for me. He may not be perfect, but he's perfect for me.

My husband's never been hung up on roles – that was probably one thing I noticed about him very early on. When we got married, I was 34, and he was 38. So he had been living by himself for a long time, and he was used to fixing his own meals, washing his own clothes, you know, taking care of himself. So he never ever expected me to suddenly take over all that, which was a huge help because I doubt we would be married if he expected me to cook dinner every night and do everything it takes to keep a house going.

For one thing, the reason I didn't get married until I was 34 was because I could tell a lot of it wasn't going to work. What was very important to me that he had was he was very fair, and he wasn't stuck in roles. He wasn't, 'I'm the guy so I have to do this; you're the girl so you have to do this.' He doesn't have a bit of that sort of thinking in him. I don't know why, but he doesn't. He just is very fair-minded.

When we started dating, we both had very busy lives. He traveled all over the place. And we had to schedule way ahead of time dates and times we were going to spend together because we were both so busy. And so it was easy early on to tell that he was going to respect the pressures and time demands on me as much as I respected it on him, whereas men I had dated before expected me to make all the compromises. They expected me to work my schedule around them, and that just didn't work."

Sharon Allen, the first woman elected to be Chairman of the Board of Deloitte, describes her situation:

"My job is all-consuming; I travel a great deal. I'm gone a lot, and it's hard. I have the pressure that goes with this job as well. And again, it's very difficult because it requires a very loving, supportive, and mutually respectful relationship with my husband. I know that I would not be able to manage this, my career as I manage it, if I didn't have that relationship.

He's very, very supportive, probably my biggest fan and also my best coach in terms of assuring that I always keep things in perspective and stay humble. But there is a lot of give-and-take, and we do a lot of talking. We do a lot of discussing, and I am very careful that I am respectful of his time and also that I am respectful of managing the time we have together. I will sometimes absolutely refuse to do a Friday event, if I can help it, unless he's part of it. I very seldom miss a Friday night with him; we call it 'date night.' We just have to make arrangements to ensure that we are spending time together. But it's still hard."

It is not common for Chinese men to be stay-home husbands. Julia Xin's husband is one of the exceptions. Julia is the Manager Director of Winterthur Insurance (Asia) Ltd., a Swiss multinational corporation. She has raised the profit as well as the profile of Winterthur as one of the best known insurance companies in China. When she moved to Shanghai for this position, her husband could not find a suitable job. Eventually, he quit his job to stay home and take care of the household and their son. He did not have a strong career aspiration and enjoyed the quiet life. He spent his time reading and investing in the stock market. He preferred to support his wife's active career. Julia believed that their mutual trust was an important foundation and they always discussed everything.

## Who Are the Supportive Partners?

Most of the women leaders concurred that finding the right husband is most important. There is one question that many young women considering their life goals of work and career would like to ask these women leaders: how do you find a husband like this?

The women leaders would not be able to give us a formula for a successful marriage. Like any good marriage, finding a compatible partner is counted as a blessing. We gathered some common characteristics from our interviewees' descriptions of their supportive spouses.

The supportive husbands were described by these women leaders as being mature, self-assured, confident, easy-going, and flexible. They are comfortable with themselves. There is mutual respect and sharing. They endorse egalitarian attitudes toward women. They are not jealous and do not have a strong ego that would be threatened by their partner's success. In the case of the Chinese men, they don't feel they are 'losing face' when their wives are successful. Instead, they embrace their partner's accomplishment with vicarious pride, and endorse the meaning of their work. Their own personality and values are important attributes that make the difference.

There may be stereotypes about cultural differences in men's endorsement of gender equality. It is commonly believed that, traditionally, Chinese men are less accepting of their wives' superior status because of the hierarchical relationship between men and women. Some of our interviewees referred to these stereotypes to explain the support they got from their husbands.

Ophelia Cheung's husband is British. She compared Chinese men with Westerners: "Many Chinese, including parents-in-law, do not like the wife to work for a salary, which is shameful to them. Compared with Chinese men who need their wives to obey them, my husband (a Scot) is more accommodating."

Alice Tai, Ombudsman in Hong Kong, is married to a senior civil servant who is British. They entered the Administrative Officer grade in the same year, and kept pace with each other in promotion. Later, Alice was promoted to a higher rank than her husband. He has been supportive of her advancement; she believes that it could have been different if he were Chinese:

"My husband did not mind; if he did, he would not have asked me to apply for the position. His personality and background meant he did not mind his wife being in a more senior position. He was happy for my achievement and success. We kept our work very separate and our professional lives apart when at home. However, because we are in the same Service, we can share our feelings and support each other mutually. Our family can serve as a sounding board for ideas.

If I were married to someone less self-assured, I might have had to exercise more self-restraint and curb my career development. In this respect, perhaps Western men are more individualistic; they have less cultural or traditional baggage; they are more broad-minded about certain gender issues. If he were Chinese, I would probably want to focus more on his feelings. If he did not want his wife to surpass him career-wise, then I would probably not let myself go."

However, from the personal stories of our interviewees from the United States, Hong Kong and Mainland China, we found more individual differences among the husbands. There were both supportive as well as unsupportive partners among the Chinese men and the American men. Ethnicity did not explain their support or lack of support for their wives.

Did the husbands learn to value the success of their wives from their family of origin? While some of our interviewees associated these egalitarian attitudes with their husband's family in which there were strong women, others attributed these attitudes to the fact that they learned to react against the power imbalance they observed in their parents. Thus, whether they came from families that supported women's success or families that abhorred it, the women tended to attribute their husband's supportive attitudes to their family life as a child.

Zhang Xin, Chairman and Co-CEO of SOHO China, explained her husband's support for her achievements:

"He always liked strong women because his mother played a very important role in the family. His mother was the center of strength that glued her family together, so he is very used to growing up and being around strong women. I think his natural character is that he likes to be with strong women. So he does not feel threatened by very strong women or very competent and independent women. In fact, I think he wouldn't feel very comfortable being with someone who relied on him all the time."

Lorna Edmundson, President of Wilson College, linked her husband's support to his childhood experience in a family in which the power was unbalanced:

> "My husband is the third of four children in his family. And as he described his three siblings, they were kind of outrageous. His older sister and older brother were very difficult, challenging people who gave his mother a hard time. So he grew up feeling that he needed to be the helper. He used to feel sorry for his mother when his sister would misbehave or his brother would get into trouble. And his father, like most fathers of the era, was away at work and not there to handle all this. And there were four children in his family only six years apart from the top to bottom so his mother had quite a lot to juggle. Because he is a third child, the 'middle child' as they often say, he had to negotiate between the sweet little baby and the first born who usually is more authoritative, and he learned how to work with people, balance things, be an intermediary.
>
> I think he observed that his father was gone too much, and his mother was sort of left with a mess all the time. He grew up seeing the imbalance in his parents' marriage. This was in the fifties. In the United States it was this period of time where post World War II families were very traditional. All the magazines had the women in the whitest shirts and the most beautiful meals. That was sort of the ethos of the time."

On the one hand, having good role models helped to socialize men to endorse egalitarian values; on the other hand, having negative role models could also account for the reaction formation. However, we did not hear from our interviewees' accounts that any of the parents of the supportive husbands explicitly taught their sons to support gender equality. This may be an important message for parents in the socialization of their sons and daughters in the next generation.

## It is Not a Fairytale Marriage; They Work Hard at It

It may sound like finding Mr. Right will be the solution. The myth of being found by Prince Charming and then living happily thereafter only happens in fairytales. If you have seen the popular movie, *Shrek the Third,* you may recall a scene in which all of the heroines from popular fairytales – Rapunzel, who was saved from imprisonment in a tower by letting down her golden hair so her prince could climb to rescue her; Snow White, who fell into a coma until awakened by a kiss from her true love; Cinderella, who found love with her tiny feet; and similar others – went from waiting to be saved by a handsome prince to "kicking butt" on their own. This is a more appropriate story for the lives of these highly successful women. The women leaders worked hard to attain a happy marriage. What do they have to do to consolidate the partnership?

There are different stages in a marriage, and the needs and tasks at each stage will vary. The women who stayed happily married emphasized that they and their husbands grew together in the marriage. They exhibit what marital counselors would call healthy couple behaviors – responsibility, alignment of goals, mutual encouragement and acceptance, commitment to equality in their relationship, empathic listening and open communication, willingness to discuss relationship, and joint conflict resolution. As Sharon Allen said, there is a lot of give and take, and a lot of discussion and negotiation.

## Carving Out Time for Intimacy

In intimate relationships, spending time together and sharing are important. Amidst their busy schedules, our interviewees create the time and space to share life with their marital partners. They mentioned how they designated evenings or weekends for the family, or special dates with their husbands. They recalled occasions when they just took off for relaxation together.

Andrea Van de Kamp, the American philanthropist from Los Angeles, and her husband both lead busy lives. But they work together to carve out their schedule and support each other's social engagements:

> "I think one of the reasons my husband was attracted to me is I had my own sense of direction. And he also shared in that. And then what we would do is sit down with a calendar on a monthly basis. And I would say, 'What are the events coming up this month where you would like to have your wife join you?' And we would work it out; I would make some choices. And he would say, 'Well I looked at

the calendar and this is where I think you might really have a good time,' or, 'you might enjoy being part of the evening.' So we made it kind of fun because one of the great things about politics, at least in America, the public is very interested in the family life of the elected official and who is the elected person's partner. And I felt it was a small way I could share and get a sense of what his responsibilities were as District Attorney of Los Angeles County and then as Attorney General of Los Angeles County."

When time was short, some women interrupted their own sleep so that they could go to bed at the same time. The former American top-level government official did it this way:

"I would frequently organize my life so that I went to bed when my husband went to bed. He needed to be in bed fairly early because he had to get up early in the morning to do surgery. I would frequently go to bed with my husband, let's say 10 o'clock, and I would sleep for four hours. I would get up at two o'clock, and I would frequently work from two until four at my desk. And then I'd go back to bed and sleep for a few more hours before I got up. So I did that; I did that many times. When I had something that I had to work on at home, those were the sort of quiet hours for me. Luckily I don't require much sleep; I never have. If I have six hours, that's fine. But I do remember thinking it was important to go to bed together and to talk and be with each other for that time and then get up later. I just organized my mind so that it happened; I woke up without an alarm clock."

Sophie Leung, the Hong Kong Legislative Councilor, had also arranged her sleep patterns this way when she had too much paperwork and she did not want to disturb her daily family schedule. When time is short, these women leaders sacrifice their own sleep so as not to sacrifice their family.

### Being Sensitive to Sensitivities

The sensitivity of a husband's feelings about his wife's exceptional success can sometimes require delicate handling. Often, the pressure comes from external social interactions. The Mainland Chinese women leaders are particularly sensitive to the normative pressure that their husbands encounter socially.

Wei Keizheng, the Board Chairman of Keili Group and Hainan Kailie Central Development Shares Co. Ltd., with major development projects in Hainan Province, is best known for setting a precedent by bringing a successfully lawsuit against the Stock Exchange of China for delaying the listing of her company. In her own life, both of her marriages ended in divorce when her ex-husbands were involved in extramarital affairs. She analyzed the roots of the problem:

> "In China, having your own career while taking care of all familial duties is very challenging to women, and options are few. Social beliefs are not easily altered. The majority of Chinese men dislike women being too strong. Men from southern China and Shanghai may be more receptive to this kind of dynamic, hence more willing to take up familial responsibilities such as taking care of children and preparing meals. In addition, being more educated will increase their sense of responsibility towards the family unit and concern for the female role.
>
> My second husband originally was the General Manager of the company, and I was the Chairman of the Board, which was a position above him. I realized that many men cannot accept women having higher status and greater achievement than they do. Someone once invited me to be the vice-mayor of Wuhan. When I told him the news, he began to cry and said he had worked hard all these years but felt very disappointed and sad because he had never even been appointed as a member of a public commission."

Chen Ying, a successful entrepreneur in the carpet industry in Mainland China, described her perception of the pressure her husband felt and how she proactively dealt with it:

> "My husband felt pressure because of my success. But the hardest period had past. In our home province, people are more likely to know me more than they know him. Therefore, when we sit around a table and introduce ourselves at a social function, I will say I am Mrs. Yang in addition to General Manager Chen. This can lighten his pressure. Although he does not speak out, there must be some pressure. There is no such feeling when we are eating at home or at work. However, when people gather around, I will become a center of attention quickly. I think many of these conflicts are subjective, and the conflicts are related to my husband's feelings. So in such situations, I am mindful of his feelings. Both of us have roles in society. Especially in this era of economic development, successful women get a lot of attention.

When we have to attend some functions together, I always pay attention to his feelings."

Having been loving and supportive of each other through the years, Ma Yuan, the Chinese Supreme Court Justice, and her husband enjoy a harmonious conjugal relationship. Yet sometimes she can still sense the pressure her husband feels:

"Sometimes my husband is reluctant to join the social gatherings related to my work. I don't know how to describe his feelings, but he is reluctant to go. Maybe he felt he was losing face. I am also very nervous in these situations because I can take care of him at home, but I can't show this caretaking in front of others. He does not talk much at these functions. Sometimes when we got home, I'd say to him, 'People there are talkative.' Then he'd say, 'You people there are the leaders and I didn't follow you.' With these words, I could feel his emotions."

Similar social strains may be experienced by the husbands of the successful American and Hong Kong women leaders, who try to bolster them or keep them away from these situations.

While many of the women leaders felt that they did not need to keep their work and family lives separate, they are specific about keeping their work and family identities separate. Many of our Chinese interviewees reminded themselves that while they would be the authoritative leader in the office making all the decisions, their identity at home is the wife/mother whose behaviors are different. They consider their family to be the priority, even though they may be spending a lot of time at work. Given their increased resources, they would show their love for their husband by taking greater care of the husband's family also. They would trust the husbands with their finances, and consider their resources and glory as shared collective property. In their own career decisions, they would consult and involve their partner in making what they consider a collective decision. When their husbands become party to their career decisions, they are more likely to support and even make sacrifices for them.

Sun Yuehuan, Board Chairman and CEO of the highly successful China Enterprise Appraisals Company, attributed the basis of her happy marriage to the mutual respect and trust she shared with her husband rather than absolute equality.

"My husband is a secondary school teacher. Our relationship remains very strong after we got married because our relationship is based on mutual understanding and respect. I may have a higher financial and political status than my husband, but I give all of my salary and bonus to him to manage because I trust him completely. We regard our family as a whole unit. In terms of career, I am more successful and have gained more public recognition. But I would not take the success as my own; rather it is the effort of the whole family. I think I could not have gone into business without my husband's support. Although he does not know how to do domestic work, he understands my needs at work and is very considerate.

At home, I can control myself. When I realize that my husband is unhappy, especially when he is under huge work stress, I would be careful, both behaviorally and verbally, in order not to let him feel inferior to me. Instead, I often praise my husband in front of others. I think if we can handle family well, our staff will take this as a role model. My husband is also very successful in his education field because he has published many books. Therefore, I think income should not be used to judge whether one is successful or not. My husband understands and trusts me and would not be affected by others. Once he told our son that he does not have a psychological burden even after I started my business. Anyway, I know that he is always good to me."

Sun Yuehuan reminded us, as did some of the other Chinese women leaders, that a happy family would constitute one important component of the role model of women's leadership. The boundary between work and family is permeable, allowing the deep meaning and joy from each of these two roles to intermingle and grow.

Mary Ma, CFO of Lenovo Group, who played a key role in the company's $1.75 billion acquisition of IBM Personal Computing Division in 2005, was asked after a public talk about her ultimate choice as a successful woman leader if she had to choose between work and family. She told the audience that by the time a woman was forced into this dichotomous choice, the outcome would no longer matter. To Mary, the woman leader could have both career and family, which constituted her success as a person. While male leaders won't be asked similar questions, Mary's answer resonates with wisdom.

# Chapter 5

---

# Cherished Children:
# Tales of Guilt and Pride

What do juvenile delinquency, the breakup of the (traditional) family, the faltering economy, drug abuse, and a myriad of other social ills have in common? Give up? They have all been blamed on working mothers – an easy scapegoat for anyone who does not let facts get in the way of their thinking. And there are many people who fall into this category.

Our beliefs about what constitutes "good mothering" run deep. We implicitly learned them at a young age and reaffirm them every time we selectively attend to information about mothers who work. Working mothers are not a new phenomenon that arose from the brow of some shrill feminist, although this is sometimes the image that is conjured up when reading comments about mothers who are employed outside the home. As an example, consider the sensational and diametrically-opposed coverage by the media of two modern tragedies. In one story, an 8-month-old baby was shaken to death by his au pair (which is the term used for a foreign-born young adult who provides residential childcare in exchange for the opportunity to live and attend school in the United States). In this horrific tragedy, the media repeatedly asked, "Where was the child's mother?" The child's mother was described in the media as "materialistic" and "negligent" because she left her infant in the care of a young woman while she went to work. It is probably not necessary to say that no one asked about the employment status of the infant's father or described him in negative and hateful terms for leaving his infant with an au pair (Warner, 2007).

By contrast, consider the tragedy of a young couple, the McCanns, who had their daughter abducted while they ate dinner at a nearby restaurant during a vacation in Portugal. The McCanns left their children unattended, despite the availability of babysitters, because "they didn't want to hand their children over to 'strangers'" (Warner, 2007). There was an unprecedented outpouring of sympathy in support of these grieving parents. Why was there such a difference in the public response to these two tragedies? Kate McCann, the mother of the abducted girl, was described as a devoted mother who had reduced her work hours as a general medical practitioner to only one and a half days a week. In support of this role of "good mother," her aunt was widely quoted as saying, "She's working to keep her career up, but spends the majority of time with her kids."

The message is clear. The mother who left her children unattended was a good mother who did not deserve the terrible nightmare of having a child abducted, but the mother whose child was killed by a live-in sitter got what she deserved because she worked (close to) full-time. In an editorial in the *New York Times*, Warner (2007) described the public's response to these tragedies as "the foul poison of working-mother-hate." These are strong words for strong emotions. How can we understand this phenomenon and what, if anything, can we do about it?

## The Origins of Working-Mother-Hate

Caring for children is hard work. When women go to work, they can usually take periodic breaks, even from the most grueling and unpleasant jobs. Mothers who care for infants or young children full-time can take their breaks only during the child's nap time, and such breaks may be nonexistent if there are several children, or if she needs to use that time for household tasks. Of course, they can park children in front of a television, but such solutions will not work for infants who need constant care. Women (and others) who care for children full-time believe that what they are doing is important. And it is. The prototypical response to questions about the decision to stay at home is that the job of raising children is too important to leave to someone else. The response of employed mothers to this insinuation that their children are not important to them is that they *are* caring for their children, but it is not necessary or desirable to be available at all times. Often the dialog turns into a battleground that sets the stage for full-scale "Mommy Wars" between mothers who work outside the home and those who do not.

Consider a lead editorial that ran in *USA Today*, a large circulation US newspaper, in response to a study conducted by the National Institute of Child Health and Human Development. The large-scale study was one of many studies on the effects of working mothers on their children. Research on this question is described in more detail later in this chapter. Like most research findings on this topic, the researchers reported that there were no negative effects for children in day-care and, in fact, they documented many positive effects of day-care for children from low-income homes. The study was conducted over a 7-year period by a team of outstanding researchers. If the research had addressed a less controversial topic, no one would have questioned the findings. But childcare remains controversial, despite reliable findings that it does not harm children and often is beneficial, because arguments about childcare are really about politics and personal choice. Somehow, the science gets lost in the rhetoric.

The editorial urged readers to "Forget day-care research – trust your instincts" (Parker, 1997, p. 15A). As you can guess from the title, the readers of *USA Today* were urged to ignore the results of the study and, instead, they were asked to rely on the author's intuition about the negative effects of day-care. The author of the editorial claimed that she cared about innocent babies and would speak for them because they cannot speak for themselves. The same message was repeated on a television talk show where the speaker posed a question that, although it is loaded with emotional language, is at the core of working-mother-hatred: "If you were an infant, would you rather be left with strangers all day in day-care or stay at home with a loving mother?" Any response that might suggest that children actually enjoy being at, or benefit from, early childhood education centers (note the difference in labeling) would be met with ridicule and a sneer. When it comes to reconciling the views of working and stay-at-home mothers, the gloves are off.

As Sandra Scarr (1997), a developmental psychologist, noted, when the results of a scientific study of day-care are pitted against intuition or the observations of a single individual, the general public tends to find these two sources of information equally compelling. We all have some experience with children and opinions about child rearing, and we believe that our personal experiences and those of people whom we trust are as valid and reliable as conclusions made from large-scale studies. Faceless statistical averages gleaned from large samples are no match for the vivid examples we personally experienced. Testimonials are compelling – a fact that advertisers use to their advantage – and a single counter-example (the "I know a person who" phenomenon) is often used to disprove a conclusion derived from a large study.

The primacy of personal experience is bolstered by the common theme that is repeated like a mantra in the popular media: anyone can lie with statistics. There is a general tendency to distrust research findings that do not agree with our personal beliefs. With this mindset, no amount of research can convince someone who believes that when mothers work there must be negative effects on their children. The criticism from both camps can be vicious and hurtful. No wonder working mothers suffer from guilt and stay-at-home mothers feel the need to defend their choices. An example of mother guilt is shown in the Sally Forth cartoon below.

Most mothers have their own personal stories about attacks lobbed from the "other" camp. Diane recalls a time when her children were young and she was at a party meeting new people. When she told someone that she was in graduate school at the time and had two young children, the response was a loud and haughty, "I stay home with my children because I love them." The implications about Diane's feelings toward her own children were loud and clear.

Figure 5.1  *Source*: King Features, Reed Brennan Media Associates

## Redefining the Good Mother

It is hard to think of any two roles that are more incompatible than being a mother to an infant or a young child and succeeding at a high-powered job. Each of these roles has expectations associated with it that drive our thoughts and feelings about the people who live these roles. The "good mother" conjures images of a woman who is married, at home, and caring for her child full-time. By contrast, the high-achieving worker is married, male, and works long into the evening and every weekend. Women who are both mothers and high-achievers must find a way to resolve the inter-role conflict. How can they be both? Is there necessarily a constant struggle between competing commitments?

In a study of the way we construct and interpret our societal roles as mothers and workers, Johnston and Swanson (2006) surveyed three groups of mothers – those who stayed at home with their children full-time, those who were employed part-time, and those who worked full-time. Unlike the women we interviewed, there was no requirement that any of these women be employed in top-level positions. They found that each group defined the role of being a mother somewhat differently. For mothers who stayed at home full-time, being available to their children at all times was a critical defining characteristic of being a good mother. Not surprisingly, the mothers in the employed groups did not define good mothers as being constantly available. The mothers who were employed (both part-time and full-time) reframed their idea of a good mother as someone who is highly involved with her children, but they did not believe that being available "24/7" was important.

The highly successful women we interviewed also redefined what it means to be a good mother, much along the same lines as the employed mothers in Johnston and Swanson's (2006) study. They described how they managed to care for children and work in extremely demanding jobs. The high-achieving women did all of the traditional activities that other mothers do with their children, but they had help with those activities that they believed to be less important for the development of their children. They explained that mothering is still about spending time together, doing everyday things together, and communicating love through your actions. They told us that their children always felt that their parents loved them even when they went to work and made other care arrangements.

Andrea van de Kamp, a philanthropist from the United States and Chair of Sotheby's west coast business activities, explained how she did it:

"I had a housekeeper. She lived in at the time, and that was hard for me. On the other hand, when I see our daughter today, she's independent, she's beautiful, she's very much her own person. She understood when I said, 'Gee, I can't do that.' She got it. But when she was growing up, anything that was major, I always made sure I was there for it. I think in her entire childhood, when I think about everything that was important to her, I missed one event. I was at every important event except for one. It's very important to be part of your child's life. [*So what would you consider as the important events?*] I think it's very important to tuck them in at night. We did not have every meal, every dinner together, but we had three or four full meals a week together when she was little. We would discuss her school work, and whatever she was working on. And then, I had a gal that was helping us out at home who also had little children and she was with Diana, my daughter, almost like a sister, so that she had other little children around her when she was growing up."

The common theme of "being there" for important events, which include tucking children in bed at night and eating meals together, is repeated by many of the other women at the top.

Jenny Ming, President of the US corporation Old Navy/Gap, also made sure that she ate most meals with her children. During the interview, Fanny commented that the emphasis on meals might be a Chinese or Chinese-American custom. Jenny replied:

"To me, this is the time that the family comes together. It is an important time to listen to what your kids have to say about their day. And, eating dinner together is very important to me. My family would not eat dinner without me. Sometimes I'd say, 'Mommy's running late. Have dinner first.' They'd say, 'No, no, we'll wait for you; we're not hungry.' So, even with a busy schedule, to me, eating together is something that we never gave up. But, if my kids had a really important event that happened to them at school, they knew they could pick up the phone right away and call me; they didn't have to wait until dinner to tell me about it. So I think the accessibility makes you feel like your mom is available even though she might physically not be there."

Jenny's comments show how she redefined mothering so that she could conform to her own definition of "good mother." As long as her children knew that she was accessible at any time, and they had meals together, she did not have to be physically present with them all day. Many of the women talked about having private phone lines that were only available for children and other family members, so they could always be reached and their family knew they were always "there," even when "there" sometimes meant available to talk on the phone.

Helena Ashby, one of the first women to achieve the post of Chief in the history of the Los Angeles County Sheriff's Department, makes a similar point, but with a different example. She told us how she managed to be a loving mother while she was working her way through promotions in the police department:

"When I worked there, we had to work different shifts [hours varied so that sometimes she had a day shift, other times a night shift], we had to work when other people have time off in order to have enough police working on each shift. There were other women working in the police department who didn't have families like mine. They didn't need to arrange their schedules so they could spend time with their kids. We all had to work some undesirable shifts. My kids didn't miss me when I worked on Christmas. I worked right down the street, and they had my mother, my sister, my husband, my brother, my cousins, to celebrate Christmas with – it was a family kind of thing. We always managed because we were a child-centered family, which meant that my husband and I never did a lot of other social things that didn't include our son. For every vacation we had up until he was 17 years old, he went too. One time we were going to the Bahamas. He had graduated from high school at 16, so he was attending a community college when we were planning a vacation in the Bahamas. We talked to him about what we would do, 'And then we're gonna . . . ' And he says, 'I'm not going; I'm busy.' We were kind of in shock. All these years, and we're spending this vacation by ourselves? And so as a family, the time we had, we spent together."

Sophie Leung, a Member of Hong Kong's Legislative Council, shared her parenting concerns and behaviors:

"I seldom worried about my children's schoolwork. Instead of concerning myself with academic results, I am more concerned about whether the children understand things, are bright and think critically about certain issues. I always pick some surrounding issues to discuss with them. Once my eldest daughter (aged 11–12) asked me why I did not behave like her friend's mother who stayed home to spend more time with her children and focused her life on her family. I turned her question around to discuss with her which type of woman she wanted to be in the future. After one year, my daughter responded that she wanted to be like me. Children may not be able to think through such sophisticated issues. I discussed complex topics with them and stimulated their thinking so that they could learn to think analytically.

Once I encouraged my husband to go fishing after his illness. Our family then used to get up at 4 a.m. and go on the outing. We did it every Sunday for a long time, which was a simple pleasure for our whole family. We did many activities together. This habit ended when my children went abroad to study. Our relationship with our children is very close. When my children got older, I offered them the authority to help me make decisions about my life. For example, they might ask me why I am not home yet on Saturday. They ask it in a nice way, which shows their concern. I also ask for their opinions. My children's school teachers and principal questioned me about my decisions regarding how I spend my time. They asked why I keep so busy with my work and do not devote time to help my children with their homework and to take care of them. My answer was that I can make a little bit of difference to society. I can hire a high school student to tutor the children. But, if I could not satisfy my own aspirations, I would become impatient, therefore it would be damaging to my children for me to give up my career to be with them all the time."

Philamena Baird is a mother of three children and an active philanthropist in Houston. When the children were young, she was working in the hospitality industry with Benchmark Corporation as a director in their hotel and country club. She described how she combined her work with her children's activities:

"I lived and worked in the same community, three minutes from my office door. A hotel never sleeps; there's always something going on. Sometimes the demands of that job and the accessibility of me living right there on that property was a little overwhelming and often overlapped a great deal. I do know that as a family, we would celebrate holidays and birthdays at the club because I needed to be there. There were no 40-hour weeks. Given my work ethic and my family life, you did not leave until the task was done. I don't know if I ever felt like it was denying a relationship with my children because we always made sure that we did something together. We did something else that signaled if this was going to be a busy week. We had a system. We started when the kids were in junior high because of homework, after school activities, golf or other sports, all those kinds of things in which the children would be involved. We would announce to everyone in the family that I am in a great place or I am having a tough time. You would put up a red flag as a type of communication, which enabled me to meet the children's needs and schedule and to maintain my responsibilities and understand how the day or week was going."

Philamena reflected on her pride about how her children have turned out as adults:

"It was just an extraordinary feeling. When they all were sitting around the table, I'm looking around and I think, 'They are so independent – politically, religiously, and in their choice of lifestyles. How can that happen with them all being from one family?' I sincerely believe that learning good communication skills early in life helped contribute to their self-confidence and their understanding of the need to respect each other.

Ophelia Cheung, the first Executive Director of Consumer Council, with a long list of achievements, including owning her own political consultancy firm in Hong Kong, explained:

"As my children were growing up, my work also became busier. Fortunately, my mother's maid and the maid's niece were loyal and reliable. They came to help me do the housework and take care of my children without pay. However, I feel that I have missed something from my role as a mother. During that time, I was the District Officer for both the Central and Wanchai districts in Hong Kong, but only received 1.5 of the usual District Officer's salary. I had to attend official functions for over 400 organizations in a year, so I might have to attend three to four functions a day, and evening functions were nearly a must. I always had to juggle time: I got up very early to take the children to school before going to work; then I returned home at around 5 p.m., bathed the children and watched them have dinner before going out in the evening for official functions. Women have a harder life than men. When my daughters were 4 years old, I took them along to attend official functions on weekends so I could keep them close by. My colleagues would help me take care of them. Besides, they would participate in my work, such as joining my media activities at the Consumer Council, which increased their exposure and educated them. Moreover, they could understand that I was out for work instead of having fun. They attended boarding school in the UK in their secondary years. However, when they came home to Hong Kong, they also came to listen to my public speeches and participated in my projects.

My daughters are grown up now. One daughter is married and has a son and a daughter. Recently, I asked them whether they missed out something in childhood when I was so busy at work; which I feel guilty about. They responded that maids could take up daily household activities; however, they could look up to me as a role model and ask me for guidance and advice. Now, both of them are professionals and do very well in their careers. Everyone has his or her own role in life. I told them it would be perfectly fine if they decided that they mainly wanted to take care of their families instead of working outside the home; however, they both chose to become professionals."

There are consistent themes that run through these stories. The women created caring and loving homes for their children and were comfortable with having others provide care when they were at work. Even missing Christmas was not seen as a problem for the children because the children were surrounded by loving family members. They are all pleased with the people their children have become as adults. Although there is some regret about missed times when they could have been together, the women believe that they made the right choice about leaving less important activities for others to do, but making sure that they were actively involved in their children's lives and present at the important events.

## Stereotypical Mothering

Despite the living evidence provided by our sample of women at the top of their professions, there are many people who believe that it is not possible to both be a good mother and have a demanding high-level career. When Sylvia Ann Hewlett (2002) studied high-achieving women without children, she found that most of these women did not make a conscious choice to remain childless. It was more that they postponed their plans for children until it was too late – either because it became biologically difficult or impossible, or because they had been promoted into positions at work that demanded extraordinary time and effort and they believed it would be impossible to fill both roles. They were passively waiting for the right time to become a mother, and that right time never happened.

It is not surprising that relatively few women with children are found in highly demanding careers. Both one's family and high-level profession are greedy. Even when women love their children and their work, it is difficult to "do" both. But as these women show us, it is not impossible to be dually successful.

There is probably no event that is more life-changing than becoming a parent. There is the realization that your life is no longer entirely your own. Something as simple as going to the dentist or joining a

**Figure 5.2** *Source*: Universal Press Syndicate, Kansas City, MO

friend at a movie has to be planned in advance when a woman becomes a mother. An infant or young child has to be prepared for an outing that needs to take into account nap cycles, diapers, and feedings (movies and many other activities are totally out) or involves finding someone you trust to care for your child in your absence. If you add to the usual difficulties of being a parent the constant chorus of naysayers and critics when mothers also achieve high-level positions, even confident women can become self-doubters.

## Hitting the Maternal Wall and How to Bounce Back

If women, in general, bump their heads on a glass ceiling that prevents them from advancing to the highest levels in their careers, then mothers run smack-dab into a wall – a maternal wall. The term was coined by Joan Williams (2000), director of the Center for Work Life Law at University of California, Hastings School of Law. She uses the term "maternal wall" to describe what happened in over 600 cases of workplace discrimination against women (and men) with family care responsibilities. Most of these discrimination cases were against mothers, with the remainder against men and women who need to care for other family members (which could include an ill parent, sibling, or spouse). The result of these discrimination cases is that large financial settlements are being paid by companies in the US which have used stereotypes about mothers to discriminate against them. The law in the US is now recognizing what have been called "implicit stereotypes" and the way in which these automatic biases and beliefs work against women's success. Williams recommends that we use the term "unexamined stereotypes" instead of "implicit" or "unconscious" stereotypes because the latter terms suggest that employers could not be held liable for their actions because the discriminatory actions are caused by beliefs that are unconscious, and so employers could not guard against them. The term "unexamined stereotypes" makes it easier to prosecute employers for discriminatory actions.

Williams documented the legal consequences of the stereotypes about women, mothers, and workers that we have been discussing throughout this book. For example, in one case, an employer was found guilty of "prescriptive stereotyping," which is the use of stereotypes to decide how people should act and what they should do based on their group membership, such as being a mother. In a case of alleged discrimination during the academic tenure process, a member of the committee that grants tenure told a professor to "stop worrying about tenure – just go home and have more babies" (Williams, 2000). In another case, Williams documented "attribution bias," which is a bias in the way behaviors are attributed or explained. For example, when a man is absent from work, his employer might assume that he is presenting a professional paper, but when a mother is absent, it is assumed that she is at home caring for her children. The third bias Williams identified is the "leniency bias," in which mothers are required to work longer hours and are held to higher standards at work because they have to prove themselves as dedicated employees. Standards for others are far more lenient.

Overwhelmingly, mothers are rated as nice, but incompetent. It is as though becoming a mother makes a woman stupid. In an experimental investigation of hypothetical candidates applying for a promotion, two different samples rated the one who was a mother as less competent than the father candidate or those without children (Heilman & Okimoto, 2008). The authors of this study concluded that "motherhood can hinder the career advancement of women" (p. 189). Other researchers agreed that, "relative to other kinds of applicants, mothers were rated as less competent, less committed, less suitable for hire, promotion, and management training, and deserving of lower salaries" (Corell & Benard, 2005).

When groups of people from different walks of life were described on a variety of dimensions and these data were then analyzed in a way that clusters similar groups, senior citizens, the disabled, the unemployed, and housewives were grouped together (Eckes, 2002). This "cluster" was rated high on "warmth" and low on "competence." This dual rating has been replicated many times and is a central component of what is known as "ambivalent prejudice." Unlike older forms of prejudice in which groups were merely good or bad, the new form allows for both positive and negative aspects to be attributed to a group. It is a fact that women face job discrimination (see Halpern, Benbow, Geary, Gur, Hyde, & Gernsbacher, 2007, for a discussion regarding job discrimination against women), yet they are also rated high on traits like "being nice." These dual ratings confirm a separation between being warm and being competent. Thus, housewives are perceived as being similar to the most stigmatized groups in the US (the elderly, disabled, and unemployed) because of their perceived incompetence.

As these data show, there are strong negative stereotypes about housewives (who are perceived as being high on warmth and low on competence) and working mothers (who are perceived as being low on warmth and high on competence). There are also negative stereotypes about women who decide not to have children. Adult women cannot avoid being negatively stereotyped, regardless of their decisions regarding children and work. Williams suggests that mothers and other caregivers be trained to understand their rights as an important way of fighting back against illegal practices, and as a way of putting a door in the maternal wall so that women can pass through on their way to positions at the top.

Laura Cha, a Member of Hong Kong's Executive Council, is one of the few women in our group of high-achieving mothers who returned to the workforce after a "stop-out" period during which she was a full-time mother and housewife. Her comments reflect the research findings perfectly:

"In the 1970s, during the era of women's liberation, I was very distressed. All my friends were professional women, but I was a stay-at-home housewife and mother. I had doubts about marrying so early and having children. It affected my self-esteem. The social norm at that time was that being a housewife is equal to a lack of ability. Because of the lack of social recognition for stay-home mothers, it did affect how I looked at myself. Even though it was a transient period, how society looks at you affects you. Society in general did not respect the housewife role very much. I waited until the children were 6 (elder) and 3 (younger) years old before I went back to law school (at University of Santa Clara). That worked out well. . . . Even though a lawyer's job was very competitive and tough, I was happy. My children understood my work when they were growing up; I talked to them about their work as well as my work. My work was very much part of our family life. They knew what I was doing. My children could see my growth in work, and I could see my children's growth physically. Therefore, I thought the timing was good, as I could take care of them when they were young."

The notion that mothers are held to a higher standard can be seen in the very public example of Katie Couric, a high-paid news anchor in the US. It was front-page news when she moved from her popular morning news program to become the first woman to anchor the evening news for a major network. Would she be up to this job, which had always previously gone to a man?

Katie Couric is a widow with two daughters. In a test of how well she would handle the position of being an anchor on the evening news, she was asked if she would go into a war zone to cover the news. Can you guess what she said? Couric replied, "I think the situation there is so dangerous, and as a single parent with two children, that's something I won't be doing" (Warner, 2006). Notice that she talked about being a single parent, not a mother. She later added that she would respond on a case-by-case basis to requests like this one. This would have been a good response from a single father as well. It tells the world that family is of primary importance and when a job makes unreasonable demands, like going into an active war zone, the needs and concerns of your children are important in determining whether you will go. We don't know how many people read this response as a sign of weakness, but we saw it as a strong statement about the roles of work and parenthood.

## The Motherhood Wage Gap

As we learned earlier, a significant proportion of people believe that mothers deserve lower pay than childless women and men. Guess what? Mothers actually do get less pay. In a study designed to find out why mothers earn less than women who are not mothers and men in general, Corell and Benard (2005) used a common research paradigm. They prepared two equivalent résumés in which both candidates were comparable in their ability to perform the job for which they applied. The résumés were then varied so that one of them had a memo attached to it saying that the candidate was the mother of two children; the other résumé did not mention children. There was also a parallel set of résumés for men, which either identified the men as fathers, or did not mention children. Can you guess the effect of this simple manipulation on decisions about hiring? As expected, it did not matter for the men whether or not they had children, but it did for the women. The childless woman was 3.5 times more likely to be recommended to be hired than the comparable woman applicant with children.

The suggested starting salaries also differed for women and men and for mothers and fathers in this study of résumés (Corell & Benard, 2005). For the men, fathers were offered approximately $152,000, compared with $148,000 for men without children. The fatherhood bonus may have been justified by the idea that they need to earn a "family wage." The childless women were offered approximately $151,000, which was 7.9 percent more than the $139,000 offered to mothers. The discrimination against mothers in hiring and wages is clearly seen in this study. Given the stereotype that mothers are incompetent, it is not surprising that fewer mothers would be offered a job or that, when salaries are determined, they are offered a lower salary.

There are several different studies which show essentially the same pattern, with the wage gap between men and women narrowing in general, and the gap between working women without children and working mothers increasing. Waldfogel (1998) explained that by "1991, the pay gap between mothers and non-mothers had become larger than the gap between women and men" (p. 148). The motherhood wage gap persists "even after controlling for differences in education, work experience, and full-time and part-time work experience" (p. 149). The difference between women without children and mothers is greatest for single mothers, a group that is most in need of better pay. They can expect the double whammy of a single-paycheck home in which the paycheck is smaller than that received when comparable work is done by married mothers or women without children.

These data showing the biases against mothers in the workplace make the success of the women whose stories we are telling even more impressive. They managed to convince the decision makers in their profession that they were the best person for the job in each of their varied and high-powered careers.

## Is Being a Working Mother Bad for Your Kids?

There is an explicit assumption that maternal employment must be detrimental to children because it takes the mother away from her child. Of course, this also assumes that constant access to one's mother is important for healthy development. Contrary to predictions, maternal employment per se is not related to child outcomes

(Gottfried and Gottfried, 2008). It is far too simplistic to study the effects of whether a mother is employed or not employed, searching for relevant developmental effects on the children. Human development is much more complicated and child outcomes depend on family circumstances, especially the quality of childcare, the home environment, and marital status. Inconsistent employment (with instability and transition being negative factors) is also important, but all of the high-achieving women had fairly consistent employment patterns, so employment instability is not relevant to this group.

There have been many studies of the effects of maternal employment on children. We know that working parents – mothers and fathers – are not detrimental to children. On the other hand, poverty, which is associated with unemployment, is harmful to children. In a study of the effect of income on the development of young children, the authors conclude that poor families cannot provide their children with the kinds of environments that promote cognitive development, and that the stress of poverty is linked to parenting behaviors that increase the probability of behavior problems in children (Yeung, Linver, & Brooks-Gunn, 2002). The broader message is clear, especially for mothers who are working their way up from the bottom or near bottom of the employment hierarchy, where the benefits of additional income are more likely to make a real difference in the lives of the children and their parents.

A major problem faced by women who are not yet at the top or cannot even see past the midway mark is the difficulty in finding affordable, high-quality childcare. It is abundantly clear that if we do not solve the crisis in childcare, the number of women with children at the top of their profession will remain low.

## The Kids are Fine

Working mothers (and fathers) really can relax. With the majority of mothers of young children in the workforce, parents can rest assured that children can develop equally well regardless of the employment status of their parents. What is important is a consistent and loving home life. As our interviewees told us, caring parents sacrifice their own personal time and find ways to adapt their schedules and their own needs to attend to their children's needs (Gottfried, Gottfried, & Bathurst, 2002).

**Working couple Phil and Liz Plethcart had
perfected the art of the 6 p.m. hand-off.**

**Figure 5.3** *Source*: Universal Press Syndicate, Kansas City, MO

Despite the overwhelming majority of evidence, occasionally there is a report in the literature documenting some negative effect of maternal employment. For example, there were two different studies which examined the effect of working mothers on children which used the same large data set from the US National Institute for Child Health and Development. One study found no negative effects, and sizable positive effects when low-income children attend early childhood education centers. The other study examined a variety of outcomes at different ages and found a slight negative effect at one age (3 years old) for one type of outcome (verbal development). A third study was then conducted to resolve the inconsistencies.

The inconsistencies were due to somewhat technical statistical analyses, but the authors of the third study concluded that there were no negative effects of having an employed mother, and warned against drawing conclusions from any single study (Burchinal & Clarke-Stewart, 2007). In the meantime, newspaper headlines scared many parents with the news that they were harming their 3-year-olds. It is no wonder that so many mothers feel overwhelmed with guilt given the tendency to blame them for nonexistent negative outcomes.

There has also been well-publicized research which reported a connection between nonmaternal day-care and children's negative behavior (Belsky, 2001). Despite a few lone studies, the vast majority of children are doing fine, and most research shows that having a working mother has positive outcomes for children, including increased academic achievement and fewer behavior problems, especially when the mother wants to work and has sufficient support at home and at work.

It is also clear from the research that the quality of early childcare is important, but "good parenting matters more" (Belsky, Vandell, Burchinal, Clarke-Stewart, McCartney, & Owen, 2007). Having loving and caring parents is the most important variable in determining positive child outcomes, but good quality childcare is also important. Children with good childcare start kindergarten with higher vocabulary skills which provide a solid foundation for learning. The problem of poor quality childcare is greater for families with low incomes than for women who are moving up the career ladder and are likely to have sufficient income and knowledge to get good care for their children.

There is an emerging consensus that the effects of maternal employment are more likely to be negative when the caretaking parent's (usually the mother) work schedule is erratic and unpredictable, the hours are long, and she faces other significant stressors such as poor health, poverty, and little control over work-related events. It is the combination of poor parenting and poor childcare that is detrimental to children. But this finding should hardly surprise anyone. Poor care is bad for children, and a double dose of poor care is especially bad. These problems are most likely to be found in low-income and low-functioning families with little support. Quality interplay among childcare, work, family, and society leads to positive long-term gains for children (Marshall, 2004).

Instead of being apologetic for employed mothers, we can acknowledge the positive outcomes they provide. This can be done without denigrating those mothers who choose to stay at home with their children, or make different choices at different stages of their life. There is no single best life choice for all people, and, in reality, most adults do not have much choice about whether or not to work for pay because, despite the positive benefits of paid employment such as enhanced self-esteem and reduced depression (Barnett & Hyde, 2001), most adults in fact work to pay for rent, food, insurance, and other necessities. The media talk-show hosts who would have us believe that the poor children of working mothers are deeply scarred from years of neglect are wrong. Although we have included only a small sample of the research on this critical contemporary issue, it is clear that the kids are doing fine. Any society that cares about the welfare of its children will make quality childcare available and affordable for all children and families. At the same time, we need to be careful not to stigmatize mothers who stay at home with their children, and respect individual choices about lifestyles and family arrangements.

## The Super Mommy Syndrome

The "Super Mommy Syndrome" requires mothers to put on home-made birthday parties with mommy-baked cakes, teach their babies to use sign language and speak French (everywhere except in France) before their first birthday, and engage in other upper-crust mothering activities which can create more stress than executive-level employment. The terms used for this new trend in mothering are "competitive mothering" or "intensive mothering," both of which imply that there is a pressure to "mother more" or "harder" so that your child can succeed at a young age. The powerful women leaders who made it to the top of their profession avoided the ridiculous and excessive demands of competitive mothering. It may seem obvious that, since more mothers are employed full-time, children are "getting the short end of the stick" and spending less time with their over-busy parents. It may seem that way, but the data across several different studies show that it just isn't so.

Parents are spending more time with their children than their own parents spent with them. Through the use of "time use diaries," researchers have found that in two-parent families, children are spending more time with their parents compared with children one and two generations ago (Gauthier, Smeeding, & Furstenberg, 2004). These results are similar across several industrialized countries. Most of the increase in time spent with children is in categories where parents interact with them in activities such as playing. These data support the idea that children are increasingly central to the lives of their parents, and doomsday predictions about ignoring children do not hold up when the data are analyzed across family types and in many countries.

## Mothers as Role Models

The outstanding women whom we interviewed consistently talked about the importance of their work as providing a role model for their children. They saw this as a critical component of the definition of a "good mother." They believed that their children learned about the possible worlds where they could be successful by watching the actions and successes of their mother.

Doreen Woo Ho, President of Wells Fargo Consumer Credit Group, the highest-ranking Asian-American woman among the top five banks in the US, received similar appreciation from her daughter: "My second daughter, who's now in college, said this to me when she was in high school: 'I'm really proud of you mom; you're really a role model for me.' So she gave me this validation by saying she can really respect what I do."

It is clear that these women believe that their success at work shows their children that everyone can have meaningful work and that it is an important dimension of a full life. The children are learning that they do not have to feel guilty or apologize when they pursue their own careers, and that they can fulfill their career aspirations and have close families, without choosing between the two. Women's real-life success is good for their families.

## Childcare and Back-up Childcare

Mothers with high-powered careers know the critical importance of having high-quality childcare and back-up care so that they are not "grounded" by unexpected childcare needs. Dependable childcare is an absolute need for any parent who needs to maintain a professional career while ensuring that their children are always in good hands.

As described in Chapter 3, Margaret York, one of the first women to achieve the level of Chief of Police for a major world city, had a difficult time when she was going through the police academy. She would take care of all her children's needs and would only try to study after they went to bed. Despite careful plans for her children, the struggles, worries, and guilt can be felt from her words. She explains how she handled last-minute sicknesses and other unexpected changes in childcare arrangements. The nature of the demands on a rising police officer caused her to worry about the effect her work had on her children:

"For the most part I had a very good support system, and that was the children's grandparents. My ex-husband's parents were retired when the children were young, so it was more convenient for them to take care of a sick child than it was for my parents who were still working at the time. My ex-husband's parents lived in the area, so help was nearby. Without a support system it's very hard to handle the last-minute problems that arise with children. At one point, when they were teenagers, I was a homicide detective. As you might expect, homicide detectives get called out when there's a homicide. So if there was a murder in the middle of the night, I would get a call and I would have to go to the scene to conduct an investigation. My children had to become self-reliant because sometimes I wasn't going to be there in the morning when they had to get up. When this happened, they would have to get themselves up, dressed, fed and to school by themselves.

When the children were teenagers, they were taking care of themselves. Even though it caused them to be very self-reliant, I had terrible guilt and regret about not being there all the time for them. It could be the evening hours that I was investigating a murder. So they would have to get themselves dinner and baths and finish their homework on their own. They were big kids; they were teenagers at that time. But I still have regrets. I said to one of my sons recently (my sons are now in their forties), 'You know, I really regret that I wasn't a better mother. I really wish that I had been able to do things a little differently.' And his response was, 'Oh, mom, stop it!' You know, 'We did just fine; don't worry about it.' I worried about it all the time. I would be at my job, and I would worry, worry, worry."

We note that, like most of the women we interviewed in the US, Hong Kong and China, Margaret concludes her tales with how well her children have turned out and how grateful the children are for having a mother who achieved as much as these women did. We subtitled this chapter about children, "tales of guilt and pride," because those are two dominant themes we found in these women's narratives. Although we do not know, we suspect that the same two themes would emerge from the stories of women who did not work outside the home. Guilt seems to be inherent in the mother role because no one can live up to the unrealistic standards of the ideal mother and, whatever life choices we make for ourselves, there are always some options that we did not select and so maybe we deprived our children of other lives – the ones they would have lived if we had made different life choices for ourselves.

## Planning for Children: Timing and Age

We do not know how many of the large number of women in top-level positions who do not have children really wanted them, and how many remained childless by choice. There is a well known cartoon in the US in which a woman exclaims, "Oh no, I forgot to have children." It is difficult for us to understand the humor in this cartoon. Perhaps it is so popular because people can read many meanings into it. It has become a slogan for many "childfree by choice" groups. The decision whether or not to have children is a personal one, although, regardless of what you decide, you are likely to get lots of advice from people who agree and do not agree with your choice. If you want to have children, you need to plan for them because the unpleasant reality is that the ticking of a woman's biological clock is real. Despite glossy magazine covers with mothers in their fifties, the reality is that fertility declines with age, and pregnancy for anyone over the age of 35 is considered high-risk. So, anyone who might want two children should be working on getting pregnant by the age of 30 to allow extra time to have the second child before the risk gets high.

We also remind everyone that there are at least half a million children in the US who need adoptive homes. Most of these children are older, part of a sibling group, or have special physical or psychological needs, but they all need a loving family. There are more young children available for adoption in other parts of the world, so there are many ways to bring children into your life.

## Some Unpleasant Truths About
### Caring for Children

One very gutsy newspaper reporter received a firestorm of criticism when she dared to write, "Sorry, but my children bore me to death" (Kirwan-Taylor, 2006). She admitted that she dearly loved her children, but she broke a societal taboo by publicly writing that being at home with her children was, in fact, boring. The idea that much of childcare is tedious was not well received by the public who responded to her article. They immediately began blogging about this selfish woman. It is interesting to compare the comments of this mother, who was able to capture widespread attention and condemnation by writing about her feelings in a newspaper, with the research findings of a distinguished team of scientists who published their work in the journal *Science*, which is among the most prestigious scientific publications in the world.

Daniel Kahneman, a US psychologist who won the Nobel Prize in economics for his work on decision making, turned his expertise to studying the daily experiences of men and women. He and his colleagues (Kahneman, Krueger, Schkade, Schwarz, & Stone, 2004) had a large sample of people fill out forms in which they documented how much time they spent on various activities throughout the day and how they felt about those activities. Close to 1,000 people reported about a working day. Each activity was rated both for how positive it was and how negative it was. They found that "having intimate relations" was both the most positive and least negative activity that people engaged in on a typical workday. What is interesting is where "taking care of my children" ranked on this list. Actually it was fairly low, coming out ahead of using the computer, doing housework, working, and commuting, but below a much longer list of activities that included socializing, relaxing, eating, watching TV, preparing food, and napping. One possible reason for the low ranking of "caring for children" is that when people think about being with children they are thinking more generally about the importance of children in their lives, but when they are rating individual interactions, the daily interactions apparently are not as positive as the global picture. In any case, there are multiple sources of data that suggest that the day-to-day care of children is less enjoyable than many other activities.

## Casualties in the Mommy Wars

The issues related to the intersection of work and childcare are not new. The idea of a full-time at-home mother whose primary job is to care for the children has been prevalent only during a short blip in human history (Coontz, 2000). Poor mothers always worked and rich mothers always had nannies. At other times in history, all women had heavy work to perform just to get through the daily chores of living such as cooking a meal, growing vegetables, or tending farm animals. The idea of mothers with substantial work commitments only sounds new, but a look at the lives of our great-grandmothers and their mothers will show us that there is a long history of mothers who worked very hard. The nature of their work differed from that of our high-achieving women, but the time and effort required was often commensurate with the 60- to 80-hour work week. The good mothers in earlier times always combined work and family and they did it without apology for their work commitments.

Although the outstanding women we interviewed all believe that combining work and mothering was the right choice, there is still enough guilt, at least for some of these high-achieving women, to suggest that we have a long way to go before mothers can create dually successful lives filled with loving families and responsible, high-level work without the added burden of guilt.

# Chapter 6

# Work–Family Spillover: From Conflict to Harmony

Have you ever known anyone who had a bad day at work and then came home and "took it out" on her spouse or kids? This is an example of negative work-to-family spillover – something happened at work that had a negative effect on the family. But there are many other kinds of relationships among the multiple ways work and family and attitudes and behaviors can combine. When the things you do at work make you a more interesting person at home or provide you with skills to deal with issues at home, the work-to-home spillover is positive. Positive spillover is sometimes called enhancement or enrichment because the emotions or activity in one role (mother or worker) strengthen the quality of the other role. Spillover also flows from home to work. The usual assumption is that children are incompatible with high-level success at work, but this assumption ignores the refuge provided by a loving family and how children can provide positive home-to-work spillover. Of course, negative home-to-work spillover also occurs, such as when a problem at home interferes with work.

Sometimes there are direct conflicts between the demands of family and work. One of the most frequent types of conflict for high-achieving mothers is time conflicts. What happens when a working mother has to be at a meeting at work and her child has a doctor's appointment at the same time? The answer, of course, is that it depends on the specifics, such as whether the doctor's appointment is for a well-child check-up or for an illness, how important the meeting is, and what can be changed and rearranged.

Unreliable childcare is a cause of much stress for most working mothers. One way in which these high-achieving mothers handle the problem of childcare is by planning for reliable care. The solution may sound obvious, but it is often difficult to find high-quality child-care. The additional income that comes with high-level careers allows these women to "buy out of" much of the stress that mothers in lower-level jobs encounter on a regular basis. High-achieving women are better able to pay someone to clean their home and provide reliable child or elder care. But, time conflicts still occur because there are some events where mothers need and want to be with their family, which may clash with times when they need and want to be at work. As with all such conflicts, choices are made which lead to a resolution. Most of these women said that their families always came first, but it is important to interpret "first" as a position that was decided upon after considering the circumstances.

Greeting her women friends as we walked to our lunch table at the Los Angeles Club, which is a private dining club in the downtown business area of Los Angeles, Andrea van de Kamp told them that we were doing an interview on work–family balance. They burst into a roar of laughter and teased her that this term must be a joke for all of them. Is it possible for women to have work–family balance?

## Beyond Work–Family Balance

What do we know about work–family balance? Are career women carrying a double burden? The balance metaphor includes the idea that any gain to one side necessarily means a loss to the other, which is one reason why some writers have suggested that we replace the balance metaphor with one that allows for integration or benefits on both sides of the scale (Halpern & Murphy, 2005). Do women with the demands of a high-level career have to give up family in order to achieve success at work? Are they more stressed out than women who stay at home? Anyone who has spent much time with children will laugh at the idea that caring for children all day is not stressful. In considering the lives and choices of highly successful women, we also need to remember that mothers who have made different choices also face their own array of stressors. Staying at home with children is stressful. The work is hard, stay-at-home moms often feel isolated, and their work is often denigrated as being unimportant.

The top women leaders we interviewed show that their overly-full lives are not necessarily more stressful than the lives of other mothers. Do they have to give up family in order to achieve success at work?

Are they more stressed out than women who stay at home? The women we interviewed show that it is not necessarily so. They may be considered atypical, but recent research also concurs. Paid employment does not have a negative effect on women's health. It may even have beneficial effects on women who have positive attitudes toward their employment (Repetti, Matthews, & Waldron, 1989; Tang, Lee, Tang, Cheung, & Chan, 2002; Warr & Parry, 1982). A lot depends on the individual's attributes and the quality of the work role and the family role.

There has been a vast literature on work–family balance dating back to the pioneering study of interrole conflict and work stress by Robert Kahn and his colleagues in the 1960s (Kahn, Wolfe, Quinn, Snoek, & Rosenthal, 1964). Rhona and Robert Rapoport (1971) raised the concern about work–personal life conflict in dual-career families in Britain. Work–family balance was originally conceptualized in terms of the presence or absence of conflict, with the issue framed from the perspective of the negative condition with work interfering with family or family interfering with work (Frone, Russell, & Cooper, 1992). These conflicts occur when there is a scarcity of time, or when the strain or the behaviors of one role make it difficult to fulfill the requirements of the other role (Greenhaus & Beutell, 1985).

Many studies have focused on women as increasing numbers break out of their traditional role in the family domain to enter the workforce, giving rise to the prevalence of dual-career families. Work and family used to be seen as separate domains, as this segregation was the typical mode of work for middle-class American males. When these boundaries are crossed, there are spillovers from one domain to the other. Early researchers assumed that work and family roles were incompatible and that conflict must ensue from having multiple roles. These studies looked at the antecedents of work–family conflicts deriving from time spent, role overload, stress and support received in each domain and how they affect the satisfaction in the other domain (Byron, 2005). Job stress, job involvement, lack of work support, and long work hours were related to work-interference-with-family conflict, which in turn was associated with poorer job satisfaction, family satisfaction and life satisfaction, higher turnover, and stress-related illness. On the other hand, family stress, family conflict, family hours and lack of family support were related to family-to-work conflict, which in turn spilled over to job satisfaction. Most of the research that used this paradigm found that there was a stronger spillover from work to family than the other way round (Allen, Herst, Bruck, & Sutton, 2000; Ford, Heinen, & Langkamer, 2007).

Recent theoretical models have taken a more balanced view and consider more complex interactions between the work and family domains, which include both negative and positive spillovers in the work–family interface. Work–family balance is not just the lack of conflict. Michael Frone (2003) articulated a two-dimensional model of work–family interface which includes the direction of influence (work to family or family to work) and the type of effect (conflict or facilitation). In addition to highlighting the interference between work and family, the positive outcome of mutual facilitation or enhancement between the work and family domains is beginning to be recognized. It is interesting to note the way in which assumptions about the negative effects of working and caring for a family have (mostly) blinded researchers to the possibility that, in fact, they may combine in positive ways.

## Alternatives to Conflict

In their book, *Beyond Work–Family Balance*, Rhona Rapoport, Lotte Bailyn, Joyce Fletcher, and Bettye Pruitt (2002) argued that the concept of work–family balance is outmoded. They show that the new approach of work–family life integration can promote a more equitable and effective workplace. Stewart Friedman and Jeffrey Greenhaus (2000) raised the overarching question in the title of their book, *Work and Family – Allies or Enemies?* They concluded that time spent working per se is not the problem. Rather, it is the "intense absorption in work that intrudes into the quality of family life" (p. 138). They found that for both men and women, when work and family are not integrated, preoccupation with work coupled with lack of involvement with the family results in dissatisfaction. On the other hand, when work and family are integrated, the two roles can enhance each other. To integrate the two roles, managing role boundaries is more important than just reducing time at work.

From their meta-analysis which reviewed 178 studies on work–family interface, Michael Ford and his associates (2007) found that support from family and work domains is positively related to cross-domain satisfaction. The experiences, skills, and opportunities gained in one domain can enhance participation in the other domain, thereby promoting greater integration of work and family. For example, women often say they excel in multitasking at work because that is what they do all the time at home. The expertise and network they accumulate at work also expand their personal skills in taking care of their home. They become more resourceful in selecting the products they want to buy or in getting advice on decisions they have to make in their family's affairs. The support they receive in one domain frees up necessary time and material resources for them to be fully engaged in the other domain.

A study using two national surveys in the US showed that women reported a higher level of positive spillover from work to family than did men (Grzywacz, Almeida, & McDonald, 2002). Ni Zhihua, Chairman of the Board of the Shanghai Sanmao Enterprise Company and Vice-Chairman and Party Deputy Secretary of the Board of Shanghai Textiles Holding Company, gave this succinct summary on the interlocking interface between work and family: "Family is a person's spiritual support; it supports you to realize your value to society."

For people working in family businesses, it may be easier to combine work and family. Work and family roles are closely interweaved, and at times indistinguishable. However, the boundaries of work and family could be enmeshed at times.

Zhang Xin is Chairman of the Board and Co-CEO of SOHO China, a real estate company in China listed on the stock exchange which is famous for its innovative architecture projects. Zhang Xin and her husband caught the golden opportunity of China's economic boom and started their company in Beijing after they got married. Before that she was an investment banker and he was a developer. She talked about how their work and family roles evolved:

"We decided to form a company together, so in addition to being husband and wife, we would become business partners. That was 10 years ago. I guess throughout the years, our roles developed to their own maturity. In the early days we had very little idea how to divide roles between us, so there was a lot of trial and error, and mistakes and quarrels. But as we progressed, we each found a niche that fit out characters, that fit our skills, and so now we are very much partners in an equal sense, in making decisions, but also very much separated in the role that we play in leading the company.

In the early days, I had a lot of discomfort, and so did he, in that I would expect him to play the role as more than a business partner, and much more like a husband. For instance, when I had difficulties, I would expect him to come in and give a helping hand; and when he didn't, I would feel terrible and think 'How could you do this, you just don't care about my feelings.' Or I would say something in front of people that he would feel was inappropriate, like me needing a husband and a man. How could I say this in front of people? So in the early days, there were a lot of mix-ups between the private roles and the business roles that we play. But as we progressed, we were able to come into the room and behave just like business partners, and it is nothing more than business partners that we expect from each other in this office or in the business environment. It actually takes years to develop this sensitivity. We're unique because we are business partners as well as husband and wife, so we are naturally woven between work and family."

Zhang Xin continued to describe how she integrated her children into her work life:

"My children are young, so they require a lot of my presence. I try to take only short trips, or when I have to make long trips, I always take them with me. Sometimes it is a little inconvenient, but all in all it works out. Like the May (Labor Day) holidays for instance. The children have two weeks of holiday and I needed to be in the US to speak at the Harvard China Review and then the Asia Society in New York. So I took them along. Some days we work and some days we play; I am so used to mixing all these trips together."

Zhang Xin's situation is unique. In the first place, her family business is very successful. But it is more due to her attitude toward family life that she insists on involving all members in it, including the children. It is also influenced by how she views her interrelated roles: "Both my family and my company are very close to my heart. It is part of seeing myself grow. In addition to my personal growth, it is also a family growth, a company growth. It is all quite interrelated now."

## Redefining Roles

Past research on work–family balance has concentrated on distinct roles and external factors such as time, demand, and stressors as predictors of outcomes in work–family balance. These external factors cannot explain why some people under similar conditions experience conflict while others do not. Increasingly, research is beginning to look at individual-level factors, such as the person's personality, attitudes, and style of coping, as well as the broader context of cultural influences. Michael Frone (2003) described the personal initiatives that individuals may take up to reduce work–family conflict. He summarizes three types of coping behavior:

> *Structural role redefinition* refers to attempts to alter external, structurally imposed expectations. Examples include eliminating role activities, negotiating a reduction in or modification of work hours, reallocating or sharing role tasks, and seeking out and fostering sources of social support. *Personal role redefinition* refers to attempts to alter one's internal conception of role demands. Examples include establishing priorities among role demands, ignoring role demands, changing one's attitude toward roles, and eliminating a role. Finally, *reactive role behavior* refers to attempts to meet all role demands. Examples include more efficient planning and scheduling and working harder and longer within each role. (Frone, 2003, p. 156)

## Structural Role Redefinition

We often hold fixed ideas without question about what we should do in order to conform to the roles prescribed by social norms. This is particularly true of women when they try to fulfill their roles as wife and mother. They have to perform all the tasks they believe a wife or mother should do and they hold themselves to the highest standards for all of the role-related tasks. They try to become supermoms or superwomen.

It did not take Jenny Ming, President of Old Navy/Gap, too long to realize that her family role could be redefined:

> "Very early on I learned that it's OK to have help. I think as women, we like to think we could do it all. I went through that myself when I first became a mother. At that time I was a buyer, and I was trying to balance traveling and spending time with my new daughter, and cleaning the house and so on. I wasn't able to do it. Then my husband said, 'Well, who said you have to do it all? Why don't you get a mother's helper to come in and help you? What about a high school student who could help you with cleaning the house a little bit. Or if

you want her to play with Kristin [our daughter], and you could clean. You know, nobody is putting that pressure on yourself except you.' I know he's here to help. It wasn't very expensive to have part-time help, even though we didn't have a lot of money at that time. So it was very workable having some help. I think she came in for four hours every Saturday morning, nine to one o'clock. And it was an incredible relief. I think that got me to understand that you don't have to do it all by yourself."

Likewise, there are times when we can, or have to, restructure our work roles.

Sue Schechter is a former Texas State Representative and Democratic Party Chair of Harris County in Texas. When she was in the Texas Congress, she had to stay in Austin most of the week when congress was in session, while her family stayed in Houston. She did not have good home help at that time:

"I was gone for those four years when I missed most of my children's activities. They were in third and fifth grade when I first ran. I quit I think when my daughter was in the eighth grade, and my son was between fifth and sixth. I've never been a very good balancer. And I'll never forget sitting one night in the lounge of the House with a female colleague. We were supporting each other over the fact that our children were just not doing well with us being gone all the time. Richard, my husband, traveled a lot. I had a housekeeper. And you know when your housekeeper calls you when you're sitting on the House floor at 11 o'clock at night and says, 'I just found your daughter. She crawled out the window and had gone down the street.' And I'm going, 'Where's Richard?' It's a terrible feeling because it's really letting someone else parent the children. So we were talking about that because she was having the same problems. And we were both lamenting about that. We both quit the same term; that was just it for us."

But Sue did not quit politics. After she returned to Houston, she ran for and became the Democratic Party Chair of Harris County. She is now a general political strategist and is actively involved in organizing campaigns for candidates and recruiting women into the office. At the time of our interview, she was also helping her husband's campaign for election to a public office. She decides how she can best fulfill her public role:

"I now realize that my time is my own. I don't have to give every minute of my time to anybody who asks. And that's why I would probably be different in public office now than when I was younger because then I didn't know how to say 'No.' It's like people owned you because you were a public servant. I'm learning now. And I spend a lot more time now devoting to a spiritual quest too as much as a professional one."

We often hold myths about how we can do a good job. Some people may think that working overtime and bringing work home will show their boss that they are good workers. Carrie Yau, the Permanent Secretary of the Hong Kong SAR government, in charge of Health and Food Hygiene, is unequivocal in debunking these beliefs:

"I seldom bring my work home because I think it is not a good habit. On one hand, it creates problems of confidentiality, and on the other hand, I find rest to be very important. I prefer to leave my office slightly later. From my earlier experience, I realize that bringing work home reinforces the tendency of slowing down the work. Therefore I prefer to make good use of my office time, e.g. reduce time on the phone or be focused on the agenda during meetings, and simplify the complicated issues. . . . Now my subordinates realize that their overtime work will not get my special recognition."

## Personal Role Redefinition

Our group of women leaders are very articulate about the way they alter their internal conception of role demands. They say that they can keep both careers and family roles, but they define these roles in ways that are meaningful and helpful to them.

Ma Yuan, former Deputy Chief Justice of the Chinese Supreme Court, aptly defines her family role: "Every one has a family and a relationship. If you cannot give more of your time, you have to give more of your affection and passion. You can grab some time to get together with your family members. You do not have to sacrifice your family to be successful in your career."

Ma Yuan values her family very much. There had been four generations living together in her family for years and she had always done her very best to be a good daughter, wife, mother, and grandmother. Her colleagues praised her for being a filial and loving daughter. Her mother passed away peacefully at the age of 100. And that is how the story of *An Extraordinary Close Relationship between Foster Mother and Daughter* (the title of her planned autobiography), mentioned in Chapter 2, came about.

Ma Yuan's family is harmonious, although there is disagreement now and then, which usually gets resolved eventually. Ma Yuan regarded family as the "warm berth for her little boat." Only with the love, care, and support of her family was she able to have a successful career and emerge as the first woman senior judge from being an ordinary teacher.

Alice Tai holds the post of Ombudsman, appointed by the Chief Executive of the Hong Kong SAR to investigate and monitor administrative complaints about the public sector. She uses the metaphor of a "safety net" to describe her work–family balance: "I think the key word is balance, not to over-emphasize either work or family. If you were too career-minded, you win some and you lose some. A safety net has to be firm on all four corners in order to hold up. I can separate my public and private lives, by putting on different hats at work and at home."

Sun Yuehuan, President of China Enterprise Appraisals, the leading assets appraisal firm in China, is a successful entrepreneur in the economic boom. She describes her attitudes toward her work and family:

"I will sacrifice my resting time in order to do things that please my family. I think it is worthwhile. At home, my role is a wife and a mother. At work, I am a leader and a CEO who enables the staff to earn a living. When I am working, I can keep my family out of my mind. There are a number of attributes that are important to my family and career. The first one is being genuine and the second one is personal competency and knowledge in my work. It is said that 'knowledge is power' because you can be empowered after you acquire knowledge. Now, I live happily because I have paid much effort, am genuine to others and contributed all I have to society, my company and also my family. My clients respect me very much, and my friends and family have much confidence in me. Therefore, I think being genuine gives you the ability to handle all relationships."

Similarly, Laura Cha, Member of the Executive Council of the Hong Kong SAR government, emphasizes the importance of attitudes toward one's career and family roles:

"I can separate work and personal matters. At home, my children keep me humble and I am a normal mother. I think it's my own personality. I always remind myself not to let it get into my head. I think it's a problem if you become very different when you are in a high position and confuse yourself with your role/position at work, but I saw a lot of people (in senior rank) like this – they become convinced of their own invincibility. At that time, this attitude will spill over into your family relationships."

Psychologists often describe cultures as being primarily collectivistic or individualistic. Collectivistic societies emphasize the good of the group, cooperation, and interdependence. By contrast, individualistic societies are more centered on the success of each individual, even at the cost of the larger group. China and Hong Kong are grouped among collectivistic societies; the US, Canada, and the UK are grouped among individualistic societies. Research in Chinese societies shows that work and family are viewed as interdependent domains, unlike the distinct segregation of these two domains in Western concepts of work and family. In individualistic societies, overwork would be considered as taking time away from the family and sacrificing the family for the advancement of one's own career. In collectivistic societies, overwork is likely to be seen as sacrificing oneself for the family, since commitment to work is viewed as a means of ensuring financial security for the family (Yang, Chen, Chao, & Zou, 2000). The needs of the self are subsumed under the needs of the collective.

It is not so much the time spent on various tasks that causes stress for high-achieving women in collectivistic societies, but it is relationships that matter. Women in collectivistic societies report that interpersonal conflict, such as a clash with a coworker, is more stressful than handling the simultaneous demands of a high-pressure job and caring for children (Lai, 1995). We explore these cultural factors in greater detail in Chapter 7 where we address the influence of culture on the way these high-achieving women fulfill their duties and engage in the joyful work of mothering and a high-level career.

## Reactive Role Behavior

There is a limit to the extent to which we can redefine our roles and change our attitudes about them. There is some flexibility in both roles, but it is not endless. We still have to meet the daily demands of the roles we fill – being a mother and being a high-level executive. As seen earlier, in order to meet all their role demands, many of our women leaders managed to fulfill both role expectations by working harder and longer, sacrificing their resting time and personal interests. They sleep less, "stealing" the extra hours to finish their own work after their family go to bed. They see fewer of their own friends and for extended periods of time, and especially when their children were growing up, they rarely did anything for their personal enjoyment outside of work and family. They also work smarter by having better planning, scheduling, and strategizing.

## Life Management Strategies

What are the practical tips for managing these demands? Recent research has examined the strategies that promote a better work–family interface. Boris Baltes and Heather Heydens-Gahir (2003) extend a general model of life management strategy to study work–family conflict. They classify the repertoire of adaptive behavior strategies as "SOC": Selection, Optimization, and Compensation.

### Selection

The primary focus of selection is on the articulation and setting of goals, which give direction to behavior. This strategy is similar to writing a mission statement for yourself because it clarifies who you are, what you care about, and how you will achieve the desirable outcomes you listed for yourself. Limited resources, including your time and your money, are then channeled to achieve these goals. This strategy is similar to Friedman and Greenhaus's (2000) first principle for creating allies of work and family – "clarify what's important" (p. 146).

Our women leaders are very clear about their goals. This is how Andrea van de Kamp looked at her work–family balance: "If you've really thought about it, you've decided what's critical and what isn't. And if you look at it that way, you will have reduced those conflicts by 80 percent, and you will be dealing with 20 percent. And you can deal and live with 20 percent."

Ann Kern, Managing Director at Korn/Ferry International, put it this way:

> "My priority was always my children. My children always came first. I never missed a basketball game or football game or anything. But I was consumed with being successful – I was consumed so that I could pay the tuition when my kids went to Harvard. I also worked very hard on the weekend and from home; the business would have to be done on the phone at night."

Betty Yuen, the first woman to become Managing Director of CLP Power Hong Kong Limited, one of the leading power companies in the world, articulates her goal:

> "Working is just a means for me to earn a living so that I can have a good family life. Therefore family was my ultimate motivation. I am very happy that I can do so well in my career. However, career is just one part of life. The most important part is my family. I work to live, but not live to work. Therefore I do not feel superior to others because of my achievement in my career. My role as a wife and a mother is even more important."

It does not mean that Betty is not giving her best to her work. She cannot afford not to do so. Otherwise, she would not have risen to the top of this traditionally engineer-dominated utilities company as a female accountant:

> "My husband always comments that I have two 'personalities' because I am active in handling problems at work while I am happy to be a follower in the family. Therefore my friends think I am an easy-going person, but it is not the case when I am at work. My husband describes me as a person who is 'careful in important things but careless in minor things.' I do not have too many views on minor things because I think it is just wasting my time."

Irrespective of background, our interviewees are unequivocal about what their priorities are. Family and children always come first. Treating family as the priority has not stalled the success of our women leaders.

Chen Ying, Managing Director of Anhui Worldbest Chemical Fibre Company and a number of joint venture companies with

American and Italian partners, is one of the new generation of successful women entrepreneurs in China. She describes her priority:

> "I know what I need. I am a person who can find happiness from work. But when it comes to major life decisions, I will put more emphasis on my family. There are no other principles concerning our family life. There may be a lot of tangible problems, but if you think clearly, they are not principles. There is only one principle, and that is related to my son. When it comes to my son's affairs, I am insistent on my principle; the others are not important."

Chen Ying started her career as a soldier in the People's Liberation Army. When she started her own business, she came across a few opportunities which would have required her to leave Anhui, her home province, to go to work in Shanghai or overseas. However, she sensed that her husband did not want her to leave home. She decided to stay behind. She eventually built up a manufacturing enterprise in her home province, which has won her many awards and honors, including being selected as one of the 10 most outstanding women leaders in the region and the exemplary woman entrepreneur award in 2006. The carpet that her company produces has become the top brand in China.

Selecting clear goals is particularly important when facing critical situations. Rita Fan has been the President of the Legislative Council in Hong Kong since the 1997 handover when Hong Kong ceased to be a British colony and became a Special Administrative Region of China. Rita had two family crises during the tumultuous period of the political transition. In the mid-1990s, Rita was serving on the Preliminary Committee set up by the Chinese central government to prepare for Hong Kong's handover. Her daughter was studying in Canada at that time. When she learned that her daughter was very ill in Canada, she dropped everything and flew to Canada to stay with her daughter. Even when she had to fly to Beijing for the Preliminary Committee meetings, she would leave right after the meeting, and not stay behind to meet the press. She believed it was important to provide spiritual support and physical comfort to her daughter when she was sick and recovering. She subsequently gave one of her kidneys for her daughter's transplant. Her daughter has since recovered and returned to Hong Kong to enroll in her medical studies.

In 2003, Rita's husband was diagnosed with terminal cancer. He died one year before our interview. Rita confided that she was very tired, both physically and psychologically, during her husband's illness:

> "I knew he had to go but he had a strong fighting spirit until the end. He was staying in a Beijing hospital [for treatment] toward the end of his life. In the last few weeks, I wanted to be with him as much as I could. I flew to Beijing every Thursday and came back [to Hong Kong] every Tuesday to attend LegCo [Legislative Council] meetings every Wednesday. When I was in the Beijing hospital, I just sat by his bedside. I felt that it was important that I spend the last part of his life journey with him. I am glad that I did it."

What kept Rita going? She said:

> "My family is priority number one. I must have a reasonably happy family before I can serve the public. Family has always been a safe harbor for me, especially when I face a lot of pressures outside. My family is a place to go back for comfort after the stormy sea. If my family has any problems, I would drop everything to be with my family."

Sandra Lee, Permanent Secretary in charge of health policies in the Food and Health Bureau of the Hong Kong SAR government, went through a similar family crisis when her husband suffered a stroke in 1998. She was resolute in giving her best to both her husband and her job:

> "In 1998 when my husband had a stroke, we faced it with courage. I have strong will-power and did not let him give up on rehabilitation. Even at difficult times, I still viewed myself as a blessed person. I only took 10 days' leave from my work, as I could not find a nurse at first. Then I hired 24-hour nurses to take care of him. I still counted my blessings – at least we can afford to hire 24-hour nurses, and I did not have to take leave all the time. Every day, I went to the hospital at 6 a.m. to bathe him and returned to visit him again after work at 8 p.m.; I spent the whole day with him during weekends. I had a strong drive, that is, my husband would not accept himself as bed-ridden. So with my encouragement, he would not give up. I trained him to walk and go out for dinner. I insisted that he would come back to a normal life. I have strong will-power. Unless I am physically incapable, I will persevere and achieve."

Sandra went on:

> "I am not the sort of person who blames others. I do not ask 'why me?' or 'why did my husband have a stroke?' I analyze situations rationally and think about what I can and can't do. I am very rational in organizing time; I set my priority and do not give up when times are difficult. I should be able to perform these two important roles (work and family). I think I am always challenging myself. I believe, psychologically, it would have made my husband feel guilty if I had taken a long leave [from work] to take care of him, as he knew how important my work was to me. My objective was to make him feel that he could have a natural recovery through the training routine used in rehabilitation for strokes, so his moods became more relaxed. I knew that if I took more leave to stay with him all day, it would create more conflict between us. At that time, I thought clearly about how I should go forward, and weighed the effects of going either way. I do not deny that I was physically exhausted, but when the goal was set, I tried my best to achieve that goal. After his stroke, I helped him regain the ability to walk, and insisted that he be mobile even though he was in a wheelchair. Whatever I did, I would give him the courage to keep trying and I would insist that he would achieve the goal to return to normal life as far as possible. For example, he would take hospital leave to go out for dinner. I think it was important for his mental health. It gave him 'dignity' by being mobile. Before I agreed to take the London posting in 2000 [Sandra was posted to the Hong Kong office in London], we agreed that since my husband could receive rehabilitation treatments on the National Health Medical Service in England [her husband was British], it was less demanding for the government than if I were posted to other countries. I brought two nurses and a maid with us to the UK. I would schedule my work and stay home more with my husband. Even with out-of-town assignments, for example, I would leave on an early morning flight in order to stay at home the previous night."

Sandra's husband died in London before she returned to take up the post of Secretary for Economic Services in Hong Kong in 2000. Despite her stoic commitment to her work even during this family crisis, Sandra is sensitive to the family needs of her subordinates:

> "There is life after work; there is a family after the office. If my colleagues have any family problem, I let them take time off to take care

of their family responsibility. For example, I had an EO [executive officer] in the London office who faced a family crisis. I allowed her to work at home via e-mail so she did not have to work at the office."

How can we determine the right goals and select our priorities? Frances Hesselbein, founding President of the Drucker Foundation, Chairman of the Board of Governors of the Leader to Leader Institute, and former Chief Executive of the Girl Scouts of the USA, has been giving sound advice to leaders who are women for a long time. She recalled a question and answer session in a retreat with eight of the highest-ranking women, all of whom were presidents of subsidiaries or vice-presidents of major functions for three of the largest American corporations. The first question these women asked her was, "I have a husband and children and a wonderful job. How do I find the balance I need in my life?"

Frances found herself telling these women that they should take time to listen to the whispers of their lives: "You have to take time, whether you call it meditation, or whether you call it finding quiet moments and just thinking. We remove ourselves from all the noise. We find a quiet corner and we think. It is amazing how the answers or maybe questions will come. It is very important; otherwise we skim along the surface of life."

Many women may complain that they do not even have time to think about themselves, yet alone find time to meditate about what is important, when work is a series of crises and family is an unending demand. Frances always finds time and uses it creatively:

"I fly twice a week, speaking somewhere in our own country. Flying so much, I find that, for me, it is a wonderful time to think because no one can get to me. There are no phones. And I always find time right before I go to sleep. I try to think, look at the day and think about what happened today and where was I helpful, where was I most productive and successful and what were the areas I could have done better."

Frances also sounded a warning:

"Now if you don't give a lot of thought about your life goals and priorities and plan for them, you can get whipped up into this hectic schedule where you're frustrated because you can't be with your family.

I think it's tragic that we hear a successful business leader saying, 'Oh, I'm having such fun with my grandchildren. You know, when my own children were growing up I hardly knew them. I was so busy. And now I'm having fun with my grandchildren.' And I think that's a very sad statement."

## Optimization

Baltes and Heydens-Gahir's (2003) second category of coping strategy is optimization. They refer to the "acquisition, refinement, and use of means to achieve the selected goals" (p. 1007). The most talked about optimization strategies in work–life balance are scheduling of time and energy and multitasking. As time constraints are the greatest concern for working women everywhere, we discussed in greater detail how our women leaders make more time in Chapter 3.

Squeezing time does not mean the women leaders sacrifice their health. Carrie Yau was the government official handling the SARS crisis in Hong Kong in 2003. She does not believe in working non-stop. During the intense crisis, she managed to balance her life:

"I was on standby 24 hours a day during the SARS period. But even at that time, I did not think I had to work without stop, like our front line colleagues [in the hospitals for example] do. I had to make important decisions, such as allocating funding. If I were too tired, I would make some wrong decisions. [During the Vietnamese boat people crisis], the police force taught me to sleep at 11 p.m. They said they would call me if any emergency arises. I also encourage my subordinates not to work overtime continuously because it just reveals the problems of the whole system or the inefficiency of individuals. Continuous overtime work also does not benefit the organization because when we need staff to handle some special situation, the staff may be burned out or sick. Therefore, I focus on keeping myself physically strong and happy in spirit. I try to avoid evening functions or sleeping late."

## Compensation

Baltes and Heydens-Gahir's third life management strategy, compensation, involves the use of alternative means when time and material resources are limited. Especially in terms of childcare, the daily tasks cannot wait. Women who hold busy executive positions often have to rely on external aids or the help of others.

Almost all of our Hong Kong women leaders have Filipino domestic helpers who take care of their housework or childcare, though they still need to supervise them. In addition, their extended family members often live close by and are able to give a helping hand with supervision. In the United States, where live-in domestic helpers are much rarer, a few of our interviewees did get helpful assistance from part-time or full-time housekeepers. Our interviewees all expressed their gratitude to these helpers, many of whom have worked for their families for a long time and in some cases are considered part of the family.

In Mainland China, part-time or live-in domestic helpers from the rural regions have now made home help more affordable. This was not the case during the time our women leaders were starting their families. Most of the women had to rely on their own parents or extended family to help out.

Gu Xiulin, Vice-Chairman of the Standing Committee of the National People's Congress, is one of the highest-ranking women in the Chinese government. She is also the President of the All-China Women's Federation. In 1983, she was elected Governor of Jiangsu Province, the first female provincial governor in China. When she assumed the post, she brought her two children along to Jiangsu while her husband stayed behind to work in Beijing. It is not unusual for couples to be posted to different parts of China. Gu Xiulin explained how she managed through the support of the social system and her extended family:

> "I joined the Party and became a leader in the seventies. The Party would arrange for my parents and family life. My mother was also responsible for the children's development, such as helping me bring my two children to school. In addition, social welfare provided nurseries and kindergartens to look after children. The most difficult time was when I was in Nanjing working as the Governor of Jiangsu Province, and my husband said he couldn't bear the responsibility of looking after the children in Beijing. Back then, my two children were in primary and middle school respectively. Although there was a cafeteria [at the work unit], where we ate most of our meals, life was still extremely busy. Things improved when my mother and sister came to Nanjing to help out."

Feng Cui, a staff member in the Ministry of Foreign Affairs at the time, did not have her extended family nearby when her children were young. Her income was low at that time. Both she and her husband were still at work when their children came home from school.

"When my elder daughter was a baby, I employed a nursemaid to take care of her, and when she turned 2 I brought her to the kindergarten. My second child was left with another family to be taken care of because employing a nursemaid was too expensive. At weekends I would bring him back home, so I was only able to see him once or twice a week. This arrangement was very common back then. I remember in those days, it took a lot of effort to find a suitable family who would baby-sit children. Usually I paid out the expenses with my salary for the two children's care, and then there was not much money left in my pocket. My husband covered all the family day-to-day expenses with his salary; all that was left each month was about 26 Yuan RMB (equivalent to US$ 3.5, enough to buy 150 kg rice at that time). In a dual-career family where both parents are working, you can send your child for boarding at the kindergarten. This way, the child will subsequently become very mature."

Feng Cui continued:

"I feel the biggest pressure was when my children were in nursery school because work was extremely busy then and I had to travel often. The places that I traveled to were far away, and I did not have any family in Beijing to help look after my children. So the children were trained to become very independent and they learned to always help each other. Both of my children helped with the housework and my husband prepared the ingredients for lunch so that my children could heat them up themselves when they came home. My daughter managed the family affairs, cooked, and protected her younger brother from being bullied. My children were also taught how to do the laundry, which was a big help in reducing the time we had to spend on household duties."

Feng Cui's husband added that, at that time, they had to tie a key around their children's necks so that they could go home from primary school on their own. It was not uncommon in their generation for children to stay at home by themselves when their parents went to work. Their neighbors would also keep an eye on the children. Readers from the US and many other countries will recognize this practice. The children are often referred to as "latchkey children" because they have keys so that they can let themselves into the house after school.

In China, the government's system of job assignment often results in family members being posted to different parts of the country. Wu Qidi, Deputy Minister of Education, is a typical example. During most of her life, she has been posted far apart from her husband. She said the longest time they had physically stayed together in one place was when both of them went abroad for further studies in Switzerland from 1981 to 1986. When she became President of Tongji University in Shanghai, her husband asked to be posted there. He finally got his posting as Vice-Director of the Standing Committee of the Shanghai Economic Council, and later became Chief Secretary in the city government in Shanghai. But, at about the same time, Wu Qidi was promoted to the Ministry of Education and had to move to Beijing. They both learned to adapt to this lifelong separation, although it was not easy. The separation is particularly difficult now that her husband is suffering from cancer. Due to his unstable condition, he has to stay in Shanghai to receive treatment. Wu Qidi has to rely on her son's family to take care of her husband during the week when she is working in Beijing:

"Personally, I value my family very much. In these days, my husband's health condition isn't good so I go back home almost every weekend, and make arrangements at home. Now, my parents have passed away, but I still have two children. One child moved overseas after graduation; another one is still going to school. My family is still in Shanghai. I am already a grandmother. I try my best to do many things, for example, I do my best to take care of my husband's health. I asked my son, daughter-in-law, grandson and granddaughter to stay with him, and I live in Beijing alone."

Wu Qidi finds this situation of being apart from her sick husband undesirable, but she has to settle for this substitute arrangement for his care for the time being. Fortunately, her husband is able to keep himself busy with, and enthusiastic about, his work in Shanghai. This gives her a bit of consolation.

There are times when the mother's role cannot be substituted. Our women leaders have found creative ways to compensate. Cordelia Chung, Vice-President of Business Partners, IBM Asia Pacific, was posted to Japan in 1996 when her daughters were in grade school in Hong Kong. While she had domestic help and her lawyer husband was there to supervise the household, Cordelia still kept a close watch over her daughters' school work, like many Chinese parents:

"The important thing is having peace of mind. I called home every day. My two children were studying Primary 2 and Primary 3, and I would prepare dictation with my children over the phone. They faxed their homework to me and then I corrected them. For the same work, their father gave them 85 marks, and I would give them 65 marks. At first, I asked them to make use of a recorder to prepare for the dictation, but they were too young to do that. So they wanted me to help them over the phone."

This was before Skype and other types of voice-over-internet technology became available. With the available communication technology at the time, Cordelia managed her mother's role.

These compensatory behaviors do not come without a cost. Our women leaders learned how to manage emotionally as well as practically. Nellie Fong, Chairman of the Chinese operation of PricewaterhouseCoopers in China, served as a Member of the Executive Council of the post-colonial Hong Kong SAR government and the China People's Political Consultative Conference. She described how she adjusted to having a maid take care of her baby daughter:

"After my daughter was born, I employed a maid to look after her. However, my child became quite attached to the maid and felt quite distanced from me. For example, when the maid was on holiday, my daughter would cry non-stop until she returned. I was really hurt because I felt my child loved the maid more than she loved me. As a mother, this has great psychological impact. Later, when my child reached the age of 2, she could identify her mother, who held the authority at home, and who really loves and cares about her. I feel women must experience the psychological conflict when they reach this stage in life. One must be able to accept and confront this challenge. Otherwise your professional career will most certainly be affected."

## Arranging Water Molecules

The children came first, but the work got done – sometimes later. Women in executive positions have the greatest leeway to reduce some of the time conflict because usually they can decide when and how to get their work done. People with the highest levels of work–family conflict also report being least satisfied with their job. Through a combination of careful planning and the autonomy of their positions, these women were able to reduce work–family conflict. They may be better able to handle work–family conflict than mothers on lower rungs in the organization because the many crises top executives encounter in their jobs have taught them how to handle difficult and unexpected problems, whether they occur at work or at home. Time-based conflict is a problem for all working mothers. This may be one area where high-level executive moms have an advantage, despite the excessive time demands of top-level careers.

Feng Lida, an immunologist holding the rank of General in the Chinese Navy Hospital, uses the metaphor of a water molecule to describe her view of the interface between work and family, and also between people and the larger society:

"I think harmony is vital to every person and society. Relationships between people should be harmonious. There can be no harmony if the family members are continually arguing and feeling tired. A harmonious family is like water molecules arranged in a particular way so that water can provide an uninterrupted flow. If you argue, you will alter the arrangement of the molecules. Every family is a system of perfectly arranged molecules that needs love and caring to maintain its careful arrangement. I think about the delicate arrangement of harmonious families that women maintain and, based on this vision, women can expand from the family to the society."

When Feng Lida adopted the water molecule metaphor, she did not have the English-language work–family spillover literature in mind. However, the metaphor is a befitting close to this chapter on work–family spillover. Only when there is harmony in the work and family interface will there be an integrated system of water molecules. Conflict results in splashes of individual water droplets.

# Chapter 7

# Culture Counts:
# Leading as the World Changes

Women made major strides in improving their status in the twentieth century. These changes were propelled by historical and sociopolitical forces that set the stage for the development of our women leaders. In this chapter, we begin by highlighting the ethos of the times in which our interviewees' leadership emerges. Affirmative action and friendly work policies have afforded American women leaders the opportunity to be in the right place at the right time. Educational opportunities and economic conditions in Hong Kong, more so than the legal and institutional mechanisms protecting women's rights, have enabled women to move into positions of power. The intertwined notions of nationhood and family in the early period of the People's Republic of China, the experience of the Cultural Revolution, and the interplay between traditional Confucianism and Communistic egalitarianism propelled the Chinese women leaders to overcome hardship and gather the strength needed to become influential leaders. The Chinese women tell historically rich stories about changes during the reign of Chairman Mao and how recent economic liberalization has had a profound effect on the status of women in China, opening up high-level positions to many of them.

## Historical Contours

The age of our group of interviewees ranges from forties to early eighties. Their life courses are shaped by different historical events of their times. Some of them have survived wartime and revolution with great resolve; others have reaped the benefits of the opportunities that arose from the historical landscape.

## Contemporary China: the Dragon Awakes

The historical epochs of twentieth-century China are most dramatic. The parents of our older interviewees grew up in the imperial Qing dynasty, which was overthrown in 1911 when a republic was established. The fledging republic was besieged by regional warlords. Poverty was prevalent. Some of the women leaders grew up during the Japanese incursion and subsequently the Second World War in the 1940s, when their fathers or brothers went to war, and they grew up in their home villages with their mothers and a community of women. The rampant corruption and extreme social inequality at that time led to the rise of the Communist Party. The civil war between the Communist Party and the nationalist government under Chiang Kai-shek's Kuomintang Party was suspended during the war years, but resumed when the war ended. In 1949, the Kuomintang government retreated to Taiwan and the People's Republic of China under the Communist Party was proclaimed.

Peacetime China was no less tumultuous. The international isolation and social movements during the early period of the People's Republic created hardship for many of our Chinese interviewees as they grew up. The greatest disruption took place during the Great Proletariat Cultural Revolution which was launched by the Communist Party Chairman Mao Zedong in 1966, officially as a campaign to rid China of its "liberal bourgeoisie" elements and to continue the revolutionary class struggle. During the 10-year Cultural Revolution, the economic and educational systems were overturned. Traditional arts and ideas were ignored, customs were condemned, and antiquities were destroyed. Young people were encouraged to criticize cultural institutions and to question their parents and teachers. Intellectuals and people with any link to capitalistic and landlord class backgrounds were persecuted. The number of people who were killed, tortured, or who committed suicide during this period was estimated to exceed a million, but the true figure could not be ascertained. A whole generation of young people missed out on education when they were sent to learn from the peasants in the countryside.

One of our interviewees, Shi Qingqi, suffered greatly during the Cultural Revolution. She was in her twenties, a mother of three, and teaching in the university at that time. Her father was a senior government official, but because he was the son of a landlord, he was persecuted by the Red Guard. Shi Qingqi was sent to the countryside for re-education through manual labor while her husband stayed in Beijing with their three children. She said her eyes would still swell with tears when she watched some television programs about the Cultural Revolution. Her pain was apparent as she recalled:

"It was tough. . . . In the Cultural Revolution, I was accused of being the 'pearl' of the Faculty Dean and 'princess' of the university [because her father was a good friend of the Dean]. But later, some of my former friends accused me of committing 72 crimes. Because my past life was so easy, it felt like being dropped from heaven into hell. I had little money at that time. I had to save up the money to send to my husband so he could pay for the children's school fees and nursery care. I learned to make their clothes and shoes myself; otherwise we could not afford it. Fortunately, I had some good friends who helped and gave me money every month. But I was tough; I would return the money to them as soon as I got my salary. Once, I was bemused with my RMB56 [equivalent to US$7] monthly salary, and I mumbled to myself that it was not enough to live on for the month. Then a friend sitting nearby quickly mentioned that she also did not have money. In fact, I did not intend to borrow money from her, but I also knew she had the money. So I decided never to complain about not having enough money in front of others. I now understand how poor people develop strong will-power. After the Cultural Revolution, I made two resolutions: one was not to become a government official; and the second was not to treat others badly. I should help others as much as possible. I think the Cultural Revolution has given me a profound education."

Mary Ma, CFO of the Lenovo Group, was 12 years old when the Cultural Revolution started. Almost 40 years later, she calmly reflected on her own gains and losses from this experience:

"Young people like me either had to go to the countryside to be re-educated, or if they came from a 'better' family or social background, they could probably stay in the city such as Beijing or Shanghai. Fortunately or unfortunately, I was one of those who were sent to the countryside. This played a very important part in developing my personality, my behavior and my way of being. The time between 12 and 18 years old is an important period when people form their personality traits. I had a very tough time during those six years. It helped me build my own life philosophy. I became very tough and independent, perhaps a little aggressive as well."

Persecutions aside, many young people at the beginning stage of the Cultural Revolution were persuaded by the utopian ideology of total equality and service to the people. Pursuing the idea of serving the people, Feng Cui, who volunteered to work in the countryside at one time, recalled the selfless attitudes shared by her young peers: "I worked very hard, and people were helping each other. Female students were eating less to save food for their male classmates, and everyone was concerned for the nation and the collective."

When asked why she would put the nation before herself and her family, Feng Cui and her husband explained conjointly:

> "In those days [before the People's Republic], the country was torn apart and families were ruined [by the long period of invasion and civil war]. After the liberation in 1949, we had to work hard in order to rebuild the country. Everyone was concerned about the nation and the collective. Without a nation, there will be no family, and there will not be us. . . . Most of the current women leaders came from that period of the Revolution."

Whether we call it the historical ethos, public education, or propaganda, the impact was enormous. Shi Qingqi reflected on the reasons for her dedication to her work and concluded: "I think the Communist Party is successful in its education because it trained us not to have our own desires, but to contribute everything, and to dedicate ourselves to our careers."

At the end of the Cultural Revolution, Deng Xiaoping assumed the leadership of the Communist Party shortly after Mao's death in 1976. He pioneered economic reforms in China with an ingenious oxymoron known as the "socialist market economy" which opened China to the global market, beginning in the 1980s. The current economic boom in China is a legacy of Deng's policies. Major shifts from state-guaranteed employment to a system of socialistic capitalism resulted in more economic freedom but also uncertainty. Restructuring of state-owned enterprises has created redundancy and unemployment on one hand, but, on the other hand, economic opportunities for private enterprises, which some of our younger Chinese interviewees have taken up, with great success. Others who fled the country during the early periods of Communist rule have since returned to invest in the booming economy.

These Chinese women leaders are not only survivors of the historical turmoil; they grew from the hardship and turned it into new resolve. In the early days of Communistic China, the state assigned jobs to everyone. It was not unusual for husbands and wives to be assigned to posts in different parts of the country, and they only got together during holidays. Children were often left to the care of the extended family or the state. The women took these arrangements as normative and regarded them as their duty to the country. They created meaning in their experience and became agents of their destiny.

## Women Can Hold Up Half the Sky in New China

Women were oppressed as a class under the feudalistic system in old China. Equal rights for women were enshrined in the constitution of the People's Republic of China in 1949. Throughout different periods of political movements, the Communist Party has consistently emphasized the ideology of liberating Chinese women from their feudalistic oppression as one of the goals of class struggle.

Ma Yuan, the Supreme Court Justice, appreciated the difference: "Now I have to thank the Party for their effort in developing the country and the liberation of women. If you have the ability, you will get the chance."

During the Cultural Revolution in the 1960s, the late Chairman Mao's motto that "women can hold up half the sky" encouraged women to participate in all walks of life. During this period, absolute equality was translated into a political movement that interrupted the social fabric. Uniformity was expressed through the unisex appearance of "Mao-suits" which downplayed femininity. With the economic liberation started by Deng Xiaoping in the 1980s, women enjoy more diversity in expressing their femininity. At the same time, gender stereotypes and commercialized objectification of women as sex objects, which were suppressed under Communist ideology, slipped back in under the influence of Western-style consumerism.

---

**Figures 7.1 and 7.2** Images of working women in China. Women were depicted engaged in more masculine pursuits during the Cultural Revolution.*Source*: IISH Stefan R. Landsberger Collection, Amsterdam

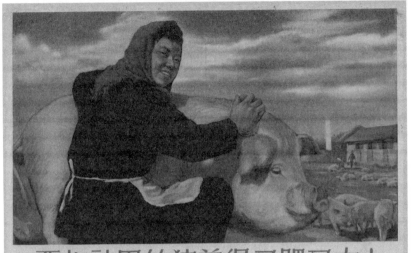

要把社里的猪养得又肥又大！

我們為參加國家工業化建設而自豪

Given its political ideology, China has a strong infrastructure to support gender equality. The All-China Women's Federation (ACWF) was established in March 1949 to promote women's advancement. Despite its official status as a non-governmental mass organization, it is a de facto machine of the Chinese Communist Party and is run by party cadres assigned at the national, provincial, county, city, and village level. It coordinates educational campaigns, promotes women's services, safeguards women's rights, and represents women's interests in government. Although not conceived of as a "feminist" organization, the ACWF has taken up a more proactive role as the advocate of women's rights since the 1980s. A dominant slogan adopted by the Sixth National Women's Congress to promote women's agency as a means to gender equality is the "Four Selfs" – "self-respect, self-confidence, self-reliance and self-strengthening" (Edwards, 2000).

At the state level, the National Working Committee on Children and Women (NWCCW) under the State Council is a coordinating body through which the State Council promotes the welfare of children and women. It urges other government departments to implement existing laws, policies, statutes, and measures to promote the cause of children and women. The first comprehensive Law on the Protection of the Rights and Interests of Women was passed in 1992, shortly before China hosted the Fourth World Congress on Women in Beijing in 1995. Specific goals are delineated in 10-year plans, the latest being the Program for the Development of Chinese Women (2001–2010).

With this infrastructure, does this mean the concept of gender equality has a stronghold in China? In terms of employment, 78.3 percent of the female working-age population between the ages of 16 and 54 are employed. Before 1949, women's illiteracy rate was 90 percent; it had been reduced to 13.5 percent by 2002. In 2000, the average number of years of education for women was 7, compared to 8.3 years for men. Women made up 44 percent of the students enrolled in institutions of higher education in 2002. There were seven women in the senior leadership of the central government and Political Bureau of the Chinese Communist Party in 2002, and 14 women at the ministerial or vice-ministerial level in the 28 ministries and commissions of the State Council, the administrative branch of the central government. At the National People's Congress, women make up 20 percent of the 3,000 delegates, and 13 percent of the 150 members of the Standing Committee, which exercises the decision-making power in between the plenary sessions of the Congress. While these figures are far from impressive in comparison to the more advanced European countries in terms of gender equality, they show that women in China have made major advances in the past 50 years under the conscious campaigns of the government.

However, even under the strong arm of the state machinery, sexism is not easily eradicated. The gap between state-supported ideology and deep-rooted cultural norms is best illustrated by the ramifications of the one-child policy introduced by the central government to control rapid population growth in the 1970s. The traditional preference for sons who carry the family name dies hard. Son-preference is not caused by the one-child policy, but is structurally rooted in the patriarchal system in which daughters are believed to be a liability rather than an asset because they marry out of the family. Chinese parents traditionally do not count on their daughters for their security and protection when they get old. Despite laws prohibiting sex selection and mistreatment or abandonment of infant girls, as well as repeated educational campaigns promoting the equal value of having daughters, many parents still try every means to attempt to have a son.

The greatest resistance to the population policy is found in the rural areas where there are reported cases of illegal abortion of female fetuses and infanticide of girl-children. In 2000, the gap in the national sex ratio reached 116.9 new-born boys to 100 girls, compared to the ratio of 108.5 boys to 100 girls in 1982 (Department of Population, Social, Science, & Technology, 2004). The gap is even wider in rural areas, where the sex ratio may reach as high as 135.6 new-born boys to 100 girls. The sex ratio increases with each additional childbirth beyond the first – additional children are allowed under the relaxation of the one-child policy for rural families, minorities, and special cases (e.g. if the first child is born with a disability). Problems of trafficking and abduction of women as brides for men in remote villages have raised the concern of the All-China Women's Federation, but poverty and low educational level, together with prejudicial attitudes toward women in these areas, complicate the problem (Committee for the Elimination of Discrimination Against Women, 10 June 2004).

Our group of Chinese interviewees may be considered atypical of Chinese women in general. We have ethnic Chinese women leaders of different age groups who are now leaders in diverse occupations in Mainland China, Hong Kong, and the US. While sharing the same cultural roots, their stories give us a glimpse of the interplay between the historical context, cultural background, and social system in shaping their experiences.

### From Colonial Rule to "One Country – Two Systems"

Hong Kong was a British colony from 1843, after the first Opium War between China and Britain, until 1997 when China resumed sovereignty. It has grown from a small fishing village to a global financial center in one century. Other than the 44-month occupation by the Japanese during the Second World War, Hong Kong has enjoyed a relatively stable administration, even over the transition period of its reunification with Mainland China. From 1949, the small local population multiplied after waves of refugees fled from China to escape the political upheaval and poverty. The richer migrants from China brought their capital and technical expertise to set up industries and trade in the colony. Hong Kong became the entrepôt for international trade with the isolated Communist China.

Among our group of interviewees, most of the older generation of women leaders in Hong Kong came from China between the late 1940s and 1960s. The local-born women leaders belong to the generation born after the 1950s, and have benefited from the economic prosperity and educational opportunities since the 1970s. With the approach of 1997, there was widespread anxiety about the political uncertainty surrounding the return of Hong Kong to China. The pragmatic Communist leader, Deng Xiaoping, introduced the principle of "One Country – Two Systems" to allow the continuity of political, economic, and social life in Hong Kong for 50 years. Hong Kong would become a Special Administrative Region (SAR) of China with its own autonomous administrative system for all local affairs other than constitutional, defense, and foreign diplomacy matters. During the 1980s to early 1990s, many professionals and small business owners who lacked confidence in the future of Hong Kong emigrated to the West.

All of our Hong Kong interviewees stayed in Hong Kong through the transition. The political transition enabled local residents to assume positions of power vacated by the British colonial government, which began a localization policy in the early 1990s. For example, Anson Chan is the first Chinese and the first woman to become Chief Secretary – head of the civil service in the colonial government – a position that she carried into the SAR government. Promotion of other Chinese women in the civil service to senior positions was also accelerated in the localization process.

The economic liberalization in Mainland China has also opened up many business opportunities for Hong Kong. Most of the manufacturing industries in Hong Kong moved to the neighboring regions in China where land and labor are cheaper. Marjorie Yang, Chairman of Esquel Group, returned to Hong Kong to help her father when China opened up, and transformed her family business into a world-leading manufacturer of shirts. She attributed part of her success to the fact that she was in the right place at the right time:

"When my father was in charge of the company, he did not trust my ability because I am a girl. But after he was admitted to hospital, he had no choice but to turn over everything to me to handle. I also need to thank Deng Xiaoping's economic and political reform because it enabled my career to develop. My grandfather was one of the first groups of Boxer scholars, but his aspiration can only be achieved now. My father also studied overseas, but his talent was unfulfilled because he was a refugee in Hong Kong. Now I want to set up my own company to return to the society and set a good example because I think an enterprise needs not exploit the employees. They can also contribute to the society. I am very lucky because I have my own country and I can set up a company to be a catalyst of change. I think I was born in a right time because it would be useless to have aspiration without chance. I am lucky because I can do what I intend to."

Doing business in China is a challenge for many people from Hong Kong, who have lifestyles and social habits which are different from those of their Mainland counterparts. Marjorie described her adjustment tactics, which are not atypical for other people doing business in China, but she had the additional role of being a young woman:

"As I was a young female, they used to treat me as a 'little girl,' which I did not want to be. I thought that I could hold my drink as well as they could, then I could find my way to communicate with the men. Among the four bad habits that men commonly had [womanizing, gambling, drinking, and smoking], I thought I could only learn to drink as they did in order to find common ground with them. So I did not think I was disadvantaged."

## Women's Advancement Rides on the
## Coat-Tails of Economic Prosperity in Hong Kong

Many people thought that under British rule, women in the more Westernized society of Hong Kong would have enjoyed more gender equality than women in Mainland China. This is an oversimplified picture. The British colonial government had established the rule of law and a Western-style administration in Hong Kong, which helped to propel its economic growth into one of the key financial centers in the world. At the same time, the colonial government allowed its subjects to preserve many of the traditional Chinese customs so as to avoid changes to the local culture and to prevent local resistance. As a result, some of the vestiges of the patriarchal systems originating in the imperial Qing dynasty were carried over to the twentieth century, including the customary marriage practice that allowed men to keep secondary wives, and the interstate inheritance of properties along the male line only. Whereas polygamy was outlawed in China when the Qing dynasty was overthrown in 1911, and equal rights were proclaimed by the People's Republic in 1949, the marriage and family laws were only changed in Hong Kong in the early 1970s after active campaigns by women's groups (Cheung, Wan, & Wan, 1994).

Equal pay for women was implemented in the civil service initially, in 1974, and for all employment sectors after the Sex Discrimination Ordinance was passed in 1995. The Equal Opportunities Commission (EOC) was set up in 1996 to investigate and conciliate complaints of discrimination in employment, education, and provision of services, on the basis of sex, pregnancy, and marital status. Sexual harassment was also covered under the Sex Discrimination Ordinance. At the time the EOC was set up in 1996, one-third of the employment advertisements in the local newspapers specified sex as a condition. These discriminatory advertisements were eliminated within six months after the EOC took up active education campaigns, warning legal action against the newspapers. The Women's Commission was later set up by the Hong Kong SAR government in 2001 as the central mechanism to promote women's status and development (Cheung & Chung, 2008).

These institutional and legislative measures resulted from decades of advocacy by different generations of women's groups. However, the advancement of women's status and their entry into leadership positions largely rode on the coat-tails of Hong Kong's overall economic development, rather than being a conscious government policy to promote women's equality.

The implementation of free and mandatory education for all children for 9 years in the 1970s and the expansion of tertiary education in the early 1990s have allowed more girls to complete secondary and tertiary education. In 1986, only 38 percent of university students were female; by 2006, the percentage of women enrolled on university degree courses had surpassed that of men at 54 percent (Census and Statistics Department, 2001, 2007). The overall labor force participation rate of women in 2007 was 52.6 percent, much lower than that of their counterparts in Mainland China and the US. Marital status affects women's employment, with only 45.6 percent of ever-married women entering the labor force. However, for women with tertiary education, most of them remain economically active during their life course, given the accessibility of foreign domestic helpers.

Many of the Hong Kong women leaders in our sample, especially those who work in the public sector, were among the early batch of local female university graduates. Their access to higher education has enabled them to enter the civil service, which operates more on meritocracy and allows these women to demonstrate their competence and advance through the ranks. Some of these women were pioneers in promoting the advancement of women, including the campaign on equal pay for women in the civil service. In 2007, women made up 29 percent of the directorate grade in the civil service, and nine out of the 19 permanent secretaries (47.4 percent) were women. There has been much progress in the past 30 years. In 1975, women made up only 3 percent of the directorate grade; and the first time a woman was promoted to the post of Secretary of a policy bureau was in 1987 when Anson Chan became the Secretary for Economic Services (Westwood, Mehrain, & Cheung, 1995).

The proportion of women in decision-making positions is still far from equal. The number of women in managerial-level occupations has risen slightly from 20 percent in 1991 to 29 percent (Census and Statistics Department, 2007), although the number of women in the boardroom or at the helm of listed companies is still under 10 percent. The percentage of women in the Legislative Council remains low (20 percent in 2007); the first woman appointed to the Legislative Council was in 1966. However, individual women have made their marks. For example, Rita Fan has presided over the Legislative Council since 1997. Betty Yuen is the first managing director of a major utilities company. Marjorie Yang is Chairman and CEO of the Esquel Group, and was named among the Fortune top 50 most powerful women in business in 2004. These are some of the Hong Kong women leaders whom we interviewed.

## United States: The Twentieth-Century World Power

The United States grew into a world power during the twentieth century. Its engagement in the Second World War changed the employment pattern for women as they filled the jobs vacated by men enlisted to fight overseas. The post-war baby boom led some women to return home as full-time homemakers, but the educational and employment opportunities for women had been opened up and the image of Rosie the Riveter, a Second World War icon with bulging biceps, assured women that "We can do it."

Alice Eagly and Linda Carli (2007) summarized the statistics on women leadership in their book *Through the Labyrinth*. Women make up only 6 percent of the Fortune 500 companies' top executives, including chairman, president, CEO (Chief Executive Officer), or COO (Chief Operating Officer); 27 percent of the federal government's Senior Executive Service; and hold only 16 percent of the seats in Congress. In 2007, Nancy Pelosi became the first female Speaker of the House of Representatives.

When we look at success in middle management, women are everywhere. In 1982, women surpassed men in college graduation rates, and the gap has been widening since then with women now comprising approximately 59 percent of college enrollments. Among females between 25 and 34 years old, 33 percent have completed college compared to 29 percent of males (US Department of Education, 2000). Women make up close to 50 percent of the workforce, but they work fewer hours per week and a large proportion are likely to stop out of the workforce when their children are young. In 2002, 66 percent of married women with a child under 2 years old were employed and 60 percent of married women with a child under 1 were employed (Media Mentions and Suse News Stanford Report, 2002). Thus, women in general are succeeding in large numbers at middle levels of organizations, but the large numbers are reduced to a trickle at the top levels.

I'm Proud... my husband wants me to do my part

SEE YOUR U. S. EMPLOYMENT SERVICE
WAR MANPOWER COMMISSION

**Figure 7.3** This US poster from the Second World War shows the complexity and conflict in women's roles at that time. Women were needed to work for the war effort, so it became the patriotic thing to do. But, as the message implies, working women did not have to give up their traditional roles as wives and mothers – it was OK to be a working woman because their husband approved.
*Source*: United States Library of Congress

Barbara Nelson and Kathryn Carver (1994) described the US as a liberal democracy within which the place of women could be evaluated in terms of programs for women, equivocal status in the law, and women's position in communal and civic life. As a country of multiracial and multiethnic groups marked by class divisions, women's lives are interlinked with these sociopolitical intersections. Since the onset of the contemporary women's movement in the 1960s, thousands of formal and informal women's groups have emerged in response to women's needs and interests. Nelson and Carver contended that despite many voices of feminism, the political infrastructure on women's issues is weak and there are few vehicles for translating women's voices into action.

## Legal Protections for Women in the United States

The US is the only major Western country that has not ratified the United Nations Convention on the Elimination of All Forms of Discrimination against Women, which was adopted by the UN in 1979 and signed and ratified by 185 countries (over 90 percent of the United Nations member states) as of 2006. Although the majority of people in the US may not have paid much attention to this fact, the rest of the world has expressed distress over the refusal of the US to endorse what they see as basic human rights for women.

There are few laws that address the rights of women specifically. The Equal Rights Amendment to the Constitution was drafted to protect equal rights for men and women; it was first introduced in 1923, and has been repeatedly defeated in Congress. Title VII of the Civil Rights Act, outlawing discrimination on the basis of race, sex, religion, and national origin, was passed in 1964. However, Nancy Baker (2005) commented that "insertion of the term sex into Title VII of the Civil Rights Act was actually the cynical attempt of some southern lawmakers to block the passage of this legislation, which would protect the rights of black Americans and outlaw the system of segregation that codified discrimination against black Americans in many southern states" (p. 37).

The Equal Employment Opportunities Commission (EEOC) is the federal body that makes equal opportunity policy and conducts enforcement litigation under Title VII of the Civil Rights Act of 1964 (Title VII) and the Equal Pay Act (EPA) in the employment sector. The EEOC has formulated directives to implement affirmative employment opportunity programs for all US federal employees as required by Title VII of the Civil Rights Act of 1964 and the Rehabilitation Act of 1973. Affirmative action programs in organizations and universities have made it possible for more women and minorities to enjoy equal opportunities on a level playing field. As Margaret York, the Los Angeles police officer who rose to the rank of Chief of Police in the Los Angeles Police Department, noted: "I frankly think that if it had not been for the Women's Movement and affirmative action, there wouldn't have been a concern about having women in upper ranks." Affirmative action has had an uneasy acceptance in the US, with several states passing their own laws that prohibit affirmative action (except where federal law would apply).

The US Labor Department set up the Glass Ceiling Commission in 1991 to study the barriers to the advancement of women and minorities within corporate hierarchies and make recommendations for the removal of hindrances blocking their access to management and decision-making positions in business. Among its recommendations are measures to create a supportive work environment for employees with family responsibilities (US Glass Ceiling Commission, 1995). Whereas many European countries have relied on the state to provide childcare support, in the US, individual employers are expected to be the primary providers of family assistance to employees, although many employers believe that individual employees are responsible for the care of their family, not the employer (Shafiro & Hammer, 2004). Some large business corporations have implemented family-friendly policies, which are slowly becoming accepted as more mainstream good management practice. The success of these policies often depends on the commitment of senior management because merely having a policy "on the books" does not ensure that employees will be able to use it.

There is a wide range of policies that could be considered "family-friendly." The underlying idea is that these policies help employees manage their family responsibilities and do their job. For example, flexible start and stop times for the workday can be a "life saver" or at the very least an "employee saver" for someone who needs to drop kids at a school that opens later than the start of the usual business day, or shift to an earlier schedule so they can be home to supervise children after school and make dinner. There are endless variations in these policies, which include compressed work weeks of 4 days, 10 hours a day, or even 3 days, 12 hours a day, which is a standard schedule for nurses. Other employers offer part-time employment, work-at-home options (usually called telecommuting), and "on and off ramps" for employees who want to take a period of time off from work and re-enter at the level they had achieved when they began their "time out." The professional literature shows benefits of flexible work arrangements for employers and employees (Corporate Voice for Working Families, 2006). But despite the "buzz" in the research literature over such arrangements, many employers remain unconvinced that they can improve their business by providing more flexibility for their employees.

The Family Medical Leave Act requires employers to provide up to 12 weeks of unpaid leave for the birth of a child, for one's own illness, or to care of a sick family member. Unfortunately, a large proportion of working adults cannot afford to take much leave time without pay, and anyone with a 3-month-old infant is sleep-deprived and will find returning to work while caring for an infant difficult to manage. Thus, while unpaid leave was a major step toward helping women manage work and children, few women, especially those at low-income levels, can afford to use it.

Few of our highly successful women took a nonconventional career track, but the American women leaders offered these advantages to their own employees when they assumed top administrative positions. The American executives in our sample are sensitive to these practices and have been supportive. Sharon Allen, who is a top executive at the "Big 4" accounting firm Deloitte and Touche, has been a supporter of a variety of programs, including Deloitte's Mass Career Customization model which addresses the fact that employees have different stages in their lives in which they must "dial" their careers up or down depending on other factors in their lives. Over the past 20 years, a few American companies have had a family leave policy whereby employees are given a certain amount of leave if they have a family situation that requires it. It is only recently that there has been more understanding of work and family issues in the workplace. Part of the reason may be that there are more women in the workplace and more women in top management positions.

Jenny Ming, President of Old Navy/Gap, demonstrated how she has made these policies a priority for her own employees now that she is in a position to set policy:

"I have created a culture that you know families are welcome. It's not a negative in someone's career. Obviously I was a very big part of creating that here. In retailing, especially in apparel, there's a lot of women. And I want to set an example that we can have a family and be successful at work. So when I hear 'Oh, it's the first day of school. A lot of moms wouldn't come in here to work because they want to go to the first day of school with their child.' I want them to do that too. So I make the opportunities available and am not afraid to create that kind of environment. Because when you hire professionals, even if they come in three hours late, I know they'll make up for it."

While these policies may have increased the number of women in managerial and administrative occupations since the 1980s, those in top executive positions are still rare. In addition, women and men who take advantage of these policies are concerned that they will be seen as less committed to their job and are likely to be passed over for promotions. It is difficult to know if their fears are justified, but we note that few of the women in our sample used these policies on their way to the top. We need to look at our next generation of women leaders to see whether these policies can help women to get to the top.

## Cultural Heritage

Culture is a universal variable. Everyone has a cultural heritage and can find meaning in the way culture shapes and constrains the choices open to women and men based on gender ideologies. Culture defines the expectations for women's and men's roles, so the ease with which a mother can combine her role with that of top leader in a demanding profession will vary with cultural values and norms.

The narratives of the women leaders whom we interviewed highlight themes that reflect these cultural ideologies. All of our women leaders consider their family roles to be as important, if not more important, than their work roles, although we personally find it distasteful to ask women (or men) whether their family or their work is more important. When asked in this manner, the only possible answer is that the family matters more, which we believe is true for most people. Yet, the very question pits family against work in the older balance metaphor where there must be a winning and a losing side.

In their descriptions of their family roles, our women leaders provide a glimpse of what they consider as an essential part of their roles. We also learn about the normative expectations of the different cultures. The American women leaders pride themselves on never missing their children's school play or soccer game; mothers in Hong Kong put more emphasis on helping their children with their school work; the Chinese mothers across the different societies emphasize family dinners, describing how they eat with their children before they go out to their own business dinners or go back to work in the office at night.

Dinner is an important activity in the Chinese family. Eating together is a symbol of togetherness. Furthermore, the wife and mother will take care of the nutritional value of the food according to the traditional Chinese beliefs. Particularly in Hong Kong and southern China, a soup is part of every dinner. Serving soups that are brewed for hours with different herbs is an expression of love and care from the wife and mother who may not communicate these feelings overtly. It is common to hear about a mother-in-law giving instructions to her daughter-in-law about making soups for the family to ensure that she is taking care of the family's health. Now, the chores of cooking and making soups may be relegated to domestic helpers under supervision. However, making sure that she is home for dinner and that the family have a good dinner is still a major role of a woman.

Irrespective of whether they are residing in Mainland China, Hong Kong or the US, the Chinese women leaders converge on the theme of eating dinner at home. Carrie Yau would decline dinner engagements so she could eat at home with her family; Ophelia Cheung would eat dinner with her children first before going out to her own dinner; Sun Yuehuan would bring food home from restaurants if she had to entertain in the evening; Feng Cui would rush to the market to make fresh dumplings for her children after a long day at work; Jenny Ming would always go home for dinner even if she was late; so would Doreen Woo Ho, and it was an implicit house rule that everyone would wait if she or her husband was late. Doreen has a modern interpretation of the importance of the family dinner:

> "We always sat down and had dinner together. So if I was late or he [my husband] was late, we waited for everyone to be home to eat together. It was a rule of the house that we must sit down and be a family at dinner every night. We are a modern family and everyone had different schedules but we made sure that we always sat down to dinner. Because in the morning, eating breakfast, we did have different schedules – with school, work or whatever. I would say, if we knew we were not going out to eat, that eating dinner together was a non-negotiable ritual. I believe that rituals like this are very important to reinforce and practice. . . . Dinner together gave us time to connect, talk and find out what each member of the family had done that day and to talk about current events."

Another dominant feature in the Chinese mother role is their children's education. Whereas all of our women leaders are proud that their children have turned out to be successful in their schooling and careers, the Chinese mothers, particularly those from Hong Kong, describe the efforts they make to supervise their children's homework. In Hong Kong, the expectation of children's school performance is very high. Children's homework is one of the sources of work–family conflict for women (Lo, 2003).

We heard from our interviewees about their detailed approach to helping their children with their school work. Betty Yuen, Managing Director of China Light and Power, spent her evenings helping her children with their homework. Fanny Law, Permanent Secretary of Education and Manpower, sent her son to special tutoring classes, asked him to practice dictation, and put him in the afternoon section of primary school so that she could supervise his homework after school. When Cordelia Chung was posted to Japan by IBM, she coached her daughters with their homework over long-distance telephone and fax because she felt that she would be a stricter supervisor than her husband.

Alice Tai, the Ombudsman in Hong Kong, describes her role during her children's examination period as "taking on another job."

"During those three months, I would announce to my colleagues that I had to leave the office at 5:30 p.m. for my 'part-time job.' I go home to help with their studies. That is a source of stress. Because of our mixed marriage, we want our children to embrace both the British and Chinese cultures. We send them to the Chinese International School to make sure they learn Chinese. I made up special worksheets to help them study Chinese. I made up volumes of text and exercises, which I prepared during lunch time. [*Alice took out a big folder of exercises that she had compiled for her sons when they were young.*] I actually improved my Putonghua [Mandarin Chinese – the official language spoken in Mainland China as opposed to Cantonese, which is the dialect spoken in Hong Kong] by learning with them. It was in 1991 when I was working at the Intellectual Property Department, and my elder son was in Primary 3 or 4. I have kept the volumes of exercises for sentimental reasons – this was a labor of love. But my husband felt these extra efforts unnecessary. As a Westerner, he is more liberal-minded and carefree about children's education. But I am a traditional Chinese mother, and hold onto many Chinese values, such as those about education, and took to pushing our children to learn. It was particularly hard for our younger son, who had to study twice as hard because of his learning difficulties. I tried to help him to get on top of his learning problems and difficulties with examinations. For example, he scored a D in Computer Studies in a mock examination in February. I persuaded him to get his exam papers from his teacher to review how he answered. We went through the exam questions together to identify where he had gone wrong in presenting his knowledge. By May, he scored A in the public examination. He is now in university, he is getting on well with his life on his own. I can now let go."

While the American women leaders also care about their children's academic achievement, their school performance is not a main theme. There is less homework in the American school system. Instead, extracurricular activities are accorded much more importance than in the Chinese schools. The American ideology of the "supermom" includes being there for their children during the important events in school. Many of our interviewees made every effort to attend their children's school plays or ball games. Flexible work schedules in the more family-friendly work settings would afford them the time to be there, although most of our highly successful women did not use any of the more traditional work plans that mothers sometimes choose, such as part-time employment or taking breaks from work.

Ann Kern, Managing Director and Partner of Korn/Ferry International in New York, recalled: "Well my priority was always my children. So my children always came first. I never missed a basketball game or football game or anything." How did she manage the time? She said:

"This is business where it's your own time. So if I left to get to a 3 o'clock football game or soccer game, nobody cared as long as the work was accomplished. As long as my work was done, and as long as I brought in the business, nobody cared. . . . I was very fortunate to have the managing partner who hired me. He was always a big fan of mine and knew I had young children and respected that. But I never would tell clients that I was off with my kids at a soccer game; I was just unreachable."

This sort of behavior is what we call "flying below the radar." Our group of highly successful mothers did what they needed to do to meet multiple demands, but they told few people about the way they managed to be at two places at the same time, and because they were highly successful employees, most supervisors would ignore these times away from work.

Having domestic helpers is the norm in Hong Kong, but we also found that many of the American women leaders we interviewed received help from part-time or live-in helpers. All of them were appreciative of the help they received, and felt lucky about the reliability and dedication of their helpers. Some of these helpers have helped to raise the children up to adulthood and are regarded as part of the family. Nevertheless, the American women expressed some uneasiness about having outside help. Jenny Ming advised other women not to try to do everything. She notes that women have the misperception that if they do not do everything in the house, they are failing in their role as mother or wife.

Lorna Edmundson, President of Wilson College, hired a housekeeper shortly after her second daughter was born. Both she and her husband were working long hours. She illustrated this uneasiness in describing her guilt at having home help:

> "I had to learn to let some things go, which isn't easy for me. That is some things around the house or in the garden or that I would normally have in much better shape. I had to learn that. I had to learn to depend on other people for cooking and that sort of thing. And that wasn't easy in the beginning. It's very easy now, but in the beginning it wasn't easy. . . . It wasn't how I was raised, so in the beginning, actually, the first time I had a housekeeper was in Algeria. I felt so guilty that this older woman was cleaning my house. It was un-American. I was raised in a home where we did everything ourselves and so was Dan [my husband]."

## Cross-Cultural Perspectives on the Work–Family Interface

The effect of culture can be seen in the way we talk about combining work and family and in the assumptions we take for granted during these discussions. The separation of work and family into two distinct domains is more congruent with contemporary Western ways of thinking. The work–family dichotomy is dualistic and individualistic – traits psychologists associate with Western cultures. Studies conducted by US researchers on the interface between work and family initially focused on conflict, interference, the double burden, and negative health outcomes. This paradigm supports the popular myth that women can choose only one or the other, but they cannot have both. This research paradigm ignores the fact that women have always worked and always had families.

Consider these reflections of Frances Hesselbein, Chairman of Leader to Leader and recipient of the Presidential Medal of Freedom:

> "I think of my grandmother, who had 10 children, seven of them lived. She had a 15-room house and cooked over a coal stove. Now she had help, but there were always blocks of time that she had to spend working in the house, taking care of children. So let's not pretend that women didn't work 100, 150 years ago. Life was very rigorous, and they had to find the time to care for large families. I remember that at four o'clock, no matter what my grandmother was doing, she and my grandfather had tea. He was born in England, and tea was very important. But four o'clock was their moment to be together. Everyone had to be very productive throughout the day, but they needed to take the time for family. Now if you don't give it a lot of thought or plan family time, you can get whipped up into a hectic schedule where you're frustrated because of the work–life balance challenge. That was just as true 100 years ago. When people preface a statement with, 'Now that women are working . . . ' I always say, 'Women have always worked.' "

It is only recently that research on family and work began to include ideas like positive spillover, balance, interface, and mutual facilitation, and also take on an international perspective (Poelmans, 2005). By contrast, cross-cultural research on the work–family interface shows that the roles of the individual and family are more blurred in Chinese culture, where work serves a utilitarian function for the long-term benefits of the family. For the Chinese women leaders, a happy family is a measure of the success of their work. Gu Xiulian, Vice-Chairman of the Standing Committee of the National People's Congress and President of the All-China Women's Federation, summarized this value in her personal motto: "To have a successful career, and to have a happy family."

In cross-cultural psychology, national cultures have been compared in terms of different dimensions of societal norms (Hofstede, 1980). Anglo cultures, like the United States, are considered to be individualistic. In these cultures, identity is based in the individual and emphasis is placed on autonomy and independence. Individuals are supposed to take care of themselves and their immediate family, which consists of the nuclear unit of the couple and their children. In contrast, Asian cultures, like China, are considered to be collectivistic in orientation.

Identity is based in the social system, an organization, or a group to which the individual belongs. People are born into extended families which take care of them in exchange for their loyalty. The concept of one's family includes members of the clan. Interdependence and harmony among group members are emphasized.

This cultural comparison may help to explain the different ways in which work and family are construed in cross-cultural research on work–family balance. Research into Chinese societies shows that work and family are viewed as interdependent domains, unlike the distinct segregation of these two domains in Western concepts of work and family. In individualistic societies, work may be viewed as a main source of self-actualization; and overwork would be considered taking time away from the family and sacrificing the family for the advancement of one's own career. In collectivistic societies, work may be viewed in terms of securing the family's well-being; and overwork is likely to be seen as sacrificing oneself for the family, since commitment to work is viewed as a means of ensuring financial security for the family (Yang, Chen, Chao, & Zou, 2000).

A cross-national comparative study (Spector, Cooper, Poelmans et al., 2004) involving 15 samples of managers across three culturally distinct regions – Anglo (Australia, Canada, England, New Zealand, and the US), China (Hong Kong, Mainland China, and Taiwan), and seven countries in Latin America – showed that for the Anglo culture, working long hours was related to work–family stress. For the Chinese and Latin cultures, this was not the case. For the Chinese managers, being married and having children were associated with higher job satisfaction and psychological well-being.

These research findings suggest that, in the Chinese culture, the needs of the self are subsumed under the needs of the collective. Women are also more likely to receive social support from their extended family. Under these social norms, it is not so much the time spent but the relationships at work and in the family which matter to Chinese women. Research on work–family stressors for Chinese women showed that the presence of interpersonal conflict presents greater stress to women than having multiple role demands (Lai, 1995).

In Hong Kong, a series of research studies conducted by Samuel Aryee and his colleagues (1999a, 1999b) on the work–family interface also showed that work and family involvement per se did not lead to work–family conflict. The sources of conflict between the work and family roles are more time-based than strain-based or behavior-based. The most frequently mentioned causes of conflict are lack of support from husbands, exhaustion and burnout, and amount of homework required of their children.

The Chinese women leaders from Hong Kong and the US highlighted the help of the spouse in a more tangible way than their Mainland Chinese counterparts. The latter group expressed less expectation of their husbands being involved in homemaking and childcare, even though during the era when everyone was poor their husbands actually had to take care of the housework and the children. Rather, it is the expectation that husbands should share that may contribute to the conflict. Aryee and his colleagues' (1999b) study in Hong Kong showed that spousal support moderated the effect of work–family conflict. Job–spouse conflict, rather than the conflict between work roles and the roles of homemaker and parent, had a greater impact on job, marital, and life satisfaction.

# The Culture of Gender

Sexism is enacted within cultures. Psychological research has identified two forms of sexist ideologies: benevolent sexism and hostile sexism. Benevolent sexism distinguishes between female characteristics and male characteristics, but considers gender differences to be complementary. Women are treated differently because they need to be taken care of and protected. Hostile sexism devalues women's characteristics and considers them to be inferior to men's. Hostile sexism is related to sex discrimination (Glick & Fiske, 1997).

Sexism is found across cultures, but may be expressed in different forms. How do these sexist ideologies come about? Cross-cultural psychological research has focused on two potential sources of sexist ideologies: family socialization and cultural contexts. A recent study compared college students' sexist attitudes in the US and Taiwan (Lee, Pratto, & Lee, 2007) and related these to parental socialization of family norms. "Deferential family norms" define hierarchical relationships within families, in which roles of parents, husbands, and older siblings are regarded as more powerful than those of children, wives, and younger siblings. Deferential family norms endorsing the idea that certain male family roles are superior to female family roles would lead to hostile sexism. On the other hand, the belief that dominant family roles (such as husbands) should support and take care of subordinate family roles (such as wives) would lead to benevolent sexism.

This study found cultural differences in the relationship between deferential family norms and the two forms of sexism. Deferential family norms predicted hostile sexism in the American students but benevolent sexism in the Taiwanese students. When the students in this study were asked to allocate limited funding resources to a men's team or a women's team in an experiment, both the American and Taiwanese students who endorsed hostile sexism were more likely to allocate money in favor of the men's team over the women's team. However, the Taiwanese, but not the American, students who endorsed benevolent sexism were also biased in favor of men in the money allocation. So, benevolent sexism, in addition to hostile sexism, also predicted sex discrimination in Taiwan. The authors referred to the Chinese cultural roots of Confucianism, which emphasizes harmony in the maintenance of hierarchical relationships, to account for the discriminatory outcome of benevolent sexism in Taiwan.

This study also illustrates that, while culture prescribes the norms and expectations of gender roles and behaviors, there are differences within the culture in the way individuals play out these roles. We recognize that there are ethnic, regional, and class differences within the larger cultural group. We have shown in this chapter how the historical and cultural contexts shape the views and experiences of our group of women leaders. Our biggest surprise in interviewing the dually successful woman in our sample was the extensive similarities across cultures. When we began our study, we thought there would be many differences between the Chinese and American women leaders in how they managed the combination of top-level work and successful family life. We found more convergence than we expected in the way that these women leaders have interwoven work and family roles on their paths to the top. One might have expected that the American women leaders would segregate their work and family roles more distinctly as shown in Western theories and research on work–family conflict. However, with their growing confidence in their own identity, professional women do not need to conform to the roles and behaviors of men in order to become leaders. They have defied the constraints of sexism which is pervasive across culture. They can embrace the multifaceted roles of being a woman. It seems that the combined roles of a woman and high-achieving leader and caregiver at this time in history are stronger than the effects of culture.

## Gender Across Cultures

In hindsight, we now see that one reason for the cross-cultural similarities is that all of the women share what we call "the culture of gender." Despite many differences in conditions of rearing, life opportunities, and political systems, there are cross-cultural gender (or sex) role norms which created opportunities and constraints for all of the women leaders. There are restrictions inherent in the role of being a woman which make it difficult to achieve at high levels in a demanding career. Here are a few that will have heads nodding everywhere around the world.

## Clothes, Makeup, Cleavage

High-achieving women are not fashion models, but they are scrutinized in the media as though they were competing for prom queen instead of corporate CEO or Supreme Court Judge (prom queen refers to a "quaint" US custom of selecting the best-looking girl and boy at the senior high school dance to serve as the queen and king). When Hillary Rodham Clinton was running for president of the United States in 2008, every outfit she wore was commented on by the press. They had a field day over "cleavage." The *Washington Post* fashion correspondent strayed into politics and psychology in a long article about Clinton's "rose-colored blazer worn over a black top. The top was a subtle V neck" that showed cleavage (Wheaton, 2007). The columnist then went on to discuss how Clinton's neckline was a symptom of her uneasiness with her femininity in her public life.

Jane Swift (2008), former governor of Massachusetts and the only governor to ever give birth while in office (she had twins!), has written about the difficulties women face when running for and holding public office in the US. Political opponents complained to the media when she worked from her hospital bed after giving birth, and her childcare decisions were a constant topic in the news.

Women have to adhere to strict standards for dress – not too frilly or feminine or too manly. According to one study: "A female candidate who is less 'tailored' – both in the way she carries herself and in her manner of dress – is perceived by both male and female voters as less qualified, less of a leader, and less professional" (Barbara Lee

Family Foundation, 2004). In a study of media coverage during the 2000 Republican primary elections, the comparisons for Elizabeth Dole, the lone female candidate, showed that when it came to coverage on policy issues, Dole received less coverage than all of the other candidates and half of the coverage that George Bush got (17 percent versus 33 percent), but when the topic was personal issues, she received twice the coverage of the least covered major candidate, Steve Forbes. The media signal what is important about female and male candidates by how and how much they present the candidate in the news. This is a critical distinction because it is through the media that the general public learn about political candidates, and what they learned was largely about Elizabeth Dole's personal life and the political views of the men she was running against.

When women first entered into the corporate world, they tried to imitate men. Marjorie Woo, who is now the CEO of Keystone Leadership (Shanghai) Inc. in China, started her career in corporate America. She remembered how she tried to dress for success:

"In the early days working in Xerox Corporation, I actually went through this stage dressing like a man – wearing a pin-striped suit, dark color suit, and pink and blue shirt or blouse or wearing a bow-tie. Those days in the 1980s, that was a corporate environment though there were no formal dress code regulations. We women thought that was how you need to behave and proceed. I think probably it is more perception. There was no formal requirement. In fact, in those days, the corporation had a certain perception about what the management people should look or act like. Even those days, there were professional women in the Bay Area from other companies whom we will meet in social life, they were also in dark and striped suits and tried to dress for acceptance. So that must be an unspoken norm for young women to think to be successful, because there are very few role models. So we imitated how men dressed and how they behaved. And we need to be dressed like them and to be very aggressive or assertive in our way of expression."

As we contend, these are cross-cultural constants that make it more difficult for women to succeed because their appearance and personal lives are scrutinized in ways that men can avoid. As we were writing this book, Anson Chan was running for an open seat on Hong Kong's Legislative Council (she won). It was a hotly contested by-election which made her "the public's most familiar political leader," known to more people than Hong Kong's Chief Executive Officer, Donald

Tsang (*South China Morning Post*, November 9, 2007, p. A4). She was representing the pro-democracy camp which was pushing for universal suffrage for all citizens of Hong Kong. She is a seasoned political leader who is over 60 years old, yet the newspaper accounts constantly referred to her dimples and her well-matched suit and cheongsam (Chinese dress), and her opponents alleged that she has had plastic surgery to make her look younger.

Anson recently spoke at a political rally and when she left a reporter followed her and later reported that she went to a hairdresser without finishing the march. It is inconceivable that we would read about a male candidate who had a haircut (except for those occasions when candidates spend several hundred dollars on one). These sorts of criticisms demean her as a serious candidate. The subtle demeaning of women in high-level positions can also be seen in the way the press described Anson and the people who work with her – describing them as the "handbag gang." Handbags are not symbols of leadership, but they are necessary and culturally appropriate for women whose clothing usually lacks pockets.

Thus, women in high-level positions need to appear young and attractive, but when they do, they are scrutinized and criticized for their appearance. Time spent on extra grooming – coloring and curling hair, painting nails, tweezing eyebrows, shopping for appropriate clothing and so on – adds many extra hours to an overpacked day. Many women who have the ability and opportunity to achieve at the highest level no doubt look at the "costs" for women high-achievers and decide that mid-level careers offer the best compromise, sparing them the constant commentary on their appearance and their families.

Those women who dared to be dually successful have done so at personal cost, including loss of privacy for themselves and, in some cases, their families. They need to fulfill the demands of multiple competing roles, appearing feminine, but without cleavage, while also appropriately tailored; having fashionable hair that seems effortless to maintain but, of course, never is; looking young and hiding any (surgical) assistance they may have had in achieving that look; and we have not yet mentioned their work as mothers and high-level achievers in demanding jobs. Women across the US, Hong Kong, and China experience the culture of gender, which makes the similarities among these incredible women more apparent than differences that may have been caused by the culture of their countries.

# Chapter 8

# Leading as Women: Styles, Obstacles, and Perceptions

The 62 powerful women leaders we interviewed are proof that the term "women leaders" is not an oxymoron. They all made it to the top of their profession, where they are making critical decisions that will have long-lasting effects on international corporations, the highest levels of government, police departments in some of the world's largest cities, legal systems, and virtually every type of influential office that can be named. Although only a few of the women we interviewed are in politics, life at the top of all hierarchies is inherently political. We are not using the term in its more usual meaning, which refers to the governing process of countries, but in its broader and more generic meaning of jockeying for power and influence regardless of the context. There are politics in the boardroom, on the judicial bench, in private and public organizations, and all along the road that leads through middle management to the executive suite or top administrative office. Leaders are powerful people who achieve their power by successfully navigating through choppy and perilous political waters. How do women, especially those with children, obtain power and how do they wield it when they make it to the top?

Every year, *Forbes* magazine lists the most powerful women in the world. They are described as "Women who make things happen" (MacDonald & Schoenberger, 2005). When we read the usual short blurbs about the professional lives of these women, their stories sound similar to those of men who made it to the top of their profession; they all weathered controversies, suffered set-backs, and, at least at the time they are being recognized, enjoy phenomenal success. But, there is little in the usual listings of who is successful in which profession that can tell us what the most powerful women did (or did not do) that allowed them entry to top-level positions, where few women have entered. Do they lead in the same way as their male counterparts? How do they achieve and maintain their legitimacy as leaders when at the end of the day they go home to change diapers and read bedtime stories?

# Is There a Women's Style of Leadership?

There is a common perception that women have a leadership style that differs from the way (most) men lead. Whenever the topic turns to women leaders, old stereotypes about men and women are inevitably raised. Most people believe that there are important differences in how women respond to the challenges of leadership. In a recent survey of approximately 300 executives, both men and women indicated their belief that male leaders "take charge" and female leaders "take care" (Catalyst, 2005). In other words, beliefs about women and men leaders mirror beliefs about women and men in general. Other research on stereotypes of male and female leaders confirms these findings and adds the optimistic perspective that these stereotypes may be changing. Increasingly, beliefs about female and male leaders are becoming more similar, although the perceived similarity is not universal (Duehr & Bono, 2006).

## Unconscious Effects of Stereotypes

It is often difficult to explain the pervasive negative effects of stereotypes on how we think and act because much of the effect is unconscious. Most readers will deny that they are limited in any way by stereotypical beliefs about women or men, but a series of experimental studies shows that we are affected in ways that escape conscious awareness. In fact, it is relatively simple to get people to alter their behavior without their awareness. For example, in one study, college students read a list of words pertaining to older adults as part of what they thought was a study of memory. These students walked more slowly as they left the laboratory than students who read a different list of words without the references to the elderly (Bargh, Chen, & Burrows, 1996). Similarly, when college students participated in a word game (scrambled sentence) in which the words described rude behavior, they interrupted the experimenter more often than when the words were polite or neutral. None of the participants were consciously aware that the words they had just read were influencing their behavior, and they would have denied it if they were asked about it. These are two examples from a large body of research literature which shows that we are often influenced by covert messages without knowing it.

Unconscious influences are important in determining whether individuals will volunteer for a leadership role and how they will perform once they are in that role. In one set of studies, researchers showed college students a series of television commercials (Davies, Spencer, & Steele, 2005). Some of the commercials depicted characters conforming to female sex role stereotypes (e.g. a college student dreams about become a home-coming queen or dances joyously after purchasing cosmetics); others did not depict sex role stereotypes (e.g. an advertisement for a cell phone). Students were randomly assigned to watch either the sex-stereotyped commercials or the neutral commercials. They were then asked to participate in a study about leadership. They could choose to be either a participant in a problem-solving group or the leader of the group. Among students who watched the neutral commercials, men and women were equally likely to select either role. Among those who watched the sex-stereotyped commercial, many fewer women selected the leader role, but there was no difference for the men. The same results were obtained with other experimental manipulations. When sex-stereotypes about women were made salient, women were less likely to take on leadership roles. None of the women were aware that their decision was affected by watching television commercials that depicted women in sex-stereotyped ways. This example is selected from a large literature on the effect of environmental messages about how we should act on how we actually do act. These demonstrations show the power of the media and other influences on our decisions, including the decision to assume the role of leader.

Our beliefs about female and male traits and behaviors comprise what cognitive psychologists call "mental schemata," which are central organizing principles that guide how we think. There is a growing body of research on the unconscious processing of information which shows that these schemata are deeply entrenched in our thinking and operate automatically and without awareness. They shape our expectations about women and men and they guide our perceptions and memories. They exert these effects even for people who claim to have no stereotyped beliefs.

Stereotypes about the way female and male leaders behave and, even more importantly, how they should behave, are clearly articulated by Wei Keizheng, who is Chair of the Board for Keili (HK) Group and for Hainan Kailie Central Development Shares Co. Ltd. She has overseen major development projects in Hainan since the province first opened up its business opportunities. Wei is the first Chinese woman entrepreneur to be listed among the "World's Outstanding Women Entrepreneurs." She set a legal precedent by bringing a successful lawsuit against the Stock Exchange of China for delaying the listing of her company. By any objective standard she is a strong and effective leader, so readers may be surprised to read about her thoughts on women leaders and her own leadership style:

"When women are working, they encounter more difficulties than men, so I needed to make the men afraid of me. At first, I would discuss matters patiently with them, but they wouldn't listen [because they did not respect me as a leader]. Later, when I produced results and earned a great deal of money, I developed a fiery temper. I developed a very strong character that I used to control the people in the corporations that I led. I would scold the people I worked with until, over time, they finally accepted me. Men are proud and thick-skinned and will bully you if you do not show them your strength. Female entrepreneurial leaders are like the old grandmother in the family where they have to be caring, loving, and helpful, but have no mercy in punishing and disciplining others. This is the only type of personality that will allow women to sustain an enterprise. It is easier for men to be leaders, whereas female leaders must keep a distance from their male subordinates, but yet not be too far away so as to maintain the role of a grandmother – respectable but not lovable."

It is interesting to note that when Wei describes her more assertive style of leadership, she is likening it to the way of influencing people that a grandmother would use, presumably with unruly children. Like an effective grandmother, she would get angry, punish naughty children, and care for them at the same time.

Shi Qingqi, the former Director of the Institute of Industrial Development under the National Development and Reform Commission, is an expert in economics who has published many influential papers on economic policies. She also uses female stereotypes, again in an unconventional way, to describe how she leads:

"They said I am not like a Department Director but a mother. I think I have to give them care and also personal space. I do not want others to govern me and make decisions for me. Therefore, I wanted to help them with their scientific research and I would bear the responsibility. . . . Compared with male bosses, I think we have more loving care. I really regard them [people who report to her] as my children. On the other hand, I would not feel bad if my subordinates excel and are better than me. I work hard in doing research because I wasted much time in my earlier years. Therefore, I always work until late at night and often just slept on the sofa."

Shi Qingqi mixes the image of the good mother with that of a competitive business person. Despite the mix of these seemingly disparate images, she makes it clear that she is caring and loving, like a mother. These are not attributes that are stereotypically associated with leaders.

Sun Yuehuan is Chair of the Board and CEO of China Enterprise Appraisals (CEA) and Board Chairman and General Manager of China Enterprise Consultants. CEA specializes in asset appraisal. The corporation assists enterprises in their reorganization and restructuring and has been ranked number one in the industry. Sun Yuehuan was one of the first Certified Public Accountants in China. Among her many achievements, she was also an officer in the People's Liberation Army of China and an official in the State Audit Administration. This is how she reflected on her leadership:

"I think I perform better than my male counterparts in this business because their teams lack cohesion; they lack the feminine emotional expression. They do not show adequate concern for their superiors and subordinates. There are two main reasons for a staff's instability at work: first is they are not convinced by their leaders; second is the members believe they are not treated fairly (e.g. they feel that their good ideas, talents, and the improvement in their performance standards have not been recognized). My staff has a strong commitment to the team. Some of them have worked with me for 10 years, but they are still hard-working because they can see their bright future.

I am the leader in this industry; my company has been at the top in terms of financial results for seven consecutive years. I think a leader should uphold a stringent principle: adhere to the truth, be decisive, able to judge, and do not do a single wrong deed or say the wrong thing. Women leaders also need to be empathetic, caring, considerate, and show respect to others. I expect my staff to be excellent in their work and harmonious in their family lives. I also set a good example for them because I am involved in my career and I handle my family well. I am very serious about my work."

I think that many readers will be surprised to see that a top female executive who served in the People's Liberation Army attributes her success to teamwork and a feminine emotional approach. She is not advocating a "mushy" or feel-good notion of what a feminine emotional approach might be. For her, a feminine approach includes being serious about your work, maintaining the highest personal standards, and being considerate and respectful of your staff.

The general consensus among the high-achieving women with families is that when women are compared to men, women have a different and even better style of leadership. They have strong opinions about what makes a good leader and they leave no doubt about the question of whether women can be just as good as men in positions of leadership. Unlike the assumption that the male leadership style results in better outcomes, many of these high-achieving women responded that women, on average, are better as leaders because:

> "We are more natural, more willing to express our feelings and thoughts, which can be an advantage. Women are more intuitive and have more collaborative skill sets. Women are better at building consensus and team spirit. I think women instinctually have leadership styles that are different from men's, but men in management today are learning more of these skills. In a crisis, I become more directive and autocratic. I can do that when I need to, but that's not my instinctive style. I guess my style would be different from the 'command and control' style of some men because I want to help others to achieve and establish relationships."

These are Barbara Franklin's (former US Secretary of Commerce) reflections on women's leadership in general and how she leads. Notice the repeated use of the word "team" by the women leaders in all three cultures. They are all communicating a sense that leadership is about the group and not the individual.

Frances Hesselbein, whose professional interests include the development of leaders, has strong opinions about this topic. She is the Chairman of Leader to Leader and former CEO of the Girl Scouts of the USA. In these roles, she has consulted extensively with leaders who are women:

"First we have to define leadership on our own terms. Mine is 'Leadership is a matter of how to be, not how to do.' It is the quality and character of the leader that determines the performance or the result that an organization is seeking. A leader should say, 'these are the principles I live by: integrity, respect for all people, and a generous spirit. I am committed to providing opportunities for other people to learn and grow and equal access to these opportunities.' When leaders look at their work, they need to ask if they are building inclusive and responsive organizations. Everything we do must embody the values and principles we espouse. You can't just talk about your integrity and values. You have to live them. There are a number of wonderful parts of Peter Drucker's leadership philosophy that should walk around with you. He says that an integral part of leadership is learning to make the strengths of our people effective and their weaknesses irrelevant."

We note here that Frances was a student of Peter Drucker, whose work we quote throughout this chapter. She worked extensively with him.

The picture of women leaders that Barbara Franklin and Frances Hesselbein portray is shared by many people. In general, women are believed to be more communal in nature than men – more concerned with the feelings of other people, more emotionally expressive, and nicer; whereas men are more agentic than women – more assertive, dominant, confident, task-oriented, and ambitious (Duehr & Bono, 2006). If you stop for a moment to think about the constellation of traits that make up our commonly held beliefs about women and men, you will realize that the traits associated with being a man are the same ones that we associate with being a leader. If you doubt that this is true, take a few minutes to read through the "Help Wanted" section of any major newspaper that lists executive-level job openings. The advertisements for executive positions state qualifications such as, "seeking aggressive deal closers," "dynamic spokespersons," and "independent thinkers and leaders." None are looking for caring executives who are nice or anyone who sees the role as similar to being a good grandmother or mother, yet these are the terms used by our women leaders to describe how they lead. Any advertisement for an executive-level opening that included these more feminine terms would most likely be met with snickers and guffaws.

By law, newspapers in the US cannot blatantly rule out women or men in their job listings (unless there is a defensible reason, such as wash-room attendant). A similar law came into effect in Hong Kong in 1996. This antidiscrimination regulation does not exist in many other countries. In a recent article about contemporary China in the highly respected journal *The Economist* (August 24, 2007), the author wrote, "I am struck by the outrageous discrimination in most of the job advertisements displayed in the exchange. If you're not a man under the age of 35, there doesn't seem to be much hope for you."

## Leadership Defined

If we want to understand the concept of leadership styles, perhaps we should take a step back to address a larger question, "What is a leader?" The most succinct definition was offered by Peter Drucker, who is generally acknowledged as a leading guru in the field of leadership: "The only definition of a leader is someone who has followers" (Hesselbein & Goldsmith, 2007). Although it would be difficult to disagree with Drucker's definition, perhaps a better question is, "What does a leader do that attracts followers?" One way to attract followers is with sheer brute force and fear, a method preferred by dictators throughout history, but one that is not recommended for a host of ethical reasons that we will not list. Our goal is not to provide a blueprint for the sort of harmful leadership that was practiced by Hitler, Stalin, and others, who oppressed people and caused massive numbers of deaths. We are interested in promoting ethical leaders, not finding ways for more women to join the ranks of what Lipman-Bluman (2004) calls "toxic leaders."

# Getting There: Leaders in the Making

The women we interviewed did not begin life at the top. As their stories show, most came from humble origins and, in some cases, extreme poverty and grew up during a time of political upheaval. How did they get where they are today? What can the rest of us, who are getting cramped necks from looking up, learn from their experiences?

There was surprising uniformity in the way the women planned their move to the top – they didn't. It is not as though there was one point early in their lives when they decided that they wanted to have more responsibility and more control, so they carefully planned how to maneuver through the labyrinth – which is a term preferred by Eagly and Carli (2007a) as an alternative to the glass ceiling.

Helena Ashby, who was chief in one of the largest sheriff's departments in the US, described her early career aspirations in this highly male-dominated field which until recently employed few men of color. Helena is an African-American woman:

> "And when I look back and I've had time to be very retrospective and introspective about the trails I've been on in my life, that [becoming chief] was like opening something that very few women, particularly women of color, would ever get to do. When I joined [the Sheriff's Department] the agreement with my husband was that I would work for five years and help him. I had no intention of making that a career because you didn't see women in positions of influence in that field, and you certainly didn't see anyone that looked like me there. So it never occurred to me that that was where I could make my career."

Sarah Weddington, the attorney in the landmark case Roe v. Wade which legalized abortion in the US, gave us this advice for becoming a leader:

> "It's what I call the step-by-step method of leadership, that you start out to do one thing, then you take that step. Then you look ahead and you say, 'Well I think I could take that other step.' So you take that step, then you take one more step, then you look around and you say, 'Well I guess I could take that next one too.' So it's a step-by-step where you don't start out . . . with the thought that you will end up at one certain place."

Anyone of us can take one step, and if we follow Weddington's instructions for the "Texas-Two-Step" (which is the name of a popular dance), we could, one day, find that instead of climbing a ladder, we danced to the top without stopping to think that we could never get that far.

Sue Schechter, a former State Representative from Texas who is currently a political strategist, comes back to the main theme of how to advance in your career when you have children:

> "When the kids were really young, in February of 89, I quit as the general manager of the CIGNA litigation office here in Houston. I had taken off that summer trying to decide what I was going to do and what I was going to do with the kids. A friend of mine suggested that I think about running against our incumbent state representative. I had

not thought of it, and I wasn't active in politics. But I was very active in my children's school through the PTA [parent–teacher association]. Of course, being a lawyer, I was active in different professional groups. And when he said this, I kind of thought, 'You know, this isn't a bad idea.' There was a tenured incumbent; so there was no hope that I could beat him. But he had moved so far to the right on issues for our representative district that I thought at least if he had an opponent then he would have to talk about things and people would kind of know where he stood on the issues. And then on the last day of filing [registering as a candidate] with the filing deadline over at six p.m., it was five til six, and he did not file. Instead, he went in and took a friend of his to file. That made it an open seat, which totally changed everything from when I was running against a tenured incumbent to running for an open seat with no incumbent. I was quite concerned about school issues. My children were in elementary school. I was concerned about what we were doing with workers' compensation because I saw a lot of that through the law practice. And that's how I became politically active."

Sue's journey seems to have begun more by serendipity than a careful plan, but by the time she was asked to run, she already had a law degree and had worked in a high-level position in the insurance industry. In addition, her concerns were education and workers' compensation – areas that showed her concern for her own children and for the way injured workers are compensated. She began to develop her leadership skills in areas where mothers typically lead – the local PTA – and she parlayed this background into a successful political career.

Rita Fan was the first woman to chair Hong Kong's Legislative Council. She oversaw many of the political transitions involved in the handover of Hong Kong from British rule to become a Special Administrative Region of China. For her, it was about serving the people of Hong Kong and helping to secure rights during this period of major change in their government. Like the others, she did not set out to become a leader:

"In 1983, in the mid of my Polytechnic career [where she was head of the student affairs service], I was appointed by the government to serve in LegCo [Legislative Council of Hong Kong]. I decided to take it up because I wanted to do something for the community. I owe Hong Kong for all that I have (e.g. a good job, quality education, and a happy family are gifts). I was not interested in politics at the time that

I joined LegCo. I saw it as a public service. I aimed to do something for education. In 1983 we were in the middle of Sino-British negotiations [the handover from British rule to China was in 1997]. I was working on many questions important to Hong Kong's future: How would we ensure that the people of Hong Kong would maintain their current lifestyle and freedoms? How would we keep economic systems and financial structures intact? During my second appointment in 1985, I got involved with the Vietnamese refugee issue. I realized that the Hong Kong community had been carrying the burden of many refugees but not getting the recognition. It was unfair that Hong Kong was criticized for its human rights policies by members of parliament in the United Kingdom. The root of the problem was in the international community, especially the attitude of the United States. It was a difficult few years because I felt that I had no chance of prevailing over those problems. But I persisted because I saw it as my responsibility as a LegCo member to speak up. I went to London, Washington, Europe, and Geneva to seek international attention on behalf of Hong Kong. The press in the US and UK would not pay attention to a woman who was appointed (there was no election at that time)."

Thus we see that Rita Fan's work in politics began with a concern for education and a desire to repay Hong Kong for the wonderful life she had there. Once she was "at the legislative table," she became a major player in the transfer of Hong Kong and in ensuring the rights of its people.

Margaret York is another interviewee from the US who became a chief of police. Margaret's department was the County of Los Angeles, also a huge department. She told us about her long road to get to the top of one of the largest police departments, a road that very few women have ever traveled. Like all of the women, she knew that she needed a strong educational background to advance, but she was a working mother. Here is how she did it:

"When I was married, and when I first came on the job, I only had a high school education. In order to be promoted to the higher ranks of supervision, you have to have both a Bachelor's Degree and a Master's Degree. And I knew – I wanted both. I wanted both degrees, but I knew that I was carrying a full load [working full-time as a police officer, later a detective, and caring for three children]. I couldn't do anything more when my children were growing up beyond being a mother and being a detective. I couldn't do anything more. So I put off my education. I didn't go back to school until my youngest child was in her later years of high school. And then I went back to night school. It took a long time, but I got a Bachelor's Degree and then I got a Master's Degree. And when I started getting my degrees, the opportunities in the upper ranks of the police department became more open for me. So I was older when I got my degrees, and I was older when I was competing in the upper ranks because most of the men – a lot of police officers get the degrees while they're on the job, but most of them started at a much younger age than I did."

This is an inspiring story about persistence.

All of the women whose stories we used, and many others whose stories we cannot include because of space limitations, did not begin their careers expecting or even necessarily considering moving into high-level positions. They each proved themselves at one level and walked through the doors they opened to the next level. There is almost no mention of ambition and the only discussions of money relate to when the women were early in their careers and had trouble making ends meet. And when they walked through the doors to the next level of responsibility, they took their children with them, focusing on family-related issues in government, improving the workplace for other women in business, and improving conditions for women and children.

## Styles of Leadership

There are many styles of leadership that have been studied by social scientists, but the two that are dominant in contemporary research are *transformational* and *transactional*. Older models were based on the "Great Man" theory, which began with the premise that we should study great men to figure out what they did as leaders and, from this, we would have a description of great leadership – it is whatever the great men did. There are many problems with this older conceptualization, not the least of which is the literal emphasis on "man," not in its more inclusive and generic meaning that includes all people, but its literal emphasis on males. There are many reasons why there have historically been few women in leadership positions – women were overtly or implicitly blocked from becoming leaders. So studying great men cannot provide insights into the question of how "great women" lead. It also provides a static vision of leadership because it is based on the past and, in this rapidly changing world, we cannot assume that what worked in the past is suited for contemporary society or societies to come.

Some people have argued that women and men must lead in the same ways because they are held to the same performance standards. This is an indirect way of saying that if we consider an individual in a context, the context will determine what that person will do. If, for example, there are uniform standards for judging the success of a CEO – which usually means financial success – then women and men in that position will adopt styles that are consistent with the standards by which they are judged. There is no doubt that the situation is important. A CEO of a corporation that is overwhelmingly masculine in its image, the people it employs, and those it serves, such as a large mining company or a machine parts manufacturer, would be expected to adopt a somewhat different style from a CEO for a corporation that is predominantly female, such as a home nursing company or a chain of preschools. The person–context match would be expected regardless of whether the CEO was a woman or a man. But there can be different routes to the same outcomes, so it does not necessarily follow that women and men must be using the same leadership styles to reach similar goals, or that they even conceptualize the goals in the same way.

## Transformational and Transactional Leadership Styles

The most influential concept in leadership studies is the distinction between transformational and transactional styles of leadership. Burns (1978) defined transformational leaders as ones who *"engage with others in such a way that leaders and followers raise one another to higher levels of motivation and morality"* (p. 20). Over the last 30 years, this concept has evolved to include leaders who are inspiring, optimistic, moral, and equitable. Judge and Piccolo (2004) built on earlier work in their study of transformational leadership and extended the concept to include charismatic individuals who provide inspirational motivation, intellectual stimulation, individual consideration, and a higher purpose in life. This style of leadership is most often contrasted with the more traditional and hierarchically organized transactional style. Transformational leaders transform others by pushing them to assume new points of view and question their prior assumptions (Goethals, 2005). They minimize hierarchies, so that they remain close to their followers instead of being separated by layers of middle-men (and middle-women).

By contrast, transactional leaders offer their followers something in exchange for the legitimacy or authority to lead. These leaders may achieve monetary gains for their followers, such as when a politician promises a tax cut if elected. According to Burns, there are no lasting bonds established between leaders and followers as a result of this exchange, so once the tax cut is enacted, the followers will readily switch their allegiance to another leader.

When Frances Hesselbein talks about women's leadership styles, it is as though she is teaching us about transformational models:

> "Today's leaders need to practice dispersed leadership, which is dispersing the responsibilities of leadership across the organization. This means throwing out your hierarchical structure and systems where you have people in little boxes, and you talk about up and down and top and bottom. We need a flat management system where the structure is circular, flexible, and fluid. Leaders need to be passionate about their mission, and mobilizing their people around mission and values."

For our sample of highly successful women, leadership is about motivating and influencing people. It is what makes their work meaningful and motivates them to work as leaders. With this definition, a leader need not be in an official position of power; the power comes from the ability to influence people, regardless of one's job title or status in an organization or society. It is practiced in a wide variety of settings where women typically lead, including as heads of parent–teacher associations, principals of elementary schools, religious leaders, and in small retail establishments. When we broaden our definition of leadership to include the ability to influence, then we see that women have always held these positions, with the difference being in the number of people being influenced (e.g. an elementary school with tens of teachers and, most likely, hundreds of students and parents, versus a large corporation with multiple offices around the world that deal with large sums of money).

## Women as Transformational Leaders

The definition of transformational leadership is more congruent with the interpersonal characteristics associated with women leaders than the aggressive and hierarchical characteristics associated with male leaders. Although it is unlikely that many of the women we interviewed are familiar with the research literature on leadership, with the exception of Frances Hesselbein who is an expert in this field, it is surprising how much their personal reflections mirror the exact language used to describe transformational leaders.

## Research on Women and Men as Leaders

There are commonly held beliefs about differences in how women and men lead, which are shared by the highly successful women we interviewed. But, are there actual data that support these beliefs? Do the commonly held stereotypes have a basis in fact?

There is a large research literature that addresses the question of sex-typed leadership. It is a complex area to study because there are many inconsistencies and the answers seem to depend on situational variables as much as individual differences in how people lead. The social psychologist Alice Eagly and her colleagues have studied women and leadership for decades and have summarized their findings in recent reviews (Eagly & Carli, 2007a, 2007b) and meta-analytic studies, where the results of many different studies are compiled and analyzed as a way of producing a single statistical summary of many different studies. We have followed the logic of her recent paper on this topic (Eagly & Carli, 2007b) as a framework for this discussion.

In a meta-analytic study of women's and men's leadership styles, Eagly and Johnson (1990) found that there was a tendency for women to be more democratic and participative in their style and for men to be more autocratic and directive. And, although many of the sex differences in leadership styles that they found in other settings tended to be smaller when they were assessed in organizational settings (e.g. corporations versus laboratory studies), this main distinction was equally strong across settings. The authors conclude that, "the view . . . that women and men lead in the same way should be very substantially revised" (p. 248). But they also go on to say that the view that there are two distinct ways of leading – a female way and a male way – is not correct either. The size of the sex differences that are found depends on the setting and how leadership styles are measured, and there is much overlap between the behaviors of women and men.

In another meta-analytic review of the research literature, Eagly and her colleagues (Eagly, Johannnesen-Schmidt, & van Engen, 2003) found that female leaders are more transformational in their style than male leaders. These researchers also found that women leaders tended to engage in more reward-contingency behaviors than men leaders. In other words, the women leaders linked employee rewards to their behaviors in appropriate ways that allowed employees to see the link between their efforts and outcomes at work and the rewards they received. Although the size of the effect that differentiated women from men leaders was small, the meta-analysis showed consistent findings that favored women leaders. Additionally, male leaders were more likely than female leaders to rely on the main components of transactional leadership, which included focusing on their followers' mistakes and waiting for problems to occur before intervening. Taken together, these two summaries of many different studies suggest that women are indeed more transformational and men more transactional in how they lead, but there are individual differences and overlap between these two types of leadership.

We ask readers to consider what type of leader they would prefer. Most people respond that they prefer a leader who is transformational. We are frequently asked if the world would be a better place if we had more women as heads of government. This is, of course, a hypothetical question, because, thus far, we have had relatively few women as heads of large governments.

Recent research on women leaders found that the situation is critical in determining if and when women really do lead differently from men. In a study of how leaders are evaluated, Eagly, Karau, and Makhijani (1995) found that, overall (across 80 different studies), men and women leaders were evaluated as being equally effective, but women were evaluated as being less effective in masculine settings, with the reverse occurring for men in feminine settings. Of course, we cannot know from these data whether women and men really were more effective when they were working in a situation that was congruent with their sex or whether they were just perceived that way – perhaps because they were violating gender norms and stereotypes when they were in settings that were more typical of the other sex. These data show that the situation is an important variable in how people perform and/or in how they are rated in their performance.

Studies of women and men political leaders show few behavioral differences, but each political situation is unique and it is difficult to generalize about high-level political positions until we have more women in top-level political ranks. The corporate and professional world may be more open for women to express leadership styles that are different from those of men. There is no doubt that people perceive differences between women and men leaders, and the leaders themselves describe their styles differently. All of the top corporate positions are international in scope or are likely to be international in the next few years. These new types of international contexts require the ability to relate to a greater diversity of people than ever before and to work with people from cultures that may be very different from one's own.

Our highly successful women leaders define the ability to relate to people as essential to leadership. The styles they describe are more congruent with contemporary interdependent organizations. In general, the women are less hierarchical in the way they structure their organizations, which is a leadership model that is at odds with the standard corporate organizational chart. The "flatter structure" they prefer may be a better fit for the "flatter world" that was described so eloquently by Thomas Friedman in his best-selling book, *The World is Flat* – a structure that is more interconnected and global than the organizations of the last generation.

Mary Ma was Chief Financial Officer of Lenovo, one of the largest computer companies in China – which means she was in a male-dominated profession within a male-dominated industry – at the time they bought IBM. She made it clear that her leadership style was both collaborative and strategic. Mary Ma described it this way:

> "It's high-level strategic leading rather than doing everything yourself. My leadership style is very much about working with people as a means to completing a task. In the past 10 years, I have participated in a lot of important decision-making for the company. Because I am not number 1, people may not agree with my suggestions right away, so I have to work hard to get my positions adopted. Sometimes I get frustrated. But by the end of the day, most of the decision makers will actually say that I was right. If you are not number 1, you have to push your position, coordinate, compromise, and convince people that you are right. You must believe you are right and prove you are right. If you choose to take a position, then you have to live with it.

Communication is the most important thing a leader can do to get her team together. You need to communicate effectively to get people motivated and to sell your ideas, your points. Out of the whole day of work – about 12 hours – I spend 8 hours on communication, talking to people and making conference calls instead of just giving instructions. I normally don't just tell people they should do something in a particular way; instead we discuss why they should do something one way, consider other alternatives, and then make our decisions."

It is interesting to note Mary's emphasis on communication, which is one of the most frequently recommended means of being an effective leader. In advice for organizations, researchers suggest that they: "Develop leaders who share information and decision-making authority, and increase leader–subordinate interactions" (Lowe, Kroeck, & Sivasubramaniam, 1996). It is as though these women have an intuitive knowledge about leadership which it has taken social scientists decades to discover.

### Are Transformational Leaders More Effective?

Lowe, Kroeck, and Sivasubramaniam (1996) examined the effectiveness of transformational and transactional leadership styles by summarizing multiple studies in a single analysis. The meta-analysis showed that transformational leadership has a greater association with effective outcomes than transactional leadership, a conclusion that held up for leaders at high and low levels in organizations. In other words, it is not just a style that works well at top levels. And any woman who is looking for ways to move up the corporate ladder or, in flatter organizations, to move across the corporate lattice, can feel comfortable that a transformational style will be effective.

### Closing the Loop: Is There a Business Advantage for Women Leaders?

So far we have argued that women's characteristic leadership style is closely aligned with transformational leadership. It is more democratic, collaborative, and inspiring, compared with the transactional style adopted by (most) men, which tends to be based on an exchange model in which the leader provides an asset, such as money, in exchange for the right to lead. We have also presented evidence that transformational styles are more effective. You may be wondering if there are data that also show that businesses that include women on their management teams are more successful. In other words, is it good business to have women leaders?

Researchers sampled over 700 businesses listed in *Fortune* magazine's list of 1,000 businesses (Krishnan & Park, 2005). They found that women constituted 6.7 percent of the "top management teams" and 2.8 percent of the line positions on these teams. Fifty-one percent of the businesses they sampled had no women on their top management teams. Although their data analyses were appropriately complex, and for that reason will not be included here, their underlying finding was a significant positive relationship between the number of women in top management and the financial performance of the company. This is a powerful and important finding. In explaining their results, these researchers believe that differences between female and male leadership styles are crucial, especially the idea that women perceive leadership as sharing information, which can drive better performance throughout the company. It is good for business to keep everyone in the know so that they can act with fuller knowledge about the entire company.

## Disadvantages for Women Leaders

If women leaders have already shown themselves to be excellent leaders, then why are there so few of them? As we have shown in the various chapters in this book, the answers are complex. It would be difficult to deny that women face discrimination as they ascend the various ladders to success. The discrimination need not be malicious or even overt. Psychologists who study prejudice and discrimination have recognized that much of it is implicit. It is common to hear people claim to have no prejudices, but when their actions are tallied over time, there is no other explanation left. For example, hiring committees may claim and may actually believe that they are fair to all applicants, but when their practices are viewed over years or decades, it turns out that they have hired very few people from certain groups, despite their availability in the hiring pool. The stereotypes we maintain about women are not compatible with those we maintain for leaders, even though, as the data in this chapter show, women's more inclusive and cooperative leadership style is actually better for business.

## Biases in Evaluation

Think about the head of the government for your country. Is this person doing a good job as a leader? As you undoubtedly know, you will get different answers to this question from different people (unless you live in a totalitarian regime that does not permit criticism of the leadership, but even then people cannot be stopped from thinking differently). The evaluation of a leader is often difficult (unless that person is unambiguously awful, which thankfully is very rare).

One experimental paradigm for studying bias in evaluations involves the use of identical information about hypothetical people, but for half of the evaluations, the person described in the materials is given a female name, and for the other half, the person is given a male name. This paradigm (or experimental set-up) was first used by Goldberg in 1968 to show that when the criteria are ambiguous (e.g. who is the better painter or better teacher), men are usually evaluated as being more competent than women by both men and women evaluators. This paradigm has been used in many experiments over the last 40 years. The results of four decades of research with this method were recently summarized by Eagly and Carli (2007a) as "not much has changed." Thus, the bias against women is alive and well despite other indicators of progress.

As suggested earlier, women are judged most harshly when they assume leadership in male-typed settings, which include contexts such as the military and police force. The norms of these organizations are based on the transactional male style of leadership – hierarchical and unquestioning. In these settings the norms associated with being a women clash with those associated with being a leader where most of the subordinates are men and the task is male-stereotyped. Women who lead in these settings tend to be disliked and judged to be inappropriate for the role.

In a series of studies, two researchers investigated ways to make these two roles (leader of a male-typed company and being a woman) more compatible so that the leader would not be placed in an impossible bind. Heilman and Okimoto (2007) found that if subordinates are given information that the leader has communal values, then she is rated more positively. For example, if the leader changes the mission statement of the workplace to include concern for the employees, or she is attributed with having created a more cooperative work environment, then she is rated higher than an identical leader without these additional attributes. Thus, overt and public communal behaviors can help women leaders in situations that call for more transactional leadership styles. It is a strategy that will signal that she has not violated the expectations associated with being a woman while leading in a masculine environment.

## Statistical Stereotypes

So far, our discussion about leadership has not been specific to mothers. Mothers face a "double whammy" of discrimination. The stereotypes of mothers are even more incompatible with those of a leader than the stereotypes of women in general. One of the authors (Diane) has taught university-level courses on the topic of work and family for many years. She always poses the same question to each class:

> "Imagine that you are on a hiring committee and you have several candidates who are well qualified for a job. No two people are ever the same, but they can have comparable experiences, education, and so on, or one can be slightly better on one criterion for the job and another slightly better on a different criterion. One of the candidates applying for the job is the mother of a young child. Would this additional information tilt your decision in any way? What if she is the mother of newborn twins? Would that matter in your selection?"

Every year, the responses from multiple classes of young adult college students are uniformly the same. The job candidate who is a mother would not be preferred even by this group of well educated students, most of whom are women – a group that might be expected to be more liberal in their outlook than almost any other group you can name. Some students feel guilty admitting their prejudice against hiring mothers; others wonder why I would even ask such an obvious question. All of them realize that discrimination against mothers is illegal in most (but not all) states in the US, but if the decision is theirs, mothers need not apply. Imagine how these attitudes come into play when we are talking about demanding top-level positions.

This example demonstrates a pervasive belief that mothers will not be as committed to their employment as women without children, and men in general (with or without children). Even mothers who may have excellent childcare arrangements, which could include a stay-at-home father to care for the children, will be discriminated against because of the widespread assumption that they will miss work for childcare commitments and be less committed in general. We are calling this statistical discrimination because an individual is being discriminated against because of a statistical association between their group membership and the target behavior.

The discriminatory disadvantage can also help us understand some of the intense animosity between mothers who are employed and those who are at home with their children. The choice of women to leave employment when they have children confirms the employers' beliefs that women are not a good investment in the workforce because they will leave after a few years. This workplace behavior hurts all women, but especially those who aspire to top levels of their profession, because they will need multiple promotions, and the cumulative effects of even small handicaps can have a massive effect.

Marjorie Yang, Chairman of the Esquel Group, was named among the Fortune top 50 most powerful women in business for transforming a small company into the world's largest cotton shirt manufacturer, producing over 60 million shirts a year. She offers an opinion that is contrary to the idea that motherhood and top-level leadership are incompatible. She believes that mothers make better leaders: "It would be better if there are more female CEOs. I think having been a mother will make you have a different feeling towards life. Male CEOs would only focus on money, but female CEOs would be concerned more about family and they may see things in a more macro way and relate more things to life." Thus, this high-powered business woman believes that the broader concerns that mothers bring with them to the workplace make them better leaders than someone who is more narrowly focused in their everyday life.

## Homosocial Reproduction

Rosebeth Kanter is the "academic mother" of the study of women and leadership. In 1977, which in psychological-social research is eons ago, Kanter coined the term "homosocial reproduction" to refer to the tendency of decision makers to promote and select people whose leadership styles are like their own. Given that the vast majority of people at the highest levels of power are men, this reproductive strategy will work against even the most qualified women. The solution to this asexual style of reproducing high-level executives is obvious, but not easy. Women need to become known to the top decision makers in their profession so that they can be perceived as similar in important ways – in how they make decisions, how they think about what is important in their setting, and how they achieve success. If you are an aspiring politician, you will need to become known to the powerful people who nominate candidates who can win an election. If you are an academic, then you need to make your work known to granting agencies, the top brass in professional societies, publishers, and journal editors. Lawyers need to become known to judges, the politicians who appoint judges, and the senior partners in law firms. You need to be perceived as a member of the same species, not necessarily the same sex, to be considered for entry into the top positions.

Some of the skills of meeting the "right" people for your career are informally taught by good mentors, a topic that we addressed in an earlier chapter. We raise it again in this context because there is a knowledge base to learning how to lead, and women who want to advance in their careers need to learn these strategies and skills.

## Leading Like a Woman is Good for People and Business

All of the data shown here and the responses from our sample of highly successful women show that "leading like a woman" should be used as a compliment for exemplary leadership. There are advantages to the financial bottom line to the transformational style that is preferred by women leaders, but prejudices against women have prevented them from benefiting from this advantage. What can we do to level the playing field so that it is fair for women?

The automatic activation of stereotypes probably cannot be changed, but with effort and education we can change the stereotypes that are activated. Women and men do tend to lead in somewhat different ways, at least in some contexts, but the more transformational style that women use is associated with better business outcomes. We expect that this effect will only continue to grow as the trend toward less hierarchical organizations continues. We also expect that it will grow as more businesses enter the global market.

Many societies around the world are collectivist in their orientation (Hofstede, 1996) – which is a popular term in psychological research used to describe cultures that are more concerned with the group as a whole, as opposed to individualistic societies, where the major emphasis is on the success of the individual. The United States is usually considered the prototype of an individualistic society; China, at least in its more socialist aspects, is considered collectivist. Several researchers have wondered if transformational leaders are better suited for collectivist societies and transactional leaders are better suited for individualistic societies. In general, the research supports this distinction, but the number of studies on this topic remains small. Even within collectivistic and individualistic societies, people with one of these two orientations prefer the type of leader that is more representative of their own orientation (Walumbwa, Lawler, & Avolio, 2007). In this recent study, workers from China, India, Kenya, and the US were compared. As predicted, the more collectivist cultures preferred transformational leaders and the more individualistic ones preferred transactional leaders. Globalization is increasingly important as businesses move across national borders. International leadership needs to be more transformational.

Another positive aspect of "leading like a woman" is that the remarkable women we interviewed created organizations where it is easier for women to succeed. We see this generosity of spirit when Jenny Ming, US President of the massive retailer Old Navy/Gap, talks about her leadership:

> "I really never thought about running a company. My ambition wasn't to be a president of a company. I don't think people think that way. My ambition was to be a buyer. And when I got there five years later, I thought that was an incredible job. I loved it. But every single step of the way, I sensed that I could do better, could do more. And that's the way that I looked at my career. It really wasn't that I had this ambition that was 20 years out. I love what I did and I was really good at it. So I never looked at it as career was a burning ambition. I think actually that has helped me because I am actually fairly relaxed about. . . . You know how sometimes really ambitious people have this

timeline and have this incredible drive. For me it's less about that; it's really making sure you're contributing and loving what you do. All those things to me are actually really important. . . . I also feel like, I also have created a culture that families are welcome. It's not a negative in someone's career."

Zhang Xin is Co-Chief Executive of SOHO China Ltd., a company that is recognized globally as a vanguard of the Chinese real estate market. She is a major player in the emerging market for high-quality architecture in China. Zhang Xin understands that a leader needs both expressive and instrumental qualities:

"Being a woman, I usually like to spend a lot of time discussing the goal, the direction, and the vision that we have, or where we want to be, with the people who work with me. So in a way, instead of just giving orders, I like to play the role as an inspiration, and I want to see everyone inspired by the goal or the vision. And then usually I leave all the details for people to do, but it doesn't end there. I will come back and check the results in a very detailed way, 10 times more detailed than a man I'm sure, down to the very last detail. So I think I spend a lot of time in the beginning, and a lot of time in the end, but in the middle it is always the people who are executing it doing most of the work. I always see the role of management as two things. One is to play the role as an inspiration, and two is to play the role as problem-solving, crisis-management."

Recent studies show that companies with more women in top management levels perform better (Krishnan & Park, 2005; McKinsey & Company, Inc., 2007). So women's style of leadership also makes business sense. We close this chapter with another quote from leadership guru, Peter Drucker (undated), whose comments on leadership sound as though they could have come from any of the outstanding women leaders we interviewed: "Leadership is not magnetic personality that can just as well be a glib tongue. It is not making friends and influencing people – that is flattery. Leadership is lifting a person's vision to higher sights, the raising of a person's performance to a higher standard, the building of a personality beyond its normal limitations." Perhaps with visions like this and women leaders like the ones we interviewed, we can look forward to a future for our children and theirs that is positive and optimistic.

# Chapter 9

# How to Lead a
# Dually Successful Life

 $W$ hat have we learned from the 62 dually successful women who shared so much of their lives with us? A great deal! They made it clear that women can thrive while maintaining high-level professional careers and caring for a family. They showed us that it is not easy to be dually successful, but it is possible. The remarkable leaders we interviewed provided advice that is inspirational and practical.

Cordelia Chung, the highest-ranking executive woman in the IBM Asia Pacific region, reminded us of the primary importance of how we feel about our roles as working mothers and caregivers:

> "Women leaders should not feel guilty. For example, I never buy gifts for my kids during my business trips. I prefer to buy things with them when we are together so they can pick out what they like. My children don't expect me to buy gifts for them every time I travel. There should not be any compensation because I have done nothing wrong. Peace of mind is important. The most important thing is first to accept yourself. If there is harmony within you, then your family will accept your choices. If you find that the way you are combining work and family is unacceptable to you, then you should make changes."

There are many changes we can all make, starting today as we move toward our own definition of a successful life. Central to having more of what we want from life is deciding on our own priorities and planning ways to achieve it. If being a loving mother and wife and having a successful career are priorities, then obligations and activities that do not contribute to these main priorities will have to be managed. Tradeoffs need to be made, and planning is essential for making home-to-work transitions as seamless as possible. House-work, cooking, and other tasks that take time away from being with your family or doing your work could be outsourced, unless it is an activity that you enjoy. Children and other family members can maintain special close bonds with you even if your workdays are long. Here are some of the suggestions we gathered from women who know how to do it. Even if you do not want to make it to the top, you can make it easier to combine all of the pieces of a hectic life with some combination of these suggestions.

## Motivation and Self-Efficacy

Psychology has a long research literature on understanding human motivation. Why do some people work late into the night and others take a look at the same job and say, "no way!"? When we look at the lives of the 62 incredible women who shared their secrets with us, we cannot help but wonder what drives their ambition and hard work. They could have chosen easier paths. They did not have to succeed at the top.

Psychological research shows that people are driven by different motives. They differ in the extent to which they pursue challenging goals, which reflects their need for achievement. As the words imply, "need for achievement" indicates how much someone strives to achieve – whether it is getting good grades in school, applying for a high-level position, accepting or seeking a promotion to CEO, or running for an elected position. People who have a high need for achievement set personal goals that are challenging but attainable, whereas those who have a low need for achievement set goals that are either extremely easy or almost impossible to attain. It is clear from their stories that the 62 high-achieving women try their best at being good mothers and achieving at work. They have aspirations to perform better at the next step and believe that with hard work they can succeed at high-level tasks – they select high-level tasks for themselves and achieve at them.

The high-achieving women leaders not only have aspirations to succeed, they also have confidence in their competence to do so. In the psychological literature, the term "self-efficacy" refers to the expectancy that your efforts will lead to success; it is your belief that you will succeed that mobilizes your energies and keeps you working hard. If you have low self-efficacy and do not believe that your efforts will pay off, you may be too discouraged to even try to achieve something as lofty as a top-notch career. People with high self-efficacy select challenging goals that lead to success. They continue to build up their self-efficacy through experiences of success. Women who achieve at the top are confident about their self-efficacy.

As we listened to the women's stories, we heard about their development of self-efficacy. As described in earlier chapters, the women told tales of supportive mothers, mentors, and others who encouraged them to recognize their own ability to excel. Along with this self-knowledge, they learned that success meant hard work. As they came to understand their own strengths and weaknesses, they developed a vision of a possible future, so that when opportunities presented themselves, they were willing to risk failure and go after the opportunities. No road through life is unmarred with set-backs and failures, and although the shorthand version of their stories may sound as though they rose up the ranks with the unimpeded speed of a meteor, in fact, they suffered losses and disappointments like the rest of us. They responded to challenges and failures with perseverance, which is another attribute of people with high self-efficacy. For people with high self-efficacy and need for achievement, failure is just a chance to learn what needs to be done differently next time.

How do you develop self-efficacy if you did not have a supportive mother and others to help you develop a "can-do" belief in yourself? Challenge yourself as you work toward a goal, but take the necessary measures to prepare for success. If you want to be a judge, you need to go to law school, study hard, begin in the legal profession, work hard, demonstrate your competence, seek out high-level assignments, become known to those who are involved in nominating judges, get further training, acquire expertise, work hard, and, well, you get the idea. Each move is one step toward your goal. Along the way you may be tapped for chief legal counsel of a large corporation or for a political office, goals that were not on your original map but which may offer an opportunity to "do good" in ways you never considered. The path may be bumpy and some backsliding is inevitable, but people with self-efficacy brush themselves off and move on to meet these challenges.

# The Motherhood Mandate: To Be or Not To Be

The Motherhood Mandate is the term for the default assumption that all women want to be and will be mothers. There has been a justified backlash against this assumption as some women do not want to be mothers. People who are childless by choice will sometimes refer to themselves as "childfree" to denote that the decision not to have children was deliberate. It seems obvious that anyone who does not want to be a parent should not have children. Everyone needs to make their own life choices, and the fact that these women succeeded as mothers (except for the few who had other significant care responsibilities) does not mean that we should denigrate women or men who make other choices. The mothers in our elite sample were all passionately positive about their children. If there were regrets concerning their children, the women did not speak about them. Like most samples of adults, these women consider children one of the most positive and important aspects of their life.

Sometimes, there is tension between employees who do not have significant care responsibilities and those who do. Unattached adults sometimes feel that they are treated unfairly when the workplace accommodates people with family care responsibilities; whereas people with family responsibilities feel their performance will be evaluated negatively if they make use of these family-friendly policies (Drago, Colbeck, Hollenshead, & Sullivan, 2008). Schisms like this at work are unfortunate and eventually hurt everyone. Workplace policies that recognize that everyone has a life outside of work are needed, so that an unmarried employee who has an elderly parent has the same right to use family-friendly policies as the single mother with two children. Policies such as part-time options, flexible start and end times, telecommuting, and others that are designed to help employees fulfill their obligations at work and at home, need to be available to all employees, even if they are used mainly by parents with young children. This way, mothers who make use of these policies will not be marginalized and regarded as less committed to work.

For those women who choose to have children, motherhood may pose as a self-imposed barrier to success. Many women who become mothers opt out of a challenging career track because they need to spend more time with their children (Hewlett, Luce, & Schiller,

2005). They believe that they have to choose between work and family. Unfortunately, women who interrupt their career often encounter difficulty in getting back into full-time work. There is a trend showing that the higher women climb up the corporate ladder, the fewer children they have (Hewlett, 2002). Not all women can have it all, or want a high-level career, or children, but from the experience of our special group of women leaders, it is possible to do so, given good preparation and strategies.

### *Preparation for Motherhood*

Just as upwardly mobile executives get the education needed for their next career move, so should future spouses or parents prepare for the next change in family status. The transition to being a new mother can be stressful. Even when the newborn is planned and wanted, a substantial proportion of new mothers experience depression (Logsdon, Wisner, & Shanahan, 2007). If a new mother returns to work while still waking several times a night with her new baby, she will be exhausted and both childcare and work will suffer. We advocate a sufficiently long parental leave, for fathers as well as mothers, so that new parents can bond with their baby and make care arrangements that are stable and dependable. New parents need the flexibility to spend more time with their newborn. A realistic plan for the transition to parenthood will help women stay at the top without falling asleep at work, while managing the joys and stress of a new baby.

The high-achieving women in our sample had occupational goals and goals for their family life. They knew the sort of family life they wanted and they pursued it with the same rigor used on the uphill path to success at work. They got their husbands involved in making the decision and got them to participate in the preparation for life as a family. For example, Jenny Ming, President of Old Navy/Gap, and her husband decided rationally that he would do the night feeding of the baby because he had no problem getting back to sleep later.

## Find the Right Husband/Partner

The women leaders all concurred that a supportive husband is essential. The support from husbands includes not only sharing the household chores, but also the emotional support, encouragement, and coaching for their career development. The research literature shows that when husbands share housework and childcare, divorce is less likely and wives report less marital stress (Frisco & Williams, 2003). So finding a husband who shares your goals and values and, at the same time, feels secure and assured about himself is the key. The question is how to find the right husband. We cannot count on stardust. Although the happily married women leaders all said they were lucky in finding a supportive husband, the reality is that they all worked hard to attain and maintain a happy marriage. As in any happy marriage, they engaged in healthy couple behavior. There was a lot of give and take, and the couples grew an emotionally strong bond in their marriage.

And there were some disappointments. There were a few tales of husbands' infidelity and of the pain of divorce. For the women who experienced broken marriages, many reported that these were agonizing times, but like everyone else they moved through them, often remarrying with a clearer idea of what they wanted in a spouse and in a marriage. Based on the sage advice we received, we heartily suggest that if you marry (and most women do), you select the right husband – one who will share your vision of what married life should be like for both of you and for your children.

## Find Mentors and Coaches

The road to the top can be more like finding your way through a labyrinth than a climb up a straight ladder (Eagly & Carli, 2007), so it is helpful to have guides to help you avoid the blind alleys and dead ends. Mentors can help you network – create a web of business associates who can help with your career. They can identify new positions that are about to become available, introduce you to Ms. and Mr. Big who can catapult the career of people they recognize have talent, provide challenging assignments where you can demonstrate and hone leadership skills, and point out smart career moves along the way.

McKinsey & Company (2007) conducted a study which showed that while companies with more women at top management levels performed better, it is generally more difficult for women to master the male code that opens doors and to find mentors or build networks in the male-centric corporate environment. Coaching, network-building, and mentoring programs are effective means to nurture women's ambition and skills to navigate through the labyrinth. One of the best practices the study cited is the cross-company mentoring programs in the UK and France which bring women high-fliers together with heads of the biggest corporations to foster mentoring and facilitate new career prospects for the women.

As suggested earlier by one of the high-achieving women, everyone can create a personal success committee – a small group of people who agree to help with your career. You would check in periodically with the committee members to see if your career is on track and if there are other possible career paths that should be explored. One of the authors (Diane) was part of one such group for a senior executive who had already been a university president and CEO of a national organization. At this point in her life, the senior executive recognized that she had one more career move before retirement. She convened a group of colleagues from a variety of disciplines and backgrounds to help her plan her next career move. The question they addressed was, "How could she use the lifetime of skills and experiences she had for one more position where she would accomplish something meaningful that took advantage of her knowledge and her passions?" A group came together, each bringing different ideas. She decided to blend two of the ideas and is happily working at her last full-time job before retirement in a way that is suited for her combination of skills and interests. Anyone can put together such a group of advisers to help them clarify goals, point out personal strengths and weaknesses, and share their knowledge of opportunities.

## Redefine Normative Roles for Good Mothers and Good Leaders

One reason that so many people are quick to say that it is not possible to have a high-level position, such as CEO, head of government, chief of police, supreme court justice, or politician, and be a good mother is that they have stereotypical beliefs of what these two roles require and they believe that the roles are incompatible. A common gender stereotype assumes that the masculine characteristic of taking charge and the feminine characteristic of taking care are mutually exclusive. Williams (2000, 2008) asks us to consider how the role of "good mother" is incompatible with the role of "ideal worker." The good mother is always available and sacrificing for her children; the good worker is always available and sacrificing for her employer. It is not possible to fulfill both of these role expectations at the same time because one person cannot always be available for two different responsibilities. For women at the top of their profession, the incompatibilities are magnified, because they are more than ideal workers – they are the leaders of the organization.

In this book we focus on the dual roles of mother (or caregiver) and employee in a top-level position. To put the challenges these women face in perspective, let us consider other life options. Consider the mothers who work at two low-wage jobs in order to make ends meet or the mothers with multiple care responsibilities in addition to their children. Many adults are finding themselves part of what is called the "sandwich generation" because they have childcare responsibilities and elder care responsibilities at the same time. These two types of caregiving are often incompatible, as harried members of the sandwich generation will explain as they travel to distant cities to care for aging parents or need to be at a hospital or nursing facility and at a parent–teacher conference at the same time. Many women and men fulfill the obligations of multiple roles that often compete, and have done so since time immemorial. Many of us can recall a grandmother who cared for the children and worked on the farm along with everyone else. No one told her it was not possible to do both, although it was undoubtedly hard work.

## Jettison Your Guilt

There are choices that we make, sometimes unconsciously, which make our lives easier or harder. For example, you can refuse to accept guilt if other people suggest that you are not a good mother because you are dedicated to your work and do not conform to *their* definition of what a good mother is. You can also refuse to believe anyone who tells you that you cannot succeed at a high-level position because you also care for children. Guilt is an emotion that we create within ourselves, and we have the ability to refuse to accept it from others. Even more importantly, working mothers have no reason for feeling guilty.

Longitudinal studies of families with working mothers show that they adapt when mothers are employed, and that there is a positive impact of maternal employment on children's development, the home environment, and other family members. Gottfried and Gottfried (2008) use the term "the upside of maternal employment" to refer to the benefits that accrue to children and families when mothers are employed. It is time to get rid of the tired notion that working mothers are bad for children and replace it with the empirically supported conclusion that there are many benefits for families when mothers are employed outside the home. To be sure, not all working mothers are loving and caring parents, but neither are all stay-at-home mothers. The quality of parenting does not depend on the employment status of the mother.

### The New Good Mother

The successful women we interviewed reported that they were all highly involved with their children. They found creative ways to keep their children central in their lives. We have presented some of their strategies throughout the book. Someone asked us if the children or husbands would paint the same positive picture of these women's highly successful lives. Would they agree that the women we interviewed were successful both at work and at home? We do not know the answer to this question, but we do know that these women leaders were happy with their lives and with their children's eventual development. We also know that the outcomes for children and husbands of stay-at-home mothers are not uniformly positive. Some of these children rebel, some of the marriages fail, and so on. The alternative of *not* working would *not* work for these women leaders. We also know from research that, on average, women who are employed outside the home are happier and less likely to be depressed, so it is not as though staying at home is a more desirable alternative for our highly successful women, and it is difficult to imagine how their families would have benefited if they had taken less ambitious paths. They talked about the pride their children took in their mother's success and the importance of being a positive role model for their sons and daughters. The highly successful women told us about the successes of their children, both in their own professions and in their relationships with their parents and others.

## An Alternative Definition of the Good Leader

Catalyst (2007), the research organization that specializes in women's issues and career advancement, conducted a series of studies on stereotypic perceptions of men's and women's leadership. Men are seen as "natural leaders" whereas women are seen as "atypical leaders" who violate either the norms of leadership or the norms of femininity. Women leaders have a narrower band-width of acceptable behaviors, because being perceived as being either too stereotypically feminine or masculine represents a violation of either the role of effective leader or the female role. These stereotypic biases create a double bind for women: they cannot take charge and take care at the same time. When they act tough, they are considered unfeminine. When they are soft, they are judged to be incompetent. These false dichotomies hinder women's advancement. Men, on the other hand, gain from adopting the caring aspects of the feminine role when they lead, which allows them greater leeway in their personal style.

Our women at the top reject these gender stereotypes. They did not have to reject their womanhood to become leaders. They are overtly competent and caring at the same time. Some of them described their leadership style as that of a mother or grandmother. They had visible, responsible positions. Yet, they managed to get home for dinner, keep in close touch with their family when they traveled, take their family with them on business trips, and stay connected via many creative strategies. They set limits to their high-level positions – limits that allowed them to have a rich and full family life. By building ways to be with their family into their workdays, they signaled to their employees and others that work is not a "24/7" commitment, regardless of the demands. They rearranged schedules, gave employees more latitude in working without supervision, and worked from home after the children went to sleep at night. In the myriad ways they combined work and family, these incredible women created a more humane workplace.

All of the available data suggest that it is good business to create flexible workplaces that can accommodate the needs of employees. We were delighted to learn about a high-level executive at Deloitte, one of the major accounting firms in the world, who told an audience of several hundred people that she was leaving early so that she could take advantage of a sale at a popular department store. What she did with this surprising announcement was to make a very public statement that she expects employees to lead full lives and if they want to leave in the middle of the day to take advantage of a sale, she is confident that they will complete their work at some other time. It was a clear message that the firm's employees are trusted professionals who can manage how and when to do their work. She was creating a humane work environment, which is good for families and the bottom line.

## Climbing One Rung at a Time

The women we interviewed concurred in their pattern of leadership development. In the early stages of their career, none of the women planned on making it to the top of their profession. As many of the women leaders told us, they never thought it would be possible. They found meaningful work that they loved and climbed one rung at a time as they rose to meet new challenges. Few of the women took career breaks or used any family-friendly policies such as part-time employment or flexible scheduling as they moved through the ranks, in part because these options were not generally available at the time. The stories are a blend of "whatever works."

As described in an earlier chapter, when an American politician from Texas quit her job as counsel for a large insurance company so that she could stay at home with her children for a few years, an opportunity immediately came up to run for a seat in the state legislature. She did not hesitate to alter her plans and to take advantage of the surprising fact that she was available to run for this office. She combined her work experiences as an insurance attorney with the leadership skills she developed as president of the PTA. Her platform highlighted education, a topic that she was concerned about for her children, and workers' compensation, an area of expertise she gained from her job. She spoke as a mother and an attorney in her successful political campaign.

It would be misleading to label circuitous and unplanned routes to the top as serendipity because the opportunities opened for women who were prepared for the uphill climb. The choices the women leaders made earlier in their careers were considered assets rather than losses. Take the example of Sarah Weddington, the former presidential adviser who did not get a job at a high-powered law firm when she got out of law school because she was a woman. She ended up with the opportunity to argue the landmark Roe v. Wade case in the Supreme Court, and then went on to higher rungs of politics and government. She called it the step-by-step method of leadership.

We used the findings from our interviews to create a model of career steps for women (or men) who want to lead dually successful lives. As shown in Figure 9.1, the lowest steps require the development of self-efficacy and self-esteem – the belief that with hard work and proper preparation, you can succeed. High self-efficacy leads to high motivation to succeed, and because we are concerned with women who succeeded in their work and family life, they were motivated in both areas. For anyone who wants to move ahead, even if the top is not within your sights, it is useful to envision the type of career and type of family life you would like to achieve. If your actions are to be goal-directed, you will need to set goals. Career and family goals will typically start with entry-level work in a field you are interested in and the preludes to marriage, which include meeting people who you think may be marriageable and ultimately marrying.

During the next steps or sometime earlier in the sequence, you will need to define a successful family life and work life for yourself. In order to have both, the definitions need to be compatible. The high-achieving women in our sample defined "being a good mother" as being someone who is highly involved with their children's lives, especially those aspects they believed to be important, but not being available "24/7" unless there was a problem or emergency. Successful careers require hard work and long hours, but there were limits set so that the women could be home for dinner or other important family events. The highly successful women developed their own strategies for making time, some of which are listed below.

As they reached the upper rungs of the ladder, a leadership style emerged that reflected both of the primary roles in their lives – a style that was relational and flatter than the standard hierarchical models. This style of leadership, which is sometimes called transformational, is associated with successful businesses. It is more compatible with the rapidly growing global economy because many cultures are inter-dependent in their orientation and expect that style to be mirrored by leaders. When they were on top, our highly successful women created work environments that were more family-friendly than traditional hierarchical workplaces typically are. As they reflected on their life's accomplishments, they looked back with pride in their children and in their career accomplishments.

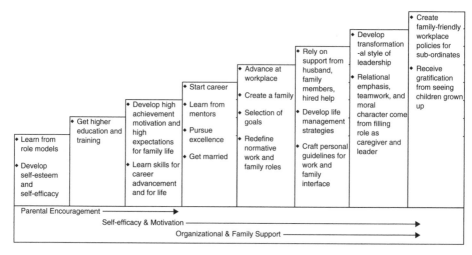

**Figure 9.1** Step-by-step model of leadership development incorporating work and family roles

# A Checklist of Ideas for Making it Easier to Combine Work and Family, and Making it to the Top

- Integrate work and family. Find ways to mix work with family so that both can benefit from the interaction. Depending on the age of your children, you could organize a work-sponsored picnic or day out for employees that includes family members, or you could bring your children to work with you one or two days a year or for a few hours at the weekend so that they can see what you do and learn about the world of work. Alternatively, you could bring your work to your family, perhaps by catching up on reading during a child's music lesson or returning phone calls during a child's visit to the dentist. There are many ways to combine the two without ruining the family event by working the entire time, or failing to accomplish work because a child is fussy and interrupting. The way these events are integrated will depend on the children's ages and the type of work that you do, but with some planning and efficient time management, you can find reasonable points of overlap.

A recent study of working adults in the Netherlands found that women were more likely to use strategies that facilitate the combination of work and family than men were (van Steenbergen, Ellemers, & Mooijaart, 2007). Instead of viewing the combination of these two spheres of life as necessarily negative, the women found ways to benefit from combining their dual roles, which was a consistent theme among our sample of women leaders.

- Make work-to-family transitions easier with the use of personal rules. It can be difficult to get back to work after spending an afternoon with the kids, so setting pre-planned rules for the transition can make it easier. As suggested in an earlier chapter, you could designate a physical location that you pass on your way to and from work. On your way in to work, it could signal that now is the time to start thinking about work, and when returning home it could signal that now is the time to start thinking about family. You could discuss your plans with your family and decide that Sunday is family day, but Sunday night after dinner is reserved for getting ready to go back to work. With pre-planned "rules" you will not have to constantly decide how to divide your time, and you can relax because you know you have planned work time and family time so that neither will suffer.
- Get and stay organized – really, really organized. A competent personal assistant who understands your multiple demands is very helpful with scheduling your work time, but you still need to coordinate your life with your family. Several organizational strategies were suggested including maintaining a family calendar. The use of one calendar for the entire family will help block off dates for shared activities and prevent you and your spouse from taking overnight trips on the same night, which might cause a crisis in childcare. Good organization also requires working well ahead of deadlines. Employees with children will inevitably have a sick child the day before a big report is due. That report should be finished a week in advance, just in case.
- Find ways to keep in touch, whenever you are needed. Depending on the age of your children and their needs, here are some of the methods that might work for you: keeping a private phone line just for family, e-mailing or using computer-based video technology throughout the day, establishing a phone time

right after school, maintaining family rituals such as vacations or weekend brunches, and arranging your work schedule so that important school events are not missed. These methods have all been used by our high-achieving women.

Most of these ways of maintaining close bonds while working in a demanding job are the prerogative of executives; working women at lower rungs of the career ladder often cannot make the sort of arrangements that allow them to keep in contact with their family throughout the day. So, in many ways, being at the top might be less stressful for women with families than working in lower-level positions. If you are a top-level executive, make sure that there are flexible work policies to help parents and caregivers at every level of the organization, and if you are not (or not yet) in a top-level executive position, propose helpful policies and, at the same time, be sure to show how they will help you do your work more efficiently and benefit your employer.

In several places throughout this book, we present data that you could use to persuade a reluctant employer that family-friendly practices are good for business. For example, you could use the studies of large companies which show that flexible work policies at all levels of employment are good for business, and the study which found higher than average financial returns for companies that are dedicated to family-friendly practices (Cascio & Young, 2005).

- Create expectations at work that you are managing a dually successful life. People who work with you should expect that you will have to leave early some afternoons, or that you will rarely accept dinner invitations, or that you will leave work three days a week no later than 7 p.m., or some combination of these, and other "rules" that fit your family needs and your work needs. Some positions require evenings at work, in which case you could arrange to have weekends free, or Tuesdays at home, or whatever works for your situation. The important point is to set boundaries so that work does not take over family time. Women in top-level positions have an unending number of important tasks which could never be completed in one lifetime, so they need to set limits that automatically signal when it is OK to leave to go home. Communicate these work-life rules to others in your organization to establish a family-friendly work culture.

- Find and use social and emotional support, especially when you face social criticism. The personal advisory committee suggested earlier is one form of social support that can help with problem solving when work and family life seem to be on a collision course. Supportive husbands, family members, and others who can provide critical physical help when you need someone to pick up the kids, and supportive staff at work who can help with last-minute deadlines are two types of physical support that are essential for overworked leaders who are also mothers and other caregivers.
- Utilize and maximize your resources. Outsource everything that you can that does not require your personal input or contribute to your family time or to your work success. Unless you are among the very few who love to do housework, find someone whose job is cleaning to do their job so that you can do what you need to do at home and at work. Of course, early in one's career there may not be enough money to pay someone to do these jobs, so find what you can afford to outsource and do it. You can also find help from other working women, and take turns cooking dinners one night a week, picking children up from school, and so on. As your salary increases and your responsibilities at work increase, you can outsource more of those jobs that do not require your personal presence, such as shopping, ironing, and getting the car repaired. When you hire help, be specific about what you want done and how you want it done. Give clear instructions, and then trust the person to do it. This way, you can build up a lasting relationship with a reliable helper.
- Prepare for the career you want. Too often women are not in a position to assume the top-level roles because they have no experience in "line positions," which are the positions that relate directly to the profit and loss or main mission of the organization. Women are more likely to rise to vice-president positions in human resources or communications, which are not the direct business of the organization. Line positions are more likely to be in sales or service delivery. When the time comes to select the next corporate president, women whose only experience is in human resources, communications, or similar roles will be passed over.
- Plan your family. We remind women about the ticking of your biological clock. If you want to have children, you need to

remember that fertility rates decline with age, and any pregnancy over the age of 35 is considered a high-risk pregnancy. It is easy to forget this biological reality when the glossy newsstand magazines are filled with stories about mothers in their fifties, but these older mothers are very rare, and many people expect that a new mother in her fifties will have a very rough time. Any woman who is turning 30 needs to carefully consider if she wants to have biological children, and, if she does, she needs to consider how to make it happen. As we noted in Chapter 5, adoption is a possibility. There are many children in the US who need loving homes, although they are likely to have special needs. Many parts of the world have children who can be adopted internationally. Just as anyone who wants to make it to the top needs to plan their career, anyone who wants to have children also needs to plan for them.

- Find work that you can love. The feeling described earlier as "flow" is a term for how people feel when they are enjoying work that is meaningful and engaging. It occurs when you are working at a task that is at the right level of difficulty and is intrinsically interesting. You will find it easier to stay motivated to work hard when you love your work and when you find it meaningful. You can identify something meaningful even in demanding tasks. Jenny Ming, President of the mammoth corporation Old Navy/Gap, did: "The fortunate thing is I really do love what I do. So I don't find it a drag or a job; I enjoy coming into work. And also with all my travel I get a chance to step away from the family. I feel that really is my time."

  Zhang Xin, CEO of an innovative architectural firm in China, reflected on her success: "Being in such a privileged position as the owner of the company, the leader of the company, you have the luxury of seeing something and putting something into practice, and that is uniquely very satisfying." Women deserve to have these sorts of satisfying work experiences, which benefits all of society.

- Discrimination against women is real, so learn how to deal with it. We need to convert those who doubt that women can be both good mothers and good leaders into believers that it can be done. The World Values Survey (2006), which is reported by the United Nations, shows that "men's discriminatory

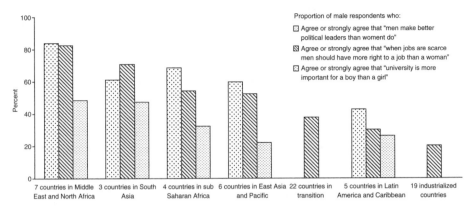

**Figure 9.2**  Men's discriminatory attitudes toward women across regions*
*Source*: World Values Survey (http://www.worldvaluessurvey.org/), accessed June 2006

attitudes toward women . . . are significant everywhere." The data from this survey are shown in Figure 9.2.

Many of the women in our sample talked about discrimination and more generally disrespect at work. They varied in the way they responded, including ignoring smirks and insults, and greeting requests to make coffee with later requests that the men now make the coffee since it was their turn. One method that is advocated by Williams (2008) is to fight discrimination against women (and men) with family care responsibilities in court, where a few large financial settlements are gaining the attention of management in large corporations. It is important to know your rights and to use your knowledge when necessary. No one should suffer in a work environment that is hostile.

*UNICEF calculations are based on data derived from the World Values Survey, Round 4 (1999-2004). Data for each country and territory in the regional aggregates are the latest year available in the period specified. The folloeing countries and territories are included in the regional aggregates cited: Middle East and North Africa: Algeria, Egypt, Islamic Republic of Iran, Iraq, Jordon, Morocco, Saudi Arabia, Latin America and Caribbean: Argentina, Bolivia, Republic of Venezuela, Chile, Mexico, Peru, South Asia: Bangladsh, India, Pakistan, East Asia and Pacific: China, Indonesia, Phillipines, Republic of Korea, Singapore, Vietnam. Sub-Saharan Africa: Nigeria, South Africa, Uganda, United Republic of Tanzania. Countries in transition: Albanian, Belarus, Bosnia and Herzegovia, Bulgaria, Croatia, Czech Reoubllc, Estonia, Hunfary, Kyrgyzstan, Latvia, Lithuania, Montenegro, Poland, Romania, Republic of Moldova, Russian Federation, Serbia, Slovakia, Slovenia, Ukraine, The former Yugoslay Republic of Macedonia, Turkey. Industrialized countries: Austria, Belgium, Canada, Denmark, Finland, France, Greece, Iceland, Ireland, Italy, Japan, Luxembourg, Malta, Netherlands, Portugal, Spain, Sweden, United Kingdom, United States.

Although many offenses can be handled by talking to human resources personnel, many of whom are women, and others can be settled by direct confrontation with the person doing the discriminating, sometimes legal action may be required to demonstrate the seriousness of the matter.

Legal action may be a last resort to remedy the situation. Proactive measures are less costly and create a win–win situation. Catalyst (2007) asked senior-level executives in Europe and the US about the strategies that they and their organizations could adopt to address the prejudice and discrimination that often put women leaders at a disadvantage. They advised that, on the individual level, the women should be able to talk openly about the issue and immediately confront the inequitable situation, and not discount their own feelings. They should make themselves visible by speaking up at meetings, showing their competence, and finding a mentor. They could use clear and effective communication to let people know what they want, but be diplomatic at the same time. While recognizing the gender discrimination, they can reframe the issue to allow practical solutions without playing up the salience of the gender dimension.

Unfortunately, some portion of the discrimination women and members of other groups face in the workplace is difficult to quantify, or it is difficult to convince others that the actions are in fact discriminatory. Political candidates are often criticized for their style of dress, the pitch of their voice, the shape of their body, and other physical attributes associated with being female. As a group (women and men concerned with competent leadership and fairness), we can band together to make sure that the media and others know that this is unacceptable. Individuals can write letters and take other personal action to ensure the dignity and integrity of women who brave the political battlefields. We all win when we elect better leaders, and the style of one's dress is not an essential qualification for selecting the best political candidate.

- Develop your own style of leadership. Do not be concerned if some criticize your leadership style as being too "feminine," if by that they mean it is based on concern for relationships rather than on giving orders and having them followed. The women talked about leadership as sharing information broadly and supporting the efforts of others. By empowering others, you are creating a work environment where top talent is retained. Leaders who are more open to sharing information with employees have good success rates. As described earlier, researchers found that the financial performance of a company is positively correlated with the number of women in management (Krishnan & Park, 2005; McKinsey & Company, Inc., 2007).

There is a positive return on investment in having women in top leadership positions. The combination of showing care for employees and demonstrating competence in leading an organization is an ideal combination that allows women to conform to both the expected female stereotype of a caring individual and the leader stereotype of enhancing the bottom line. Both of these stereotypes can be combined for a competent and caring model of how to lead. Women can "have the best of both worlds" by taking what is best from each of these stereotypes. In addition, just as meaningful work is important for you, it is important to let employees know why their work is meaningful. Employee appreciation is good for business.

Business organizations are beginning to recognize the contributions of women's representation in senior management to corporate performance. For example, IBM Corporation sponsored Catalyst to study the impact of stereotyping on women's leadership. The Catalyst (2007) study advised that while individual strategies can help women handle these daily hassles, women should not be made the only party responsible for addressing these problems. If organizations do not want to lose their top women talent, they need to develop and promote institutional mechanisms to remove these barriers. Catalyst recommended giving employees tools to raise awareness of women's leadership skills and the negative effects of stereotypes. Human resource practices to avoid gender bias should be implemented and monitored. The management also needs to create an organizational climate that fosters diversity, by discarding the stereotypic "ideal worker" norms based on traditional masculine norms and promoting a more inclusive leadership style than the masculine style of authoritative and hierarchical leadership.

We can all benefit from the wisdom of Frances Hesselbein, Chairman of the Leader to Leader Institute: "We need to listen to the whispers of our lives" – a phrase Hesselbein used in her advice to young career women. She talked about three kinds of whispers:

> "the whispers of the body, the whispers of the heart and the whispers of the spirit. For women, finding the right work–life combination is the greatest challenge. It takes time. But we're so busy sometimes we don't hear those inner voices, the little whispers. It is those little whispers that tell us how to set our own priorities to create a successful life."

The insights into combining work and family give readers the option of deciding whether they want to "have it all" with a career at the top of their profession and a successful family life, or whether they just want to have more of the many options that can create a successful life. The powerful women leaders who shared their life stories with us have shown us how to combine work at the top of one's career with a happy and healthy family. They have made it easier for the rest of us to create our own successful lives filled with meaningful work and close family relationships – a dually successful life.

# Closing Thoughts

## *Meaningful Work, Deep Relationships, and Happiness*

It has been over 100 years since the field of psychology emerged as an independent discipline, and during most of that time it has been primarily concerned with mental illness and fixing unhappiness. More recently, the focus has shifted to the positive aspects of human existence, especially the scientific study of happiness. There are now hundreds of studies that focus on what is important in making people happy. A first guess might include money, but actually money is an important contributor to happiness only for people who are living in poverty. Money is important when there is not enough to eat, or you cannot pay the heating bills during the cold winter months, or you cannot afford medical care. For most people who are living above the dark line of poverty, money is relatively unimportant in determining their level of happiness. All the big lottery winners, who are definitely very happy at the time they win, return to their pre-win levels of happiness within a few months, and even those who face life's difficulties, which might include losing a limb or the tragic death of a loved one, return to pre-loss levels or close to them after a period of mourning. Life is a diverse collection of positive and negative events, and while a major gain or loss can offset the balance for a while, in the long run the rest of life takes over and most of us return to where we were.

Cai Jing, Chairwoman of the Shanghai Pudong Women's Federation, came to the same realization:

> "I always have that feeling: what brings a person success is a happy life. A happy life is a successful life. If you want to be happy, you need to solve the difficulties in life. If you want to solve the difficulties, you need to have enough knowledge, scientific point of view and open and balanced attitudes. All these things need to work out over a period of long time. You need to go through it to learn it."

Happiness researchers have identified two major areas where people find or create lasting happiness. One is in deep relationships with other people, usually our closest family members and friends. The other is in meaningful work (Arnold, Turner, Barling, Kelloway, & McKee, 2007; Seligman, 2002). These are two areas of life where we can use our strengths to contribute to something that is "bigger" and more lasting than we are. It is in our interactions with people we care deeply about and when doing meaningful work that we experience our most positive emotions and gratifications. These are the components of a good life. We should not ask women to choose between them because both are important.

## A Crisis in Leadership

In a 2006 National Study of Confidence in Leadership conducted by the Center for Public Leadership (Pittinsky, Rosenthal, Bacon, Montoya, & Zhu, 2006), the authors found a "crisis in leadership" among Americans. Over 70 percent of a random sample responded that they agreed or strongly agreed that "We have a leadership crisis" (p. 4). With so few women in top leadership positions, we are only using half of our national talent as leaders, a fact that is true everywhere around the world. *The Global Gender Gap*, a report published by the World Economic Forum in 2006 (Hausmann, Tyson, & Zahidi, 2006), benchmarked gender equality in 115 countries. The authors report that "no country in the world has yet managed to eliminate the gender gap" (p. 3). They assert that this inequality is not a women's issue, but a human rights issue that should concern everyone.

The Nordic countries achieved the highest overall rankings in gender equality, with Sweden, Norway, Finland, and Iceland in the top four spots respectively. The United States ranked twenty-second and China was sixty-third. Overall, women have made the greatest gains in educational attainment and the least gains in politics. One conclusion from this study is that well educated women are ready to take additional positions of leadership. But, as long as women remain primary caregivers and they cannot "see" a way to be both a mother and a high-achieving professional, both caregiving and professional leadership will suffer.

We hope that readers have seen for themselves that it is possible to be successful in one's career and in one's family life. No one ever asks if men can successfully combine work and family. The women who so generously shared their life stories with us have shown that women can also be dually successful. They do not have to give up their hopes and dreams for a happy family or for a top-notch career. They redefine success as work and family and are fully involved in both life domains. We believe that everyone benefits when all members of society have a real opportunity to develop to their fullest potential, at home and at work. We sincerely thank the 62 women who have invited us into their lives and have provided guideposts so that others who may want to follow them to the top can find the way. For anyone who has set her sights on the half-way mark, the many strategies used by these women at the top will help you combine work and family regardless of how far you ultimately climb.

In listening to these women tell the stories of their lives, we are reminded of Ginger Rogers, the dance partner of Fred Astaire who has been variously described as the man who "danced on air" and the "silver screen's greatest song-and-dance man." Ginger Rogers never gained the acclaim that Fred Astaire did, yet, as others have already noted, she did everything Fred Astaire did; she just did it backwards and in high heels. All women dance backwards and in high heels; these are the universal norms of women's dance. But these mothers and caregivers at the top of their profession redefined the norms by taking the lead, and we may never dance the same way again.

# References

## Preface

Equal Opportunities Commission (1999). *Formal Investigation Report on Secondary School Places Allocation (SSPA) System.* www.eoc.org.hk/eoc/graphicsfolder/inforcenter/investigation/list.aspx?itemid=1210& investigationname=1 (retrieved November 30, 2007).

Halpern, D. F., Benbow, C., Geary, D., Gur, D., Hyde, J. and Gernsbacher, M. A. (2007). The science of sex-differences in science and mathematics. *Psychological Science in the Public Interest*, 8, 1–52.

## 1 For Women at the Top

Arnold, K. A., Turner, N., Barling, J., Kelloway, E. K., and McKee, M. C. (2007). Transformational leadership and psychological well-being: the mediating role of meaningful work. *Journal of Occupational Work Psychology*, 12, 195–203.

Aryee, S., Luk, V., Leung, A., and Lo, S. (1999). Role stressors, interrole conflict, and well-being: the moderating effect of spousal support and coping behaviors among employed parents in Hong Kong. *Journal of Vocational Behavior*, 54, 259–278.

Barnett, R. C. and Hyde, J. S. (2001). Women, men, work, and family. *American Psychologist*, 56, 781–796.

Bennetts, L. (2007). *The Feminine Mistake: Are We Giving up Too Much?* New York: Hyperion.

Boushey, H. (2005, November). Briefing paper: Are women opting out? Debunking the myth. Center for Economic and Policy Research. www.cepr.com (retrieved December 12, 2005).

Bureau of Labor Statistics Current Population Survey (2005). Table 25. Wives who earn more than their husbands 1987–2003. www.bls.gov/cps/wlf-table25-2005.pdf (retrieved November 10, 2007).

Catalyst (2006). *Different Cultures, Similar Perceptions: Stereotypes of West European Business Leaders*. New York: Author.

Census and Statistics Department (2007). *Women and Men in Hong Kong: Key Statistics*. Hong Kong: Census and Statistics Department, Government of the Hong Kong Special Administrative Region.

CNNMoney.com (2006, April 17). Fortune 500 2006: Women CEOs for Fortune 500 Companies. http://money.cnn.com/magazines/fortune/fortune500/womenceos/

Council of Economic Advisers (1998). Explaining trends in the gender wage gap. clinton4.nara.gov/WH/EOP/CEA/htm/gendergap.html (retrieved November 12, 2007).

Department of Population, Social, Science, and Technology (2004). *Women and Men in China: Facts and Figures 2004*. Beijing: National Bureau of Statistics.

Diener, E. and Seligman, M. E. P. (2004). Beyond money: toward an economy of well-being. *Psychological Science in the Public Interest*, 5, 1–31.

European Commission (2006). *Report on Equality between Women and Men 2006*. http://ec.europa.eu/employment_social/publications/2006/keaj06001_en.pdf (retrieved November 30, 2007).

Families and Work Institute (2006). Dual-centric: a new concept of work-life. www.familiesandwork.org/site/research/reports/dual-centric.pdf (retrieved October 4, 2007).

Fish, S. (2007, November 11). It depends on what the meaning of makes sense is. *New York Times*. http://fish.blogs.nytimes.com/2007/11/11/it-depends-what-the-meaning-of-makes-sense-is/?8ty&emc=ty (retrieved November 12, 2007).

Forbes (2005). The 100 most powerful women. http://www.forbes.com/lists/2005/11/22J7.html (retrieved December 13, 2007).

Fortune (2006). Fortune 50 most powerful women in business. http://money.cnn.com/popups/2006/fortune/mostpowerfulwomen_intl/10.html (retrieved December 13, 2007).

Friedan, B. (1963). *The Feminine Mystique*. New York: W. W. Norton.

Government Accounting Office (2003, October). *Women's Earnings: Work Patterns Partially Explain Difference between Men's and Women's Earnings*. Washington, DC: United States Printing Office.

Heilman, M. E. and Okimoto, T. G. (2008). Motherhood: a potential source of bias in employment decisions. *Journal of Applied Psychology*, 93, 189–198.

Hewlett, S. A. (2002). Executive women and the myth of having it all. *Harvard Business Review*, 80, 66–73.

Lee, C. M., Li, H. B., and Zhang, J. S. (2008). Gender earnings differentials in Hong Kong. In F. M. Cheung and E. Holroyd (eds.) *Mainstreaming Gender in Hong Kong Society*. Hong Kong: Chinese University Press.

Mason, M. A. and Goulden, M. (2004). Do babies matter? Part II: Closing the baby gap. Academe. www.eric.ed.gov/ERICWebPortal/recordDetail? accno=EJ727479 (retrieved May 1, 2005).

McKinsey & Company, Inc. (2007). Women matter: gender diversity, a corporate performance driver. www.epwn.net/pdf/mcKinsey_2007_gender_ matters.pdf (retrieved November 30, 2007).

National Association of Women in Law Firms (2006, October). National survey on retention and promotion of women in law firms. *Women Lawyers Journal*, 92, 1–12.

Ozanian, M. K. and MacDonald, E. (2005, May 9). Executive pay: paychecks on steroids. *Forbes*. http://www.forbes.com/free_forbes/2005/0509/134. html (retrieved November 15, 2007).

People's Daily Online (2007, May 18). People take 45% workforce in China. http://english.people.com.cn/200705/18/eng20070518_375703.html (retrieved November 10, 2007).

Roberts, S. (2007, January 16). 51% of women now living without a spouse. *New York Times*. www.newyorktimes.com/ 2007/01/16/us/16census. html?ei=5087%OA&em=&en (retrieved January 17, 2007).

Schwartz, F. (1989). Management women and the new facts of life. *Harvard Business Review*, 89, 65–75.

Singh, V. and Vinnicombe, S. (2006). The Female FTSE Report 2006. www.som.cranfield.ac.uk/som/research/centres/cdwbl/downloads/ FTSE2006full.pdf (retrieved November 9, 2007).

Statistics Canada (2006, August). Statistics on labour and income, vol. 7, no. 8.

Tang, C. S., Lee, A. M., Tang, T., Cheung, F. M., and Chan, C. (2002). Role occupancy, role quality, and psychological distress in Chinese women. *Women and Health*, 36, 49–66.

US Census Bureau (2004). Fertility of American women: June 2004. www. census.gov/prod/2005pubs/p20-555.pdf (retrieved November 13, 2007).

US Census Bureau (2007, August 9). Facts for Features: Women's history month. www.census.gov/Press-Release/www/releases/archives/facts_ for_features_special_editions/003897.html (retrieved November 9, 2007).

US Department of Education (2005). The condition of education. Postsecondary participation rates by sex and race/ethnicity: 1974–2003. nces. ed.gov/programs/quarterly/vol_71/1_2/5_6.asp (retrieved December 17, 2007).

Willams, J. (2008). Messages the courts are sending about workplace flexibility. In A. Newhall-Marcus, D. F. Halpern, and S. Tan (eds.) *The Changing Realities of Work and Family: An Interdisciplinary Approach*. New York: Wiley/Blackwell.

Xinhua New Agency (2002, July 6). Marriage most stable when husband earns twice as much as wife: survey. http://news.xinhuanet.com/english/2002-06/07/content_429388.htm (retrieved November 2007).

# 2 Learning from Mothers

Allen, T. D., Eby, L. D., Poteet, M. L. Lentz, E., and Lima, L. (2004). Career benefits associated with mentoring for protégés: a meta-analysis. *Journal of Applied Psychology*, 89, 127–136.

Baruch, G. and Barnett, R. C. (1983). Adult daughters' relationships with their mothers. *Journal of Marriage and the Family*, 45, 601–606.

Cianciolo, A. T., Antonakis, J., and Sternberg, R. J. (2004). Practical intelligence and leadership: using experience as a "mentor." In S. M. Halpin, D. V. Day, and S. J. Zaccaro (eds.) *Leader Development for Transforming Organizations: Growing Leaders for Tomorrow*. Mahwah, NJ: Lawrence Erlbaum Associates.

Dweck, C. S. (1999). Self-Theories: Their Role in Motivation, Personality and Development. Philadelphia, PA: The Psychology Press.

Ensher, E. and Murphy, S. (2005). *Power Mentoring: How Successful Mentors and Protégés Get the Most out of Their Relationships*. San Francisco, CA: Jossey-Bass.

Fischer, L. R. (1986). *Linked Lives: Adult Daughters and Their Mothers*. New York: Harper and Row.

Fischer, L. R. (1991). Between mothers and daughters. *Marriage and Family Review*, 16, 3/4, 237–248.

Higgins, M. C. and Kram, K. E. (2001). Reconceptualizing mentoring at work: a developmental network perspective. *Academy of Management Review*, 26, 264–288.

Higgins, M. C. and Thomas, D. A. (2001). Constellations and careers: toward understanding of the effects of multiple developmental relationships. *Journal of Organizational Behavior*, 22, 223–247.

Jones, D. (2000). Teaching/learning through Confucius: navigating our way through the Analects. www.aasianst.org/EAA/jones.htm (retrieved December 17, 2007).

Kram, K. E. (1985). *Mentoring at Work: Developmental Relationships in Organization Life*. Glenview, IL: Scott, Foresman.

Ragins, B. R. (1989). Barriers to mentoring: the female manager's dilemma. *Human Relations*, 42, 1–22.

Ragins, B. R. and Cotton, J. L. (1999). Mentor functions and outcomes: a comparison of men and women in formal and informal mentoring relationships. *Journal of Applied Psychology*, 84, 529–550.

## 3 Saving and Spending Time

Barnett, R. C. (2005). Dual-earner couples: good/bad for her and/or him? In D. F. Halpern and S. E. Murphy (eds.) *From Work–Family Balance to Work–Family Interaction: Changing the Metaphor*. Mahwah, NJ: Erlbaum.

Bianchi, S. M. (2006). What gives when mothers are employed? Parental time allocation in dual earner and single earner two-parent families. www.socialscience.cornell.edu/0407/Bianchi%20What%gives%20April202006.pdf (retrieved December 1, 2007).

Bond, J. T. (with Thompson, C., Galinsky, E., and Prottas, D.) (2002). Highlights of the National Study of the Changing Workforce Executive Summary. www.familiesandwork.org/summary/nscw2002.pdf (retrieved December 4, 2007).

Census and Statistics Department (2003). *Thematic Household Survey Report No. 14*. Executive summary. Hong Kong: Hong Kong Special Administrative Region Government. www.women.gov.hk/eng/research/research.html (retrieved October 16, 2007).

Department of Population, Social, Science, and Technology (2004). *Women and Men in China: Facts and Figures 2004*. Beijing: National Bureau of Statistics.

Fair Labor Standards Act (1938). www.flsa.com/coverage.html (retrieved December 5, 2007).

Galinsky, E. (2005). *Overwork in America: When the Way We Work Becomes Too Much*. New York: Families and Work Institute.

Greenhaus, J. H. and Beutell, N. J. (1985). Sources of conflict between work and family roles. *Academy of Management Review*, 10, 76–88.

Hewlett, S. A. (2007). *Off Ramps and On Ramps: Keeping Talented Women on the Road to Success*. Cambridge, MA: Harvard Business School Press.

Hewlett, S. A. and Luce, C. B. (2006). Extreme jobs: the dangerous allure of the 70-hour work week. *Harvard Business Review*, 84, 49–59.

Hochschild, A. R. (1997). *The Time Bind: When Work Becomes Home and Home Becomes Work*. New York: Metropolitan.

Hochschild, A. R. (1989). *The Second Shift*. London: Penguin.

Institute for Women's Policy Research (2005; updated 2006). The gender wage ratio: women's and men's earnings. IWPR #C350. www.iwpr.org/pdf/updated2006_C350.pdf (retrieved December 17, 2007).

International Labour Organization (1999). Americans work longest hours among industrialized countries, Japanese second longest. Europeans work less time, but register faster productivity gains. www.ilo.org/global/About_the_ ILO/Media_and_public_information/Press_releases/lang-en/WCMS_071326/index.htm (retrieved December 15, 2007).

International Labour Organization (2007). Working time around the world: one in five workers worldwide are putting in "excessive" hours: new ILO study spotlights working time in over 50 countries. www.ilo.org/global/About_the_ILO/Media_and_public_information/Press_releases/lang–en/WCMS_082827 (retrieved December 4, 2007).

Levine, J. A., Weisell, R., Chevassus, S., Martinez, C. D., Burlingame, B., and Coward, W. A. (2001). *Science*, 294, 812–813.

Morgenstern, J. (2000). *Time Management from the Inside Out*. New York: Holt.

Slaughter, A.-M. (2007, September 27). Moon cakes in Shanghai. http://kristof.blogs.nytimes.com/2007/09/27/moon-cakes-in-shanghai/ (retrieved September 27, 2007).

## 4  Happy Homemaker, Happy Marriage

*10 Downing Street: PM: Margaret Thatcher*. www.number10.gov.uk/output/Page126.asp (retrieved November 3, 2007).

Bianci, S. M., Milkie, M. A., Sayer, L. C., and Robinson, J. P. (2000). Is anyone doing the housework? Trends in the gender division of household labor. *Social Forces*, 79, 191–228.

Burley, K. A. (1995). Family variables as mediators of the relationship between work–family conflict and marital adjustment among dual-career men and women. *Journal of Social Psychology*, 135, 483–498.

Gilbert, L. A. (1988). *Sharing it All: The Rewards and Struggles of Two-Career Families*. New York: Plenum Press.

Gupta, S. (2005). Her money; her time: women's earnings and their housework hours. *Social Science Research*, 35, 955–999.

Schoen, R. and Weinick, R. M. (1993). Partner choice in marriage and cohabitations. *Journal of Marriage and the Family*, 55, 408–414.

Vannoy-Hiller, D. and Philliber, W. W. (1991). *Equal Partners: Successful Women in Marriage*. Newbury Park, CA: Sage.

Yang, J. and Short, S. A. (2007). Investigating China's stalled revolution: husband and wife involvement in housework in the PRC. http://paa2005.princeton.edu/download.aspx?submissionId=50773 (retrieved November 9, 2007).

## 5  Cherished Children

Barnett, R. C. and Hyde, J. S. (2001). Women, men, work, and family. *American Psychologist*, 56, 781–796.

Belsky, J. (2001). Emanuel Miller Lecture: Developmental risks (still) associated with early child care. *Journal of Child Psychology and Psychiatry*, 42, 845–859.

Belsky, J., Vandell, D. L., Burchinal, M. K., Clarke-Stewart, A., McCartney, K., and Owen, M. T. (2007). The NICHD Early Child Care Research Network: are there long-term effects of early child care? *Child Development*, 78, 681–701.

Burchinal, M. R. and Clarke-Stewart, K. A. (2007). Maternal employment and cognitive outcomes: the importance of analytic approach. *Developmental Psychology*, 43, 1140–1155.

Coontz, S. (2000). *The Way We Never Were: American Families and the Nostalgia Trap*. New York: Basic Books.

Corell, S. J. and Benard, S. (2005, January 25). Getting a job: is there a motherhood penalty? http://news.cornell.edu/stories/Aug05/soc.mothers.dea.html (retrieved May 26, 2006).

Eckes, T. (2002). Paternalistic and Envious Gender stereotypes: testing predictions from the stereotype content model. *Sex Roles*, 47, 99–114.

Gauthier, A. H., Smeeding, T., and Furstenberg, Jr., F. F. (2004, October). Do we invest less time in children? Trends in parental time in selected industrialized countries since the 1960s. Center for Policy Research Working Paper no. 64. http://cpr.maxwell.syr.edu/cprwps/wps64abs.htm (retrieved October 24, 2007).

Gottfried, A. E. and Gottfried, A. W. (2008). The upside of maternal and dual-earner employment: a focus on positive family adaptations, home environments, and child development in the Fullerton longitudinal study. In A. Marcus-Newhall, D. F. Halpern, and S. J. Tan (eds.) *The Changing Realities of Work and Family: An Interdisciplinary Approach*. New York: Wiley-Blackwell.

Gottfried, A. E., Gottfried, A. W., and Bathurst, K. (2002). Maternal and dual-earner employment status and parenting. In M. H. Bornstein (ed.) *Handbook of Parenting*, 2nd edn (Vol. 2, pp. 207–229). Mahwah, NJ: Lawrence Erlbaum Associates.

Halpern, D. F., Benbow, C., Geary, D., Gur, D., Hyde, J., and Gernsbacher, M. A. (2007). The science of sex-differences in science and mathematics. *Psychological Science in the Public Interest*, 8, 1–52.

Heilman, M. E., and Okimoto, T. G. (2008). Motherhood: a potential source of bias in employment decisions. *Journal of Applied Psychology*, 93, 189–198.

Hewlett, S. (2002). *Creating a Life: Professional Women and the Quest for Children*. New York: Hyperion.

Johnston, D. D. and Swanson, D. H. (2006). Constructing the "Good Mother": the experience of mothering ideologies by work status. *Sex Roles*, 54, 509–519.

Kahneman, D., Krueger, A. B, Schkade, D. A., Schwarz, N., and Stone, A. A. (2004). A survey method for characterizing daily life experience: the day reconstruction method. *Science*, 306, 1776–1780.

Kirwan-Taylor, H. (2006, July 26). Sorry, my children bore me to death. *Daily Mail.* www.dailymail.co.uk/pages/live/femail/article.html?in_article_id=397672 (retrieved August 5, 2006).

Marshall, N. L. (2004). The quality of early child care and children's development. *Current Directions in Psychological Science,* 13, 165–168.

Parker, K. (1997, July 17). Forget the research – Trust your instincts. *USA Today,* p. A15.

Scarr, S. (1997). Rules of evidence: a larger context for the statistical debate. *Psychological Science,* 8, 16–17.

Waldfogel, J. (1998). Understanding the "family gap" in pay for women with children. *The Journal of Economic Perspectives,* 12, 1, 137–156.

Warner, J. (2006, August 1). Mom's balancing act. *New York Times.* http://select.nytimes.com/2006/08/01/opinion.01warner.html (retrieved November 9, 2006).

Warner, J. (2007, May 24). Words that wound the working mother. *New York Times.* www.newyorktimes.com (retrieved May 24, 2007).

Williams, J. (2000). *Unbending Gender: Why Family and Work Conflict and What to Do about it.* New York: Oxford University Press.

Yeung, W. J., Linver, M. R., and Brooks-Gunn, J. (2002). How money matters for young children's development: parental investment and family processes. *Child Development,* 73, 1861–1879.

# 6   Work–Family Spillover

Allen, T. D., Herst, D. E. L., Bruck, C. S., and Sutton, M. (2000). Consequences associated with work-to-family conflict; a review and agenda for future research. *Journal of Occupational Health Psychology,* 5, 278–308.

Baltes, B. B. and Heydens-Gahir, H. A. (2003). Reduction of work–family conflict through the use of selection, optimization, and compensation behaviors. *Journal of Applied Psychology,* 88, 1005–1018.

Byron, K. (2005). A meta-analytic review of work–family conflict and its antecedents. *Journal of Vocational Behavior,* 67, 169–198.

Ford, M. T., Heinen, B. A., and Langkamer, K. L. (2007). Work and family satisfaction and conflict: a meta-analysis of cross-domain relations. *Journal of Applied Psychology,* 92, 57–80.

Friedman, S. D. and Greenhaus, J. H. (2000). *Work and Family – Allies or Enemies? What Happens When Business Professionals Confront Life Choices.* New York: Oxford University Press.

Frone, M. R. (2003). Work–family balance. In J. C. Quick and L. E. Tetrick (eds.) *Handbook of Occupational Health Psychology* (pp. 143–162). Washington, DC: American Psychological Association.

Frone, M. R., Russell, M., and Cooper, M. L. (1992). Antecedents and outcomes of work–family conflict: testing a model of the work–family interface. *Journal of Applied Psychology*, 77, 65–78.

Greenhaus, J. H. and Beutell, N. J. (1985). Sources of conflict between work and family roles. *Academy of Management Review*, 10, 76–88.

Grzywacz, J. G., Almeida, D. M., and McDonald, D. A. (2002). Work–family spillover and daily reports of work and family stress in the adult labor force. *Family Relations*, 51, 28–36.

Halpern, D. F. and Murphy, S. E. (eds.) (2005). *From Work–Family Balance to Work–Family Interaction: Changing the Metaphor*. Mahwah, NJ: Lawrence Erlbaum Associates.

Kahn, R. L., Wolfe, D. M., Quinn, R., Snoek, J. D., and Rosenthal, R. A. (1964). *Organizational Stress*. New York: John Wiley.

Lai, G. (1995). Work and family roles and psychological well being in urban China. *Journal of Health and Social Behavior*, 36, 11–37.

Rapoport, R. and Rapoport, R. N. (1971). *Dual-Career Families*. Harmondsworth, England: Penguin.

Rapoport, R., Bailyn, L., Fletcher, J. K., and Pruitt, B. H. (2002). *Beyond Work–Family Balance: Advancing Gender Equity and Workplace Performance*. San Francisco, CA: Jossey-Bass.

Repetti, R. J., Matthews, K. A., and Waldron, I. (1989). Employment and women's health. *American Psychologist*, 44, 1394–1401.

Tang, C. S., Lee, A. M., Tang, T., Cheung, F. M., and Chan, C. (2002). Role occupancy, role quality, and psychological distress in Chinese women. *Women and Health*, 36, 49–66.

Warr, P. and Parry, G. (1982). Paid employment and women's psychological well-being. *Psychological Bulletin*, 91, 498–516.

Yang, N., Chen, C. C., Chao, J., and Zou, Y. (2000). Sources of work–family conflict: a Sino-U.S. comparison of the effects of work and family demands. *Academy of Management Journal*, 43, 113–123.

# 7 Culture Counts

Aryee, S., Field, D., and Luk, V. (1999a). A cross-cultural test of a model of work–family interface. *Journal of Management*, 25, 491–511.

Aryee, S., Luk, V., Leung, A., and Lo, S. (1999b). Role stressors, interrole conflict, and well-being: the moderating effect of spousal support and coping behaviors among employed parents in Hong Kong. *Journal of Vocational Behavior*, 54, 259–278.

Baker, N. L. (2005). Women, work, and discrimination. In A. Barnes (ed.) *The Handbook of Women, Psychology, and the Law* (pp. 37–63). San Francisco, CA: Jossey-Bass.

The Barbara Lee Family Foundation (2004). Cracking the code: Unlock the door: The guide for women running for governor [Brochure]. Cambridge, MA: Barbara Lee.

Census and Statistics Department (2001). *Women and Men in Hong Kong: Key Statistics* (2001 edn). Hong Kong: Hong Kong SAR Government.

Census and Statistics Department (2007). *Women and Men in Hong Kong: Key Statistics* (2007 edn). Hong Kong: Hong Kong SAR Government.

Cheung, F. M. and Chung, P. (2008). Central mechanisms: the Equal Opportunities Commission and the Women's Commission. In F. M. Cheung and E. Holroyd (eds.) *Mainstreaming Gender in Hong Kong Society*. Hong Kong: Chinese University Press.

Cheung, F. M., Wan, P. S., and Wan, O. C. (1994). The underdeveloped political potential of women in Hong Kong. In B. Nelson and N. Chowdhury (eds.) *Women and Politics Worldwide* (pp. 326–346). New Haven, CT: Yale University Press.

Committee for the Elimination of Discrimination Against Women (2004, June 10). *Combined 5th & 6th Periodic Report of State Parties: China*. http://daccessdds.un.org/doc/UNDOC/GEN/N04/403/05/PDF/N0440305. pdf?OpenElement (retrieved October 29, 2007).

Corporate Voice for Working Families (2006). Business impacts of flexibility: an imperative for expansion. www.cvworkingfamilies.org/downloads/ Business%20Impacts%20of%20Flexibility.pdf (retrieved November 7, 2007).

Department of Population, Social, Science, and Technology (2004). *Women and Men in China: Facts and Figures 2004*. Beijing: National Bureau of Statistics.

Eagly, A. H. and Carli, L. L. (2007). *Through the Labyrinth: The Truth about How Women Become Leaders*. Boston, MA: Harvard Business School Press.

Edwards, L. (2000). Women in the People's Republic of China: new challenges to the grand gender narrative. In L. Edwards and M. Roces (eds.) *Women in Asia: Tradition, Modernity and Globalization* (pp. 59–84). St. Leonards, NSW, Australia: Allen & Unwin.

Glick, P. and Fiske, S. T. (1997). Hostile and benevolent sexism. *Psychology of Women Quarterly*, 21, 119–135.

Hofstede, G. (1980). *Culture's Consequences: International Differences in Work-Related Values*. Beverly Hills, CA: Sage.

Lai, G. (1995). Work and family roles and psychological well being in urban China. *Journal of Health and Social Behavior*, 36, 11–37.

Lee, I. C., Pratto, F., and Lee, M. C. (2007). Social relationships and sexism in the United States and Taiwan. *Journal of Cross-Cultural Psychology*, 38, 595–612.

Lo, S. (2003). Perceptions of work–family conflict among married female professionals in Hong Kong. *Personnel Review*, 32, 376–390.

Media Mentions and Suse News Stanford Report (2002, April 10). By Lisa Trei. http://ed.stanford.edu/suse/newsbureau/displayRecord.php?tablen ame=notify1&id=10 (retrieved April 4, 2005).

Nelson, B., J. and Carver, K. A. (1994). Many voices but few vehicles: the consequences for women of weak political infrastructure in the United States. In B. Nelson and N. Chowdhury (eds.) *Women and Politics Worldwide* (pp. 738–757). New Haven, CT: Yale University Press.

Poelmans, S. A. Y. (ed.) (2005). *Work and Family – An International Research Perspective*. Mahwah, NJ: Lawrence Erlbaum Associates.

Shafiro, M. and Hammer, L. (2004). Work and family: a cross-cultural psychology perspective. *Sloan Work and Family Encyclopedia*. Boston, MA: Boston College: Sloan Work and Family Research Network. http://wfnetwork.bc.edu/encyclopedia_entry.php?id=226&area=academics (retrieved October 30, 2007).

*South China Morning Post* (2007, November 9). Ip and Chan head Chief Executive on recognition, p. A4.

Spector, P. E., Cooper, C. L., Poelmans, S., Allen, T. D., O'Driscoll, M., Sanchez, J. I., et al. (2004). A cross-national comparative study of work–family stressors, working hours, and well-being: China and Latin America versus the Anglo world. *Personnel Psychology*, 57, 119–142.

Swift, J. (2008). Politics, motherhood, and Madame President. In A. Marcus-Newhall, D. F. Halpern, and S. Tan (eds.) *The Changing Realities of Work and Family: An Interdisciplinary Approach*. New York: Wiley-Blackwell.

US Department of Education (2000). National Center for Education Statistics. *Trends in Educational Equity for Girls and Women*. NCES 2000–030. By Y. Bae, S. Choy, C. Geddes, J. Sable, and T. Snyder. Washington, DC: US Printing Office.

US Glass Ceiling Commission (1995). *A Solid Investing: Making Full Use of the Nation's Human Capital*. Washington, DC: US Glass Ceiling Commission. http://digitalcommons.ilr.cornell.edu/key_workplace/120/ (retrieved October 29, 2007).

Westwood, R., Mehrain, T., and Cheung, F. M. (1995). *Gender and Society in Hong Kong: A Statistical Profile*. HK Institute of Asia-Pacific Studies Research Monograph No. 23. Hong Kong: HKIAPS.

Wheaton, S. (2007, July 27). Campaigning with "cleavage." *New York Times*. http://thecaucus.blogs.nytimes.com/2007/07/27/campaigning-with-cleavage (retrieved July 27, 2007).

Working Women. National Working Committee on Children and Women (2001). *The Program for the Development of Chinese Women (2001–2010)*. Beijing: People's Republic of China: State Council. www/isg.ml/~landsberger/ww.htm (retrieved December 16, 2007).

Yang, N., Chen, C. C., Chao, J., and Zou, Y. (2000). Sources of work–family conflict: a Sino-U.S. comparison of the effects of work and family demands. *Academy of Management Journal*, 43, 113–123.

# 8 Leading as Women

Bargh, J. A., Chen, M., and Burrows, L. (1996). Automaticity of social behavior: direct effects of trait construct and stereotype activation on action. *Journal of Personality and Social Psychology*, 71, 230–244.

Burns, J. M. (1978). *Leadership*. New York: Harper & Row.

Catalyst (2005). Women "take care," men "take charge": stereotyping of U.S. business leaders exposed. www.catalystwomen.org/files/full/Women%20Take%20Care%20Men%20Take%20Charge.pdf (retrieved October 15, 2007).

Davies, P. G., Spencer, S. J., and Steele, C. M. (2005). Clearing the air: identity safety moderates the effects of stereotype threat on women's leadership aspirations. *Journal of Personality and Social Psychology*, 88, 276–287.

Drucker, P. (undated). *Thinkexist.com* http://thinkexist.com/quotation/leadership_is_not_magnetic_personality-that_can/294628.html (retrieved October 15, 2007).

Duehr, E. E. and Bono, J. E. (2006). Men, women, and managers: are stereotypes finally changing? *Personnel Psychology*, 59, 815–846.

Eagly, A. H. (2007). Female leadership advantage and disadvantage: resolving the contradictions. *Psychology of Women Quarterly*, 31, 1, 1–12.

Eagly, A. C. and Carli, L. L. (2007a). Women and the labyrinth of leadership [Electronic version]. *Harvard Business Review*. www.hbr.org (retrieved October 15, 2007).

Eagly, A. H. and Carli, L. L. (2007b). *Through the Labyrinth: The Truth about How Women Become Leaders*. Boston, MA: Harvard Business School Press.

Eagly, A. H. and Johnson, B. T. (1990). Gender and leadership style: a meta-analysis. *Psychological Bulletin*, 108, 233–256.

Eagly, A. H., Karau, S. J., and Makhijani, M. G. (1995). Gender and the effectiveness of leaders: a meta-analysis. *Psychological Bulletin*, 117, 125–145.

Eagly, A. H., Johannesen-Schmidt, M. C., and van Engen, M. (2003). Transformational, transactional, and laissez-faire leadership styles: a meta-analysis comparing women and men. *Psychological Bulletin*, 95, 569–591.

*The Economist* (2007, August 24). Another cultural revolution [Electronic version]. www.economist.com/displaystory.cfm?story_id=9674048 (retrieved October 15, 2007).

Friedman, T. L. (2005). *The World is Flat*. New York: Farrar, Straus and Giroux.

Goethals, G. R. (2005). Presidential leadership. *Annual Review of Psychology*, 56, 545–570.

Heilman, M. E. and Okimoto, T. G. (2007). Why are women penalized for success at male tasks? The implied communality deficiency. *Journal of Applied Psychology*, 92, 81–92.

Hesselbein, F. & Goldsmith, M. (eds.) (2007). *Leader to Leader Institute*. San Francisco, CA: Jossey-Bass.

Hofstede, G. (1996). Gender stereotypes and partner preferences of Asian women in masculine and feminine cultures. *Journal of Cross-Cultural Psychology*, 27, 533–546.

Judge, T. A. and Piccolo, R. F. (2004). Transformational and transactional leadership: a meta-analytic test of their relative validity. *Journal of Applied Psychology*, 89, 901–910.

Kanter, R. M. (1977). *Men and Women of the Corporation*. New York: Basic Books.

Krishnan, H. A. and Park, D. (2005). A few good women – on top management teams. *Journal of Business Research*, 58, 1712–1720.

Lipman-Bluman, J. (2004). *The Allure of Toxic Leaders: Why We Follow Destructive Bosses and Corrupt Politicians – And How We Can Survive Them*. New York: Oxford University Press.

Lowe, K. B., Kroeck, K. G., and Sivasubramaniam, N. (1996). Effectiveness correlates of transformational and transactional leadership: a meta-analytic review of the MLQ literature. *The Leadership Quarterly*, 7, 385–425.

MacDonald, E. and Schoenberger, C. R. (2005). The 100 most powerful women. www.forbes.com/2005/07/27/powerfull-women-world-cz_05powomen_land.html (retrieved October 14, 2007).

McKinsey & Company, Inc. (2007). Women matter: gender diversity, a corporate performance driver. www.epwn.net/pdf/mcKinsey_2007_gender_matters.pdf (retrieved November 30, 2007).

Walumbwa, F. O., Lawler, J. J., and Avolio, B. J. (2007). Leadership, individual differences, and work-related attitudes: a cross-cultural investigation. *Applied Psychology: An International Review*, 56, 212–230.

## 9  How to Lead a Dually Successful Life

Arnold, K. A., Turner, N., Barling, J., Kelloway, E. K., and McKee, M. C. (2007). Transformational leadership and psychological well-being: the mediating role of meaningful work. *Journal of Occupational Health Psychology*, 12, 193–203.

Cascio, W. F. and Young, C. E. (2005). Work–family balance: does the market reward firms that respect it? In D. F. Halpern and S. E. Murphy (eds.) *From Work–Family Balance to Work–Family Interaction. Changing the Metaphor* (pp. 49–64). Mahwah, NJ: Erlbaum.

Catalyst (2007). The double-bind dilemma for women in leadership: damned if you do, doomed if you don't. www.catalystwomen.org/files/full/2007%20Double%20Bind.pdf (retrieved November 28, 2007).

Drago, R., Colbeck, C., Hollenshead, C., and Sullivan, B. (2008). Work–family policies and the avoidance of bias against caregiving. In A. Newhall-Marcus, D. F. Halpern, and S. Tan (eds.) *The Changing Realities of Work and Family: An Interdisciplinary Approach*. New York: Wiley/Blackwell.

Eagly, A. H. and Carli, L. L. (2007). *Through the Labyrinth: The Truth about How Women Become Leaders*. Boston, MA: Harvard Business School Press.

Frisco, M. and Williams, K. (2003). Perceived housework equity, marital happiness, and divorce in dual-earner households. *Journal of Family Issues*, 24, 51–73.

Gottfried, A. E. and Gottfried, A. (2008). The upside of maternal employment. In A. Newhall-Marcus, D. F. Halpern, and S. Tan (eds.) *The Changing Realities of Work and Family: An Interdisciplinary Approach*. New York: Wiley/Blackwell.

Hausmann, R., Tyson, L. D., and Zahidi, S. (2006). *The Global Gender Gap: Report 2006*. Geneva, Switzerland: World Economic Forum.

Hewlett, S. A. (2002). Executive women and the myth of having it all. *Harvard Business Review*, 80, 66–73.

Hewlett, S. A., Luce, C. B., and Schiller, P. (2005). The hidden brain drain: off ramp and on ramp in women's careers. *Harvard Business Review*, 83, 31–57.

Krishnan, H. A. and Park, D. (2005). A few good women – on top management teams. *Journal of Business Research*, 58, 1712–1720.

Logsdon, M. C., Wisner, K., and Shanahan, B. (2007). Evidence on postpartum depression: 10 publications to guide nursing practice. *Issues in Mental Health Nursing*, 28, 445–451.

McKinsey & Company, Inc. (2007). Women matter: gender diversity, a corporate performance driver. www.epwn.net/pdf/mcKinsey_2007_gender_matters.pdf (retrieved November 30, 2007).

Pittinsky, T. L., Rosenthal, S. A., Bacon, L. M., Montoya, R. M., and Zhu, W. (2006). *National Leadership Index 2006: A National Study of Confidence in Leadership*. Center for Public Leadership, Harvard University. Cambridge, MA. leadershipcrisis2006.pdf (retrieved November 26, 2007).

Seligman, M. E. P. (2002). *Authentic Happiness*. New York: Free Press.

Van Steenbergen, E. F., Ellemers, N., and Mooijaart, A. (2007). How work and family can facilitate each other: distinct types of work–family facilitation and outcomes for women and men. *Journal of Occupational Health Psychology*, 12, 279–300.

Williams, J. (2000). *Unbending Gender*. New York: Houghton Mifflin.

Willams. J. (2008). Messages the courts are sending about workplace flexibility. In A. Newhall-Marcus, D. F. Halpern, and S. Tan (eds.) *The Changing Realities of Work and Family: An Interdisciplinary Approach*. New York: Wiley/Blackwell.

The World Values Survey (2006). 2005–2006 World Values Survey. www.worldvaluessurvey.org/statistics/WVSQuestRoot.pdf (retrieved December 15, 2007).

# Appendix: Biography of the Women Leaders

## Women Leaders in the USA

### Sharon ALLEN

Sharon Allen is Chairman of the Board of Deloitte LLP, leading the firm's governance process, and a member of the board of directors of the global organization Deloitte Touche Tohmatsu. Allen is the first woman elected as Chairman of the Board and the highest-ranking woman in the organization's history as well as in her profession. With 30 years of experience in auditing and consulting, Allen has worked with many high-profile clients. She has been twice named as one of the 100 Most Powerful Women in the World by *Forbes* magazine. She is also involved in her community, serving on the Women's Leadership Board at Harvard University's John F. Kennedy School of Government, the President's Export Council, the boards of the Los Angeles Area Chamber of Commerce, United Way of Greater Los Angeles, and the national board of the YMCA. In addition, Allen has received numerous awards for business and community leadership.

### Helena ASHBY

Chief Helena Ashby was promoted to the rank of Chief in 1995 and became at that time the highest-ranking woman in the history of the Sheriff's Department of Los Angeles County, which not only ran jails and courts, but patrolled over 40 independent cities. (The Sheriff is the top law enforcement officer of Los Angeles County and is assisted by Division Chiefs who are civil servants.) Starting her career as a deputy, Chief Ashby was a member of the Los Angeles County Sheriff's Department for more than 30 years and retired in 2000.

During her time in the Sheriff's Department, she served in the Custody, Detective, and Administration Divisions, the Detective, Administration, and Technical Services Divisions, and Field Operations. Recognized by the National Organization of Black Law Enforcement Executives (NOBLE) for her contributions to law enforcement, Chief Ashby is also a past recipient of the Soroptimist Club's Woman of the Year and the YWCA's Woman of the Year and Woman of Achievement Awards. She has served on the board of the Youth Intervention Project as well as on the committee of the Los Angeles County Management Council. A Harvard University alumna, Chief Ashby received her Master's degree in Public Administration from the Kennedy School of Government.

### Philamena BAIRD

Philamena Baird is a leading figure in philanthropy in Texas. She is the founding Chairman of the Education Foundation of Harris County, Texas and now serves on its Board of Directors. She also serves on the Board of Directors of Children at Risk in the Greater Houston area and as a board member of Greater Houston Community Foundation. She was named as one of the 2006 Women of Distinction by the ABC Channel for her dedication to community service. Honoring her commitment as a teacher to help children of minority groups, developing a curriculum called "Life Skills," Baird was presented with the "2006 Teacher of the Year" award by Former First Lady Barbara Bush at the annual "Excellence in Education" gala hosted by the Education Foundation.

### Kim CAMPBELL

The nineteenth Prime Minister of Canada, Kim Campbell is the first female to hold the position. Before her election as leader, some of the important posts she has held include Minister of State for Indian Affairs and Northern Development, Minister of Justice and Attorney General of Canada, Minister of National Defense and Minister of Veterans' Affairs. She was the first woman to hold the Justice and Defense portfolios and the first woman to be Defense Minister of a NATO country. An elected Leader of the Progressive Conservative Party of Canada, Campbell was sworn in as Canada's first female

Prime Minister in 1993 but left office later that year when her government was defeated in a general election. During her government, Campbell participated in major international meetings including the Commonwealth, NATO, the G7 Summit and the United Nations General Assembly. After her tenure as Prime Minister, Campbell served as the Canadian Consul-General in Los Angeles from 1996 to 2000 and from 1999 to 2003 Chair of the Council of Women World Leaders (CWWL) whose membership consists of women who hold or have held the office of President or Prime Minister in their own country. In 2002, Campbell was a founder of the Club of Madrid, an organization of former heads of government and state who work to promote democratization through peer relations with leaders of transitional democracies. She served as Acting President and Vice-President until she assumed the position of Secretary General from 2004 to 2006. From 2003 to 2005 Campbell was also president of the International Women's Forum, a global organization of women of significant and diverse achievement. A graduate of the University of British Columbia with a Bachelor of Arts degree and a Law degree, she did doctorate studies in Soviet Government at the London School of Economics where she is an Honorary Fellow. She is also an Honorary Fellow of the Centre for Public Leadership at John F. Kennedy School of Government, Harvard University, where she taught from 2001 to 2003.

### Wilma CHAN

Wilma Chan is a member of the California State Assembly, bringing her 25 years of community service and 10 years of hands-on legislative experience to the Legislature. Chan represents the cities of Oakland, Alameda, and Piedmont in the Assembly. Prior to the appointment, Chan served on the Board of Supervisors and chaired the Health Committee. She was the first Chair of the Alameda County Children and Families Commission, which distributes $20 million annually to new funds for children's services. She was the Assembly Majority Leader, the first woman and the first Asian-American to hold the position, and has served on a variety of Assembly Committees on Health, Education, and Economic Development, among others. Chan was also the Chair of the Select Committee on California Children's School Readiness and Health. She has been honored by the National Association of Social Workers (California Chapter), the American Association of University Women, California Hunger Action Network, Alameda County Tobacco Control Coalition, and the Soroptimists. Chan also received the Paul Harris Award, the Rotary's highest honor, from the Alameda Rotary. She holds a BA from Wellesley and a Master's degree in Education Policy from Stanford University.

## Lorna Duphiney EDMUNDSON

Lorna Duphiney Edmundson is the eighteenth President of Wilson College, an all-women college in Pennsylvania. She has dedicated her life to education, women's education in particular. Upon graduation, she taught in a Head Start program, served with the American Friends' Service Committee, and served as a consultant with the New York City Schools in minority communities. In addition, Edmundson developed internship programs for women at the American University in Paris. Later in her career, she served as a Fulbright Scholar in residence at Tokyo Women's Christian University, Japan. She has held senior positions at the American University in Paris, Columbia University Teachers College School of General Studies, and Columbia University, Marymount, and Colby-Sawyer College. Prior to heading Wilson College, Edmundson served as President of the Association of Vermont Independent Colleges and Trinity College of Vermont. Edmundson has been honored by the Alumni Association of Rhode Island College, her alma mater, as Outstanding Alumna.

## Ada EDWARDS

Ada Edwards is a member of Houston City Council District D and chairs Housing and Community Development, the State of Emergency HIV/AIDS Task Force, and the Flooding and Drainage Issues Committee. She also serves on six other committees of the City Council. Edwards owns a production distribution company which produces educational video- and audiotapes on African history, culture, economics, and politics. A widely published freelance writer and broadcast journalist, she produces and hosts a news and weekly public affairs program, *Dialogue with Ada Edwards*. Edwards is greatly involved in community affairs. Being the founder of several coalitions which help minorities – e.g. the Houston Chapter of the "Free South Africa Movement" – she is currently a member of the

NAACP, the Union Community Fund (AFL-CIO), the American Indian Movement, and the African Community Organization. Affiliated with the Houston Area Women's Center, she also serves on the Board for the Joint City County Commission on Children and Youth and the Advisory Board for Mothers for Clean Air. In addition, she is a member and bishop of the Pan African Orthodox Christian Church. She has also served as a community relations consultant to three Houston Police Chiefs. Locally, Edwards has worked for the Harris County Democratic Party as well as being the campaign treasurer for Sue Schechter in her successful bid for Harris County Democratic Party Chair.

### Barbara FRANKLIN

Barbara Hackman Franklin is President and CEO of Barbara Franklin Enterprises, a private investment and management consulting firm. She served as the twenty-ninth US Secretary of Commerce in the administration of President George H. W. Bush. As Secretary of Commerce, she led the historic mission to China in 1992 to normalize commercial relations and resume ministerial contact, which the United States had banned since the Tiananmen Square uprising in 1989. In her career in the government, she has worked with five US presidents and was one of the original Commissioners and the Vice-Chair of the US Consumer Product Safety Commission as well as Staff Assistant to President Richard Nixon charged with recruiting women for high-level jobs in the federal government. Franklin founded Franklin Associates, a management consulting firm in which she served as President and CEO. She also served as a public member of the Board of the American Institute of Certified Public Accountants and of the Auditing Standards Board. She received the John J. McCloy Award for contributions to audit excellence, the Director of the Year Award from the National Association of Corporate Directors, and an Outstanding Director Award from the Outstanding Directors Exchange. She is Chairman Emerita of the Economic Club of New York, a Director of the National Association of Corporate Directors and the National Committee on US–China Relations, Chair of the Asian Studies Center Advisory Council of the Heritage Foundation, and a member of the Public Company Accounting Oversight Board Advisory Council. She is also past Vice-Chair of the US–China Business Council. She graduated with distinction from Pennsylvania State University and was one of the first women graduates of Harvard Business School.

## Ginny GONG

Ginny Gong is National President of the Organization of Chinese Americans, the first to be elected by general membership. Formerly the Montgomery County Public Schools (MCPS) administrator, she now serves as the Director of the County's Community Use of Public Facilities, working with MCPS principals and administrative staff to oversee and coordinate procedures for scheduling public facilities for community use and to survey community needs to ensure appropriate and efficient use of public facilities. She has worked for the MCPS in various positions, being responsible for planning and implementing comprehensive community and, in her latest position, human relations programs for the community. In addition, she has served, and currently serves, in leadership positions on boards and commissions, including the Board of Advisors to University of Maryland Systems, Montgomery Community Television, Leadership Montgomery, the Mid-Atlantic Equity Consortium, the Arts and Humanities Cultural Plan Steering Committee, and MC Police Chief Advisory Council. For her active involvement in the community, Gong received the Outstanding Service Award from the National Association of Professional Asian American Women. In 1996, she was nominated to the Maryland Women Hall of Fame and subsequently recognized as one of Maryland's distinguished "Women Leading the Way." Prior to her public service in Montgomery County, Gong was a mathematics teacher in secondary schools in New York State and Pennsylvania.

## Frances HESSELBEIN

Frances Hesselbein is the Chairman of the Board of Governors of the Leader to Leader Institute, formerly the Peter F. Drucker Foundation for Nonprofit Management, and served as its founding President and CEO. She serves on many nonprofit and private sector corporate boards, including the Veteran's Corporation Advisory Board, and the Boards of the Center for Social Initiative at Harvard Business School and the Hauser Center for Nonprofit Management at the Kennedy School. She was the Chairman of the national board of directors for the Volunteers of America. Hesselbein is Editor-in-Chief of the quarterly journal *Leader to Leader* as well as a co-editor of the three volumes of the Drucker Foundation Future Series, with the best-selling *The Leader of the Future* being translated into 16 languages. Hesselbein was awarded the Presidential Medal of Freedom, the USA's highest civilian honor, in 1998. The award recognized her leadership as Chief Executive Officer of Girl Scouts of the USA from 1976 to 1990, as well as her role as founding President of the Peter F. Drucker Foundation for Nonprofit Management, "as a pioneer for women, diversity and inclusion." Her contributions were also recognized by former President Bush, who appointed her to two Presidential commissions on community service, the Board of Directors of the Commission on National and Community Service, and his Advisory Committee on the Points of Light Initiative Foundation. Hesselbein was awarded the Legion of Honor Gold Medallion from the Chapel of the Four Chaplains, the Distinguished Alumni Fellows Award from the University of Pittsburgh, and the International ATHENA Award. Hesselbein was also awarded the Henry A. Rosso Medal for Lifetime Achievement in Ethical Fund Raising from Indiana University's Center on Philanthropy and was the first recipient of the Dwight D. Eisenhower National Security Series Award, presented by US Army Chief of Staff, General Eric K. Shinseki. Junior Achievement established a Frances Hesselbein "How To Be" Leadership Award for ethical leadership. In addition, Hesselbein was presented with the Juliette Award from the Girl Scouts of the USA and the 2004 Visionary Award from the American Society of Association Executives Foundation.

### Doreen Woo HO

Doreen Woo Ho is President of Wells Fargo Consumer Credit Group, the highest-ranking Asian-American woman among the top five banks in the United States. She has been a successful business woman for over two decades, and under her leadership Wells Fargo has become America's leading provider in consumer finance. For her professional contributions to the financial community and her many contributions to culture and education in San Francisco, Ho was selected for *US Banker*'s inaugural list of the "25 Most Powerful Women in Banking" and has remained on the list for the past five years. She was also named the "Financial Woman of the Year" in 2004, the highest honor of the Financial Women's organization. In addition, *Money* magazine named her one of "America's Most Powerful Women Executives." Named as 2007 Person of the Year by the Asian Real Estate Association of America, she was also honored by Leadership Education for Asian Pacific Inc. A community-minded leader, she has also been recognized by the Chinese Historical Society of America and the Chinatown Community Development Center. She also serves on the board and executive committee of the San Francisco Opera. A graduate from Smith College, Ho holds a Master's degree in East Asian studies from Columbia University.

### Ann KERN

Ann Kern is the Managing Director and Partner and former Vice-President of Korn/Ferry International, which provides executive human capital solutions, with services ranging from corporate governance and CEO recruitment to executive search, middle-management recruitment, and Leadership Development Solutions (LDS). Kern specializes in executive searches in the not-for-profit and education fields. Beginning her career as an occupational therapist, she later joined the fundraising profession and worked with New York University Medical Center. She then became the Director of Development for the Stern School of Business. Kern now serves on the Leadership Council of Tanenbaum Center for Interreligious Understanding and on the advisory board for the George H. Heyman, Jr. Center for Philanthropy and Fundraising, New York University. She is also a member of the Women's Forum, Inc. of New York. As a nonprofit leader, Kern received a Special Tribute from Reynold Levy, President of Lincoln Center for the Performing Arts, who noted the role Kern has played in building the Tanenbaum Center and the entire nonprofit sector through her professional leadership at Korn/Ferry International.

### Jenny MING

Jenny Ming is the former President of Old Navy, a division of Gap Inc., a leading international specialty retailer under the Gap, Banana Republic, and Old Navy brand names, and once oversaw everything from the retailer's store operations to marketing and advertising. She started her career in the industry as merchandise manager of Gap brand active wear and after that was promoted through the ranks. As part of the executive team that introduced Old Navy in 1994, Ming helped Old Navy to make history as the first retailer ever to reach $1 billion in annual sales in less than four years, and Old Navy is now the biggest contributor to the parent company's overall growth. Ming received the Award for Leadership in Business and Community Service from Merage Foundation for the American Dream in 2007. She was named in *Fortune* magazine's list of the 50 most powerful women in business for two consecutive years (2003 and 2004) and was also named by *Business Week* magazine as one of the nation's top 25 managers in 2000. Ming has served on the board of Big Brothers Big Sisters, San Francisco & Peninsula, and is now a board member of the Committee of 100 and the Merage Foundation for the American Dream. She received her Bachelor's degree from San Jose State University.

### Sue SCHECHTER

Sue Schecher is a former Texas State Representative and Democratic Party Chair of Harris County, Texas. Before starting her career in politics, she worked as a lawyer and later as General Manager of the CIGNA litigation office. Schechter is now a general political strategist and is actively involved in organizing campaigns for candidates and recruiting women into office.

### Valari D. STAAB

Starting her career in a clerical position, Valari Staab is now President and General Manager of the TV station KGO-TV, ABC-7. She has worked for five different television stations in marketing and research, new business development, and creative services departments. In the community, Staab serves on the Board of Directors for the United Way of the Bay Area, the San Francisco Chamber of Commerce, the California Association of Broadcasters, and the Bay Area Council. She also launched a multi-year television campaign called "End Hunger Now" to keep area food banks full year-round. A graduate from the University of Texas at Tyler, she holds an MBA degree from Baylor University.

### Andrea L. VAN DE KAMP

Andrea Van de Kamp is the former Chairman of Sotheby's west coast business activities and oversaw development and operation. She now serves as the Director of Maguire Properties, Inc. Currently serving as the first Chairman Emeritus of the Music Center of Los Angeles County, the second largest performance arts center in the United States, she also directs the operations of Walt Disney Concert Hall. Having served on the Board of Directors of City National Bank, Van de Kamp was the Senior Vice-President for Sotheby's North America, and a member of its Board of Directors. Prior to joining Sotheby's, she was the President and CEO of the Independent Colleges of Southern California where she administered annual fundraising campaigns for 15 independent colleges. Earlier in her career, Van de Kamp served as Director for Public Affairs for Carter Hawley Hale Stores, Director of Development of the Museum of Contemporary Art, Executive Director of the Southern California Coro Foundation, and Associate Director of Admissions for Dartmouth College. In addition, Van de Kamp was appointed by the Mayor as Co-Chairman for the Los Angeles Arts Task Force. She served on the Board of Directors of Jenny Craig, Inc. and the Walt Disney Company.

## Sarah WEDDINGTON

Sarah Weddington, founder of the Weddington Centre, is a nationally-known attorney and spokesperson on leadership and public issues. She is particularly well known for her work on issues affecting women through her many roles as attorney, legislator, presidential adviser, professor, and expert called upon by the national media. She is thought to be the youngest woman ever to win a case in the Supreme Court, with the landmark case Roe v. Wade making abortion legal in the United States. As the first woman from Austin elected to the Texas House of Representatives, she served three terms before becoming the US Department of Agriculture's General Counsel, the first woman ever to hold that position. Weddington later served as Assistant to the President of the United States. She was designated by President Carter to direct the Administration's work on women's issues and leadership outreach. She also directed White House efforts to extend the time for ratification of the ERA and to assist in the selection of women for federal judiciary appointments. Weddington has received numerous honors and awards, as *Texas Lawyer* named her as "One of the Most Influential Lawyers of the 20th Century," and the *Houston Chronicle* named her as one of "The Tallest Texans

– Those who left their mark on Texas and the rest of the world in the 20th Century." Weddington holds honorary doctorates from McMurry University, Hamilton College, Austin College, Southwestern University, and Nova Southeastern University. A Distinguished Alumna of McMurry University, she received her JD degree from the University of Texas School of Law, where she is currently an adjunct professor.

### Margaret A. YORK

Margaret A. York is the Chief of Los Angeles County Office of Public Safety, commanding the fourth largest law enforcement agency in the county and one of the largest in the state of California. Beginning her law enforcement career at the Los Angeles Police Department, Chief York became the first woman in the history of the Los Angeles Police Department to hold the rank of Deputy Chief and was responsible for five police stations in the heart of Los Angeles. Chief York is very involved in community affairs and was named a "Woman of the Year" by the Congress Representative Adam Schiff of California's 29th District in 2007. She is a member and former vice-chair of the Metropolitan Board of the Salvation Army and is a founding member of the Army of Angels. She is also a member of the LA5 Rotary Club, a board member of Women Against Gun Violence, and a trustee of the YWCA of Greater Los Angeles. Chief York has a Master's degree in Public Administration from USC and a Bachelor's degree in Management from the University of Redlands. She is also a graduate of the FBI National Academy and the Southern California Leadership Network.

### Anonymous

Former United States Commissioner of Social Security.

### Anonymous

President of a state university.

### Anonymous

President of a liberal arts college.

## Women Leaders in Mainland China

### CAI Jing

Currently Chairman of the Supervising Committee of Shanghai Pudong Development (Group) Co. Ltd., Cai Jing is the first Director of the Shanghai Pudong Women's Federation and the representative of the 2nd People's Congress of Pudong New District. Starting as a guidance officer of the Junior Propaganda Troop, she was later admitted into the regimental committee of Chuansa County which is now incorporated into the Pudong region, Shanghai. She was promoted through the ranks and became Director of the Women's Federation of Chuansa County. Committed to community affairs, especially promoting women's and children's rights, she plays an active role in helping their development. Some of her plans include a family-based access-to-internet campaign and setting up vocational training centers for women. She has also set up employment agencies which assist women domestic workers in finding jobs. She is also a member of the Executive Committee of the Shanghai Women's Federation and the Putong Region Council. She has been named as "Shanghai Outstanding Worker in Women's Affairs" for her dedication.

### CHEN Naifang

Chen Naifang is former President of the Beijing Foreign Studies University. She started her academic career as a faculty member, and later became Deputy Dean of the English department, and Vice-President of the University. At the University, Chen was committed to English language teaching and research as well as the school's management. She has published articles covering a wide range of topics in education. She was assigned by the State Education Commission to serve as the Education Counselor in the Chinese Embassy in Belgium and in the Chinese Commission to the European Union. Chen is now a member of the 10th National Committee of Chinese People's Political Consultative Conference and of its Foreign Affairs Committee, Vice-Chairperson of the Chinese Higher Education Management Research Association, a member of the Standing Committee, China Education Association for International Exchanges, a member of the Chinese People's Association for Friendship with Foreign Countries, and Editor-in-Chief of *International Forum* magazine. A graduate of

Beijing Foreign Languages Institute (which has now been renamed Beijing Foreign Studies University), Chen holds an honorary doctoral degree in Law conferred by Lancaster University, UK, and an honorary doctoral degree in Education from Rajabhat Institute Chiang Mai, Thailand.

## CHEN Ying

Chen Ying is General Manager of Anhui Worldbest Chemical Fibre Co. Ltd., a leading carpet fiber manufacturing and listed company in China. She also serves as Chairman of the Board of affiliated companies, which include Hubei Worldbest Carpet and Tianjin Worldbest Carpet. She is Vice-President of the China Association of Women Entrepreneurs and the China Chamber of International Commerce, Anhui Chamber of Commerce. For her entrepreneurship, she was named among the "100 Best Chinese Female Entrepreneurs." Prior to her career in the business sector, Chen served in the military and was the only female lieutenant-colonel at the time.

## DONG Jianhua

Dong Jianhua served as Board Director and General Manager of Hongta (Hong Kong) International Tobacco Co. from 1999 to 2006. Currently a Senior Engineer (technical title; 1995–), she was previously General Manager (2003–2006) as well as Deputy Chief Engineer (1993–2003) of the Hongta Group, a listed state-owned enterprise in China. Dong started her career in the company in a technical position and finally reached the management level. She obtained her Bachelor's degree and MBA degree from Yunnan Industrial University.

## FENG Cui

Feng Cui is a Vice-President of China Children and Teenagers' Fund and a National Committee Member of the Chinese People's Political Consultative Conference. An advocate of women's rights, she has served on the Executive Committee and the Secretariat of the All-China Women's Federation (ACWF). Feng was the former Director General of the International Department of the ACWF and an Expert

Committee Member of the Convention on the Elimination of All Forms of Discrimination against Women of the United Nations. In her diplomatic career, Feng has worked at the United Nations office in Geneva and served in the Permanent Mission of China to the United Nations (in Geneva as well as in New York). In addition, she is a Vice-President of the China Association of Women Entrepreneurs.

### FENG Lida

A world-renowned immunologist, Feng Lida is the former Deputy Director of the General Navy Hospital, China and currently Director of the Chinese Immunology Research Center. She also serves as a National Committee Member of the Chinese People's Political Consultative Conference. She held the rank of General in the military hospital system. Feng has put forward innovative directions for scientific research in the areas of immunology and Chinese Qigong. She was the first to study the effects of Qigong on bacteria, viruses, and cells. She has worked for the Ministry of Public Health of China on prevention of diseases. Feng is Vice-President of the World Medical Qigong Association, Honorary Consultant of the American Qigong Institute, and Vice-President of the International Qigong Science Association. In recognition of the significance of her study of immunology in children, she won the Leningrad prize from the Soviet Union. In addition, she was honored as an Expert with Special Contribution to Medicine and Public Health by the Chinese government. The book *Chinese Traditional Recovery Medicine*, co-written by Feng and others, won the first prize for "Books of Civilization and Progress." Feng received her Bachelor of Science degree from the University of California, Berkeley and holds a PhD degree from the Medical College of Leningrad University.

### GONG Qiaoyu

Gong Qiaoyu is General Manager of Beijing Shuau Technology Development Co. Ltd. and serves as a Director of the Standing Committee of the China Association of Women Entrepreneurs. Educated as a geologist, her work on underground water sources has been recognized by the government and has won her national awards. Developing an interest in the business sector in her later career, Gong started her own consultancy firm specializing in technology. She received the Outstanding Women Entrepreneurs Award from the China Association of Women Entrepreneurs. A graduate of Xi'an Institute of Geology, she holds an MBA degree from Renmin University of China.

## GU Xiulian

Gu Xiulian is President of the All-China Women's Federation, where she has previously served as Vice-President and First Secretary. She is also the Vice-Chairman of the Standing Committee of the tenth National People's Congress, the top legislature in China, which makes her one of the most senior women political leaders in China. Gu began her career in politics by joining the Chinese Communist Party and has been a long-standing member of the party's Central Committee. She has served as Vice-Chairperson of the State Family Planning Commission and the first female Governor of Jiangsu Province. She later became Minister of the Ministry of Chemical Industry. Gu has been actively involved in promoting children's and women's rights and was awarded the Song Qingling Award by the Chinese Welfare Association in 2006.

## Mary MA

Currently Managing Director and Partner of Texas Pacific Group (TPG), Mary Ma is the former Senior Vice-President, Chief Financial Officer, and a Member of the Board of Directors of Lenovo Group, the largest manufacturer of personal computers in China and the world's third-largest. She now serves as Non-Executive Vice-Chairman of the Group. At TPG, she now focuses on its China business and helps the firm build long-term relationships with Chinese business leaders. In her previous position at Lenovo, Ma played a key role in Lenovo's landmark acquisition of IBM's Personal Computing Division in May 2005. Before joining Lenovo, Ma held positions at the Chinese Academy of Sciences. She is also an Independent Non-Executive Director of Standard Chartered Bank (Hong Kong) Ltd. and Sohu.com Inc., both publicly listed companies. Ma was elected by Forbes one of "the World's 100 Most Powerful Women" in 2004 and 2005. She was also named one of "the 50 Most Powerful Women in Business" by Fortune in 2004–2006. Named by *Finance Asia* magazine as one of the best CFOs in 2002 and 2006 respectively, Ma received the Outstanding Women Entrepreneurs Award in 2002, and was selected by *Asia Money* magazine as the Top Executive of 2005 (China). She graduated from Capital Normal University with a Bachelor of Arts degree and continued her studies at King's College, University of London.

## MA Yuan

Currently Honorary President of the Women Judges Association of China and specially appointed Professor of the State Judge College, Ma Yuan is the former Deputy Chief Justice, the first woman Senior Judge of the People's Supreme Court, President of the Women Judges Association of China, and Honorary Professor of the Law School of the Renmin University of China. Having finished her postgraduate work in the Faculty of Law of the Renmin University of China, she became an instructor at Peking University and practiced as a part-time lawyer. Ma was later transferred to the People's Supreme Court to be a judge and promoted through the ranks. She was elected a Member of the National Congress of the Chinese Communist Party and a Member of the Executive Committee of the All-China Women's Federation.

## NI Zhihua

Ni Zhihua is Board Chairman of Shanghai Sanmao Enterprise (Group) Co., Ltd. She also serves as Vice-Chairman and Party Deputy Secretary of the Board of Shanghai Textiles Holding Co., a listed company. She is an engineer by training and holds the rank of a senior engineer. She was the Party Deputy Secretary and Director of the former Shanghai Textile Industry Bureau.

## SHI Qingqi

Shi Qingqi is Vice-President and Secretary General of the China Association of Women Entrepreneurs (CAWE). She is the former Director of the Institute of Industrial Economy and Technical Economy under the National Development and Reform Commission. As an expert in economics, she helped to formulate policies and developed tools to measure economic growth. Her research project in cooperation with the World Bank has received the American International Management

Science Franz Maurice Edelman Award, which is hailed as the "Nobel Prize" for Management Science. Her work was awarded the first prize and third prize of the Science and Technology Development Award at ministry and commission level several times, and the second prize of the National Science and Technology Development Award. In addition, her efforts in applying the model of transportation system of coal-based electricity from the US Energy Department in China gained her the Best Application Award from the American Association of Geography. A graduate from China University of Geosciences, Shi holds a Master's degree from the Institute of Economics, China Academy of Social Sciences.

**Nora SUN**

Nora Sun is Chairman and President of Nora Sun Associates Ltd., a firm specializing in business formation, government relations, and management consulting in China. Prior to setting up this top-level consulting firm, Sun was President of BLC Consulting Group Ltd. Sun began her career in financial management with the Raytheon Company, a US-based high-technology firm with global operations. Later, as a diplomat working for the US Foreign Service, she was assigned as the Principal Commercial Officer to the US Consulates in Shanghai and Guangzhou. During her diplomatic assignments in China, Sun was responsible for facilitating major US investments as well as assisting and resolving issues for US companies in China. She then served in the same position in Washington, DC, and as the Commercial Attaché in the US Embassy in Paris, France. A graduate of the University of Arizona with a Bachelor of Science degree in Finance, Sun also did graduate studies at Babson College in Massachusetts.

**SUN Yuehuan**

Sun Yuehuan is the founder, Board Chairman, and CEO of China Enterprise Appraisals (CEA), a listed company in Beijing. Her company specializes in asset appraisal in terms of assisting enterprises in their reorganization and restructuring for listing and has been ranked number one in the industry. As one of the first approved Certified Public Accountants in China, Sun now serves as Standing Director of the Beijing Association of Certified Public Accountants, and Board Chairman and General Manager of China Enterprise

Consultants Co., Ltd. Sun was once an officer of the People's Liberation Army of China and an official in the State Audit Administration. She holds a Bachelor's degree from the Beijing Normal University.

## WEI Keizheng

Wei Keizheng is the Board Chairman of Keili (HK) Group and Hainan Kailie Central Development Shares Co. Ltd., with major investment and development projects in Hainan Province. She served as Vice-President of the China Association of Women Entrepreneurs and Vice-President of Wuhan University of Economics and Trade. Wei has received numerous awards and honors in China for her entrepreneurship and is the first Chinese woman entrepreneur to receive the World's Outstanding Women Entrepreneurs Award. She holds a Bachelor's degree in Hydraulic and Electrical Engineering from Wuhan University.

## Marjorie WOO

Marjorie Woo is CEO of Keystone Leadership (Shanghai) Inc. and Master Licensee of Leadership Management International Inc. (LMI), China. Starting her career at Xerox's American headquarters, her later position in the international operations division of the company allowed her to participate in the negotiations of the joint venture between Xerox and the Shanghai government, which resulted in the biggest joint venture program of the company at that time. Woo was also Implementation Director of the new joint venture operation, liaising with top Chinese government officials. The founder of Option Consultants International Ltd., she was on the Board of Governors of Shanghai's American Chamber of Commerce (AmCham). Her dedication to developing global leaders and managers in China made her the first Chairman of its Education and Training Committee. She is also an active board member of the Shanghai Rotary Club International. Woo has a Master's degree in Business Administration from St. Mary's College, California.

## WU Qidi

Wu Qidi is Vice-Minister of the Ministry of Education of the People's Republic of China. Wu was former President of Tongji University and was the first university president in China to be chosen by a democratic election. Currently Vice-President of the All-China Women's Federation, she has served as an Alternate Member of the 16th Central Committee of the Communist Party of China, Deputy Director of the Degree Awarding Committee of the State Council, and Vice-Chair of Shanghai Association of Science and Technology. An expert in electrical engineering, she is committed to high-quality research and her research projects have won provincial, ministerial, and state awards. Her outstanding work has gained her the Outstanding Young and Middle-Aged Expert Award from the Ministry of Personnel, the Excellent Overseas Returned Scholar Award, and the National Ten Outstanding Women Award. In addition, the German Federal government awarded her with the Grand Cross of the Order of Merit of the Federal Republic of Germany. Wu received her Bachelor's degree in Radio Engineering and Master's degree in Automation from Tsinghua University, and holds a doctoral degree in Automation from the Federal Institute of Technology, Zurich, Switzerland.

## Julia XIN

Julia Xin was Managing Director of Winterthur Insurance (Asia) Ltd., the Shanghai branch of the Swiss multinational corporation which is now a member of the AXA group. She is currently Head of Corporate Solutions and is responsible for the AXA corporate business subsidiary in China. At Winterthur, Xin introduced international standards and management systems to produce outstanding performance results, raising the company's profile in China as well as overseas. Prior to joining Winterthur, Xin worked with PICC Property and Casualty Company Ltd. Xin is a graduate of Central University of Economics and Finance and China Europe International Business School. She is fluent in English and German.

## ZHANG Xin

Zhang Xin is Chairman and Co-CEO of SOHO China, a real estate company in China famous for its innovative architecture projects. Prior to starting her own company, Zhang joined Wall Street and worked for Goldman Sachs and Travelers Group. Following the concept of SOHO (Small Office Home Office), Zhang and her husband have shown their determination in providing high-quality multifunctional spaces for the rising middle class in China and shaping the future of modern Chinese cities. Some of Zhang's projects include Jianwai SOHO, Commune by the Great Wall, and SOHO New Town. She has worked with some world-renowned architects. For her creativity, passion for art and architecture, and accomplishments, Zhang has been selected by the World Economic Forum as a Young Global Leader, and won *Business Week*'s Stars of Asia Award. She was also the only winner from Mainland China of the 2004 Mont-blanc Arts Patronage Award and was named one of the "100 Most Powerful Women in China" in the same year. A special prize for an individual patron of architectural work was awarded to Zhang at the 2002 Biennale di Venezia. A graduate in Economics from the University of Sussex, Zhang holds a Master's degree in Development Economics from Cambridge University.

**Anonymous**

A top-level banker.

# Women Leaders in Hong Kong

**Laura CHA**

Laura Cha Shih Mei-lun is currently a Non-Executive Deputy Chairman of the Hong Kong and Shanghai Banking Corporation Ltd. and a Member of the Executive Council of the HKSAR which advises the Chief Executive of the Hong Kong SAR government. She was appointed Vice-Chairman of the China Securities Regulatory Commission (CSRC) by the State Council in 2001 and became the first person outside Mainland China to join the Chinese government at the vice-ministerial rank. At the CSRC, Cha's major efforts were in the reform of the public offer mechanism and improvement of corporate governance in Chinese listed companies. Before her post at the CSRC, Cha was with the Securities and Futures Commission (SFC) in Hong Kong and headed the Corporate Finance Division at the SFC before being appointed Deputy Chairman. Cha played a key role in all the major reforms of the Hong Kong securities market, including the establishment of the regulatory framework for the listing of Chinese state-owned enterprises in Hong Kong, as well as the demutualization and merger of the stock and futures exchanges and clearing houses of Hong Kong. Cha is currently an independent Non-Executive Director of Johnson Electric Holdings Ltd., Hong Kong Exchanges and Clearing Ltd., BaoShan Iron and Steel Company Ltd., Bank of Communications in China, and Tata Consultancy Services Ltd. in India. She is also a member of the International Council of the Asia Society in New York, a senior adviser to Investor AB, a Swedish conglomerate, and a former member of the Committee of 100 in the United States. Prior to these appointments, she practiced law in San Francisco and in Hong Kong. She was awarded a Silver Bauhinia Star Medal by the HKSAR government for her public service. A graduate of the University of Wisconsin with a Bachelor of Arts degree, and the University of Santa Clara with a Law degree, Cha received an honorary doctoral degree from the Hong Kong University of Science and Technology.

### Anson CHAN

Anson Chan was the Chief Secretary, head of Hong Kong's civil service, before and after the territory's handover to the People's Republic of China from British colonial rule, before she retired in 2001. She is the first woman and the first Chinese to hold the second-highest governmental position in Hong Kong. As the head of the civil service, Chan played a key role in ensuring a stable and effective civil service as well as a smooth transition in 1997. As Chief Secretary for Administration of the Hong Kong SAR government, Chan advised the Chief Executive on matters of policy, deputized for him during his absence, and was responsible for the effective implementation of the full range of government policies. Chan joined the civil service as an administrative service cadet and then became a senior administrative officer. During her civil service career, she helped set up the Association of Female Senior Government Officers to fight for better rights for women civil servants. She was later appointed Director of Social Welfare and Secretary for Economic Services, before becoming the thirtieth and the last Chief Secretary to oversee the localization of the civil service in the colonial government. In recognition of her 34 years of public service to Hong Kong, Chan has been appointed by Her Majesty Queen Elizabeth II to be an honorary Dame Grand Cross of the Most Distinguished Order of St Michael and St George.

She was also appointed Commander of the Most Excellent Order of the British Empire and awarded the Grand Bauhinia Medal of the Hong Kong SAR. Chan has received honorary degrees, professorships and fellowships from both local and overseas universities. In December 2007, Chan won a hotly contested by-election for a seat on the Legislative Council, representing the pan-democracy camp.

### Ophelia CHEUNG

Chairman and Managing Director of Cheung Macpherson & Co., Ltd., Ophelia Cheung Look-ping started her career as an Administrative Officer and was later appointed the first Executive Director of the Consumer Council of Hong Kong, which aims to protect consumers from unscrupulous suppliers and manufacturers. For her contribution to society, Cheung has been named among the "Ten Outstanding Young Persons" by Junior Chamber International Hong Kong. After leaving the civil service, Cheung joined the international accounting firm Arthur Anderson and then established her own political lobby consultancy. For many years, she has been active in community affairs, serving on many advisory committees to the Hong Kong government, and on school and university boards. She was the Chairman of the Royal Commonwealth Society. She has served on the Board of Directors of the International Women's Forum and has been its Global Vice-President for two terms. She serves on the Board of Directors of the Leadership Foundation, an international organization dedicated to the training of women leaders. She was also a founding member of the Women's Commission established by the Hong Kong SAR government.

### Sein CHEW

Sein Chew is the Founder-President and CEO of Unity Asset Management (UAM), a global investment firm with offices in Hong Kong and London. In the early stage of her career, she was trained in chartered accountancy in Australia. Chew then developed her career in banking and was the first woman Vice-President and the first woman to hold a line management position in the Bank of America in Hong Kong. She later joined Merrill Lynch, an investment firm, and became the first woman to top the revenue-earner chart in the Asia Pacific.

She was offered a management position in their New York office which she turned down to start the very successful asset management firm, UAM. Chew was presented with the "Outstanding 50 Asian Americans in Business" award in 2006 by the Asian American Business Development Center for her entrepreneurship. The US-based award honors Asian-American entrepreneurs and business professionals, and celebrates the spirit of cultural diversity and excellence in business. Chew was the only Hong Kong person to be presented with an award at the New York ceremony. Chew holds a Master's degree from Oxford University.

### Alice CHIU

Alice Chiu Tsang Hok-wan is Director of Henyep Development (Holdings) Ltd., one of the most established financial services and investment management companies in Hong Kong. She founded the Sheen Hok Charitable Foundation, which has helped over 300 organizations both in Hong Kong and in the Chinese Mainland, and is an active supporter of local education development. Chiu also actively participates in various community services. She is the Vice-Chairman of China Medical Mission and was in charge of the International Campaign of Operation Smile. She is President of Hong Kong Marrow Match Foundation, founding fundraising Chairman and Vice-Chairman of the Hong Kong AIDS Foundation, and a member of the Hong Kong Housing Authority Appeal Panel. A leading community member and tireless fundraiser for the past 20 years, she was appointed Justice of the Peace and was named "Outstanding Philanthropist" on the fiftieth anniversary of the Hong Kong Council of Social Service. She was also recognized as "The Most Amazing Woman in Hong Kong," as well as being honored with the "Knight in the Leopold II Order" by the Belgium government, in recognition of her enormous contribution to the underprivileged and needy. In addition, she was selected as one of the "Leading Women Entrepreneurs of the World," being identified as an outstanding woman entrepreneur and role model for other women in business.

### Cordelia CHUNG

Cordelia Chung is Vice-President of Marketing and Channels, Greater China Group of IBM. She started her career in IBM as General

Counsel for China and Hong Kong, and later General Counsel for the Greater China Group – China, Hong Kong, and Taiwan – and Vice-President of Business Partners, IBM Asia Pacific. As Vice-President and General Counsel of IBM Asia Pacific, Chung is responsible for legal and security affairs in the region. As General Manager of IBM China/Hong Kong Ltd. in her last position, she is now a member of the IBM senior leadership team. She has also served on the IBM Asia Pacific Women's Council and Global Workforce Diversity Council. Prior to joining IBM, Chung practiced law in an international law firm and specialized in corporate commercial law with an emphasis on advising foreign companies doing business in the emerging markets. Chung has served as Vice-President on the Board of Governors of the Hong Kong American Chamber of Commerce. She also serves as a member of various committees of the Hong Kong government, namely the Digital 21 Strategy Advisory Committee (formerly known as the Information Infrastructure Advisory Committee), the Appeal Board on Closure Orders (Immediate Health Hazard), and the Citizens Advisory Committee on Community Relations of the Independent Commission Against Corruption. In addition, Chung is a member of the Court of the Hong Kong University of Science and Technology, and a member of the General Committee of the Hong Kong Arts Festival Society. A graduate with a law degree from the University of Hong Kong, she holds a diploma in Chinese law from the University of Law and Politics of the People's Republic of China.

**Audrey EU**

Audrey Eu is a Member of the Legislative Council of Hong Kong and the House Leader of the Civic Party, a newly established political party. Eu was admitted as a barrister in Hong Kong and later appointed Queen's Counsel (Senior Counsel after 1997). Before her entrance into politics, Eu was Chairman of the Hong Kong Bar Association. Her firm stance on the interpretation of Hong Kong's Basic Law by the National People's Congress on the issue of right-of-abode in 1997 made her known to many Hong Kong people. Becoming a politician by gaining a Legislative Council seat at a by-election, some of her most important political achievements include the setting up of the Basic Law Article 23 Concern Group, and, later, the Basic Law Article 45 Concern Group. Eu has served as the Chairman of the Review

Board Panel of Consumer Goods Safety and the Law Reform Commission – Sub-Committee on Civil Liability for Unsafe Products. A graduate from the University of Hong Kong with an LLB degree, she received her LLM degree from the University of London.

### Rita FAN

Rita Fan Hsu Lai-tai is President of the Legislative Council of Hong Kong, the first President after the transfer of sovereignty and the first woman to hold the post. Fan serves in a number of roles in the public sector, including Hong Kong Deputy to the tenth National People's Congress of the People's Republic of China and an elected member of the Standing Committee of the eleventh National People's Congress, Chairman of the Board of Trustees of the Association for Celebration of Reunification of Hong Kong with China Charitable Trust Fund, and Supervising Advisor of the Hong Kong Federation of Women. She is also a Council Member of the Family Planning Association of Hong Kong. Prior to the establishment of the HKSAR, Fan was appointed by China as a member of the Preparatory Committee for the Hong Kong SAR and a member of the Preliminary Working Committee for the Preparatory Committee for the Hong Kong SAR. During the British rule, she was a Member of the Executive Council and of the Legislative Council. Fan also served as Chairman of the Education Commission and the Board of Education. With a Bachelor of Science degree (Chemistry and Physics) from the University of Hong Kong, she holds a Master's degree in Social Sciences (Psychology) and was awarded an honorary doctoral degree in Law from China University of Political Science and Law, People's Republic of China, and an honorary doctoral degree in Social Science from the City University of Hong Kong.

### Barbara FEI

Barbara Fei Ming-yee is a world-renowned choral master. Dedicated to the development of the arts in Hong Kong, she plays an active role in promoting musical exchange among Hong Kong, Mainland China and the international arena. In recognition of her contribution to the arts, Fei was awarded the Bronze Bauhinia Star by the Hong Kong SAR government. She has given numerous performances in Hong

Kong as well as in Europe and America, and was the first Hong Kong choral master to be invited to a solo performance in Mainland China. Fei founded the Allegro Singers and is now its Music Director and Conductor. She serves in many cultural organizations, including as a member of the Arts Promotion Committee and the Arts Support Committee of Hong Kong Arts Development Council, and Vice-President of the Chinese Culture Promotion Society, among others. Fei took a major in Piano at the predecessor of the Central Conservatory of Music and later went to Schola Cantorum in Paris, France for training in Vocal Music.

### Nellie FONG

Nellie Fong Wong Kut-man is Chairman of the Chinese operation of PricewaterhouseCoopers in China, and practices as a chartered accountant. She has also been an active member in the public sector, as a former Member of the Executive Council of the Hong Kong SAR government and the Chinese People's Political Consultative Conference (CPPCC). Fong is the Special Advisor, the former Executive President of the Lifeline Express Committee, and the Founding Chairman of Lifeline Express Hong Kong Foundation which helps restore the sight of cataract patients in rural China. She is also a member of the Advisory Council of the Hong Kong Society for the Protection of Children. She was awarded a Gold Bauhinia Star by the Hong Kong SAR government.

### Peggy LAM

Peggy Lam Pei Yu-dja is a former Member of the Legislative Council and the Chinese People's Political Consultative Conference. She is currently Chairman of the Hong Kong Federation of Women. Lam has an impressive record of social service for the elderly, women, social welfare, education, the environment, and hygiene. She worked as the Executive Director of the Family Planning Association of Hong Kong before she retired, and has served as a Member of the Executive Committee of the All-China Women's Federation in China. She has also served as a member of the Women's Commission, a member of the Equal Opportunities Commission, a member of the Salvation Army Advisory Board, a Board Director of the Hong Kong Tuberculosis, Chest and Heart Disease Association, President and founding

Chairman of Hong Kong Girl Guides Wan Chai District Association, and founding Chairman of the Hong Kong AIDS Foundation and of the Environmental Campaign Committee, among others. In recognition of her commitment to community affairs, she was awarded the OBE and MBE (Officer and Member of the Order of the British Empire, respectively) by the British government, and later the Silver Bauhinia Star and Gold Bauhinia Star by the HKSAR government. A graduate from the University of Shanghai with a Bachelor of Arts degree, Lam received diplomas in Family Planning and Public Health Administration from the University of Chicago and the University of Michigan and is a fellow in Family Planning at the American University. She was also made an Honorary Professor by the University of Shanghai for Science and Technology in 2006.

### Emily LAU

Emily Lau Wai-hing is a Member of the Legislative Council and was the first woman to be directly elected to the Council. She is also a founding Member and the current Convenor of Frontier, a pro-democracy lobby group in Hong Kong. Lau began her career as a journalist and has worked with *South China Morning Post* (SCMP), Hong Kong TVB news, and the BBC in the UK. She has also served as the Chairperson of the Hong Kong Journalists Association. Lau is famous for her firm stance on promotion of democracy in Hong Kong and human rights, and for her efforts in the area of equal opportunities. She has received the Human Rights Award from the Bruno Kreisky Foundation, Austria. A graduate of the University of Southern California with a Bachelor of Arts degree, she earned her Master of Science degree in International Relations from the London School of Economics and Political Science, University of London.

### Fanny LAW

Fanny Law Fan Chiu-fun was the Commissioner of the Independent Commission Against Corruption (ICAC) in Hong Kong prior to her retirement from the civil service. Prior to this appointment, she was Permanent Secretary of the Education and Manpower Bureau of the HKSAR government. She was responsible for formulating and implementing policies related to education and manpower planning. She joined the civil service as an Executive Officer and later became an Administrative Officer. Throughout her career in the government, she has served in several bureaus including the former Civil Service Bureau, the Housing Authority, and the Transport Department. She was Director of the Education Department under British colonial rule. Law obtained a Master's degree in Public Administration from the John F. Kennedy School of Government, Harvard University, and was awarded a Littaur Fellowship for her excellent academic attainment and leadership. She also holds a Master's degree in Education from the Chinese University of Hong Kong.

### Sandra LEE

Sandra Lee Suk-yee is currently Permanent Secretary for Health. Formerly she was Permanent Secretary for Health and Welfare, and Permanent Secretary for Economic Development in the Hong Kong SAR government. Lee joined the government as an Executive Officer and later became an Administrative Officer. Lee has served in various bureaus and departments, including the Information Services Department, the former Trade and Industry Branch, the former City and New Territories Administration (and later the Home Affairs Department), and the Hong Kong Economic and Trade Office in Washington. She has been Deputy Secretary for the Civil Service, Director-General of the London office, and Secretary for Economic Services. Lee holds a Bachelor of Arts degree from the University of Hong Kong and a Master's degree from Harvard University.

### Shelley LEE

Shelley Lee Lai-kuen was the Permanent Secretary of the Home Affairs Bureau prior to her retirement. She joined the civil service as an Executive Officer and some of her important posts include being the first woman to take on the post of Private Secretary to the former Governor, Lord MacLehose, and being the first female Director of Home Affairs, who helped see the community through the transfer of sovereignty in 1997. During her posting as Deputy Secretary for Health and Welfare, she played a key role in pushing through the policy on traditional Chinese medicine. In addition, Lee has been active in promoting women's and children's rights and welfare within and outside the civil service. She is Honorary Advisor of the Hong Kong Federation of Women and a founding Member and former Chairman of the Association of Female Senior Government Officers, set up to fight for equal remuneration terms for married women in the civil service.

Together with three other senior female civil servants, Lee set up the "We Care Education Fund" to show support and concern for children orphaned by the SARS epidemic in Hong Kong. Her sincere concern for the underprivileged makes Lee fondly known to the public as the "Community Godmother." A distinguished alumna of the University of Hong Kong, Lee obtained a Master of Public Administration degree from Harvard University and attended the Advanced Management Programme at Harvard Business School.

### Sophie LEUNG

Sophie Leung Lau Yau-fun is a Member of the Legislative Council of Hong Kong and a Hong Kong SAR Deputy of the tenth and eleventh National People's Congress of China. A director of a number of large textile conglomerates in Hong Kong with businesses extending to the world market, she plays an active role in the development of the textile and garment industry. She is the Honorary President of the Federation of Hong Kong Garment Manufacturers and a Director of the Textile Council. She serves as a member of the Textiles Advisory Board, a member of the Steering Committee on the Development of the Fashion Industry, and a member of the Hong Kong Institute of Directors' Council. Leung is widely recognized for her public service contributions to the development and implementation of the health care system in Hong Kong. She is a founding member of the Hospital Authority and serves on the governing committees and management boards of major hospitals. She was appointed by the HKSAR government as the founding Chairperson of the Women's Commission. She is also the Founder and Chairman of the Young Entrepreneurs Development Council, which seeks to cultivate entrepreneurial and leadership qualities and skills in Hong Kong, and the former Vice-Chairman of the United Nation Children's Fund (UNICEF) in Hong Kong. In recognition of her dedication to community service, Leung was awarded the Silver and Gold Bauhinia Stars by the Hong Kong SAR government.

### Alice TAI

Alice Tai Yuen-ying is the Ombudsman of the Hong Kong SAR, responsible for investigating public complaints about alleged maladministration of government departments as well as 18 public organizations, with the objective of improving public administration. Starting her career as an Administrative Officer, she has served in many government departments and policy branches in Hong Kong as well as in the Hong Kong Government Office in London. She was later appointed the first Director of Intellectual Property and then the first Judiciary Administrator to assist the Chief Justice in the overall administration of the Judiciary. Tai is active in international ombudsman activities, serving as Secretary of both the International Ombudsman Institute and the Asian Ombudsman Association, which aim to promote the principles and practice of ombudsmanship. Tai holds a Bachelor of Law degree from the University of Hong Kong and a Master of Law degree from the University of London. She is an Unofficial Justice of the Peace in Hong Kong and was awarded an OBE.

## Rosanna WONG

Rosanna Wong Yick-ming is the Executive Director of the Hong Kong Federation of Youth Groups, one of the largest nonprofit multifaceted youth work agencies in Hong Kong. Wong is also a member of the National Committee of the Chinese People's Political Consultative Conference and a member of the Judicial Officers Recommendation Commission and the Commission on Strategic Development, both under the government of the HKSAR. Among the former public offices she has held are: Member of the Executive Council, Member of the Legislative Council, Chairman of the Education Commission, and Chairperson of the Hong Kong Housing Authority, the Commission on Youth, and the Social Welfare Advisory Committee. She is also a Working Group Member of the United Nations High Level Commission on Legal Empowerment of the Poor and a former Member of the United Nations High Level Panel on Youth Employment. Wong is committed to a number of welfare organizations and charities, including World Vision Hong Kong, World Vision International, Mother's Choice, the Asia Foundation Hong Kong Leadership Council, and the English Speaking Union (Hong Kong). She serves as Non-Executive Director of the Hong Kong and Shanghai Banking Corporation Ltd. and Cheung Kong (Holdings) Limited. She was honored as Officer, Commander, and Dame Commander of the British Empire, and was a recipient of the "Ten Outstanding Young Persons" award. Wong holds a Bachelor's degree in Social Science from the

University of Hong Kong, a Master of Social Work degree from the University of Toronto, and a Master of Science degree from the London School of Economics and Political Science, University of London. She has also received a Master of Arts degree and a PhD from the University of California, Davis.

### Marjorie YANG

Marjorie Yang is Chairman of the Esquel Group. She is one of the world's most successful business women, named among the Fortune top 50 most powerful women in business in 2004 and 2005. She started her career with the First Boston Corporation (now Credit Suisse First Boston) in New York, before returning to Hong Kong to help her father set up Esquel. Yang succeeded in transforming a small company into one of the world's leading high-quality cotton shirt manufacturers, supplying such household-name brands as Polo Ralph Lauren, Hugo Boss, Tommy Hilfiger, Nordstrom, and Abercrombie & Fitch. Her company now produces over 60 million cotton shirts a year – more than any other company in the world. Hoping to set an example in Asia, Yang has placed huge emphasis on ethical business practices, social and environmental responsibility, and worker welfare. Besides Esquel, she also serves on the Board of Novartis, HSBC Asia Pacific, Swire Pacific, and the MIT Corporation. A graduate of Massachusetts Institute of Technology with a Bachelor of Science degree in Mathematics, she holds a Master of Business Administration degree from Harvard Business School.

### Carrie YAU

Carrie Yau Tsang Kar-lai is Permanent Secretary for the Home Affairs Bureau and former Permanent Secretary for the Health, Welfare and Food Bureau of the HKSAR government, where she controlled a fiscal budget of over 14.5 percent of the total recurrent expenditure of the government. Yau is a keen advocate of building a healthy and caring society through measures such as ensuring food safety and promoting the interests of people with disabilities and the underprivileged. During the SARS outbreak, she played an important leadership role in the containment of the disease in the community and communication with the international society. During her career in the civil service, Yau was the youngest Head of Department appointed by the HKSAR government and became the youngest policy secretary upon her appointment as Secretary for IT and Broadcasting. She spearheaded the Electronic Service Delivery Scheme which won the Stockholm Challenge Award. Yau also has experience in coordinating major state visits and hosting international events (e.g. ITU Telecom Asia 2000 and Global Summit of Women 2001). She holds a Bachelor of Social Science degree from the University of Hong Kong.

## Betty YUEN

Betty Yuen So Siu-mai is Managing Director of CLP Power Hong Kong Ltd., the first Chinese ever appointed to this position and also the first woman chief executive in the company. She is also Chairman of CLP IT Solutions Ltd. The CLP group is one of the leading power companies in the world. She is also a member of its Regulatory Affairs Committee, China Committee, and Finance and General Committee. Yuen overlooks the operations of the Hong Kong business, which includes a vertically integrated electricity utility serving over 5.7 million people. Prior to her appointment as Managing Director, Yuen was Director – Finance and Planning – of CLP Power Hong Kong, with responsibilities for government relations and regulatory affairs, corporate strategy and planning, finance, accounting, and legal matters. A qualified chartered accountant by training, Yuen began her career in public accounting in Canada and worked for ExxonMobil, CLP's joint venture partner in power generation in Hong Kong. She is also a Director of a number of subsidiary companies of the CLP group. Yuen was named "Business Woman of the Year" in 2004 by Veuve Clicquot, for her entrepreneurship.

# Index

abortion (of female children) 161
achievement, need for 209–10
adaptive behavior strategies 142–52
adoption 128, 224
affirmative action 168–9
age
  of interviewees 5
  of marriage 2
  planning for children 128–30
aging population 15
All-China Women's Federation
  (ACWF) 25, 43, 44, 68, 160,
  161, 176, 258, 260, 261, 264,
  271
Allen, Sharon 38–9, 59–60, 97,
  101, 170, 246
Allen, T. D. 44–5, 134
Almeida, D. M. 135
"ambivalent prejudice" 118
Antonakis, J. 38
Arnold, K. A. 11, 229
Aryee, S. 11, 177, 178
Ashby, Helena 30–1, 66, 112, 191,
  246–7
"attribution bias" 118
Avolio, B. J. 206

back-up childcare 126–8
Bacon, L. M. 229
Bailyn, L. 134

Baird, Philamena 113–14, 247
Baker, N. L. 168
Baltes, B. B. 142, 148
Barbara Lee Family Foundation
  180–1
Bargh, J. A. 184
Barling, J. 11, 229
Barnett, R. C. 10, 31, 47, 125
Baruch, G. 31
Bathurst, K. 122
behavior, adaptive (strategies)
  142–52
belief systems 32
Belsky, J. 124
Benard, S. 118, 120–1
Benbow, C. 118
benevolent sexism 178–9
Bennetts, L. 15, 17
Beutell, N. J. 53, 133
Bianchi, S. M. 67, 73
bias 118, 202–3
biological clock 115–16, 223–4
birth rate 19
Bond, J. T. 49
Bono, J. E. 184, 189
Boushey, H. 2
Brooks-Gunn, J. 122
Bruck, C. S. 134
Brundtland, Gro Harlem 35
Burchinal, M. R. 124

Burley, K. A. 83
Burlingame, B. 50
Burns, J. M. 195, 196
Burrows, L. 184
Byron, K. 133

Cai Jing 229, 257
Campbell, Kim 13–14, 19, 33–4,
    94–5, 247–8
career
    dual-career families 95–7, 133
    -related support 37–8
    track 6–9, 211–12
career development
    role of husband 86–100, 213
    role of mentor 37–42, 44–6,
        213–14
    step-by-step approach 191,
        218–20
Carli, L. L. 166, 190, 197, 202,
    213
Carver, K. A. 167
Cascio, W. F. 222
Catalyst 9, 184, 217, 226, 227
Center for Work Life Policy 64–5,
    117
CEOs 195, 204
Cha, Laura 51, 63–4, 65, 119,
    140–1, 265–6
Chan, Anson 29–30, 42, 58, 83–4,
    162–3, 165, 181–2, 266–7
Chan, C. 11, 133
Chan, Wilma 79, 248–9
Chao, C. 141, 177
checklist (of integration ideas)
    220–8
cheerleader, husband as 86–9
Chen, C. C. 141, 177
Chen, M. 184
Chen Naifang 62, 81, 257–8
Chen Ying 103–4, 143–4, 258
Cheung, F. M. 11, 133, 164, 165

Cheung, Ophelia 65–6, 98, 114–15,
    172, 267
Chevassus, S. 50
Chew, Sein 267–8
Chiang Kai-shek 26, 155
childcare 7, 215
    back-up 126–8
    effect on children 108, 121–8
    by extended family 78–9, 127,
        149–50, 177
    life management strategies
        148–51
    mothers' attitudes 108, 129, 130,
        152
    reliable/unreliable 131–2
    by spouse 79–82, 213
    SuperMom Syndrome 75–7,
        125–6, 174
    US system 169
    working-mother-hate 106–9
childlessness 4–5, 115–16, 128, 211
children
    abortion (of females) 161
    adoption 128, 224
    effects of maternal employment
        121–8, 215–15
    family size 2, 4–5
    good mothers 106–7, 110–15,
        126, 130, 214–18, 219
    mother–daughter bond 31–2
    planning for 128–30, 223–4
    stereotypical mothering
        115–21
    working-mother-hate 106–9
    see also daughters
China
    colonial rule 162–4
    Communist Party 3, 25, 26, 43,
        154, 155, 157–8, 160, 162, 264
    contemporary 155–8
    Cultural Revolution 22, 27, 88,
        154, 155–7, 158

China (*Cont'd*)
  Health and Nutrition Survey 74
  "One Country – Two Systems"
    162–3
  women's rights 158–62
  women leaders (biographies)
    257–65
  *see also* Hong Kong
Chiu, Alice 268
Chung, Cordelia 152, 173, 208,
  268–9
Chung, P. 164
Cianciolo, A. T. 38
Civil Rights Act (USA) 168
Clarke-Stewart, K. A. 124
cleavage (culture of gender) 180,
  182
Clinton, Hillary 15, 180
clothes (culture of gender) 180–2,
  226
coach/coaching
  finding 213–14
  husband as 86–9, 97, 213
  parental role 34
Colbeck, C. 211
collectivistic societies 141, 176–7,
  206
colonial rule (China) 162–4
commitments (outsourcing) 58–60,
  62–3, 208–9, 223
Committee for the Elimination of
  Discrimination Against Women
  161
  communications 40
  maintaining contact with family
    110–15, 221–2
Communist Party (China) 3, 25,
  26, 43, 154, 155, 157–8, 160,
  162, 264
compensation 39, 45, 52
  strategy (life management) 142,
    148–52

competence ratings 118–19
"competitive mothering" 125
conflict (work–family) 12, 79, 83,
  177–9
  alternatives to 134–6
  time conflicts 131–2, 153
  *see also* work–family spillover
Confucianism 21, 154, 179
Confucius 32
Convention on the Elimination of
  All Forms of Discrimination
  against Women 168, 259
cooking/food 62, 68, 75, 111–12,
  171–2
Coontz, S. 130
Cooper, C. L. 177
Cooper, M. L. 133
coping behavior 137–42
Corell, S. J. 118, 120–1
Corporate Voice for Working
  Families 169
Cotton, J. L. 39
Council of Economic Advisers
  16
Council of Women World Leaders
  34, 248
Couric, Katie 119–20
Coward, W. A. 50
crisis in leadership 229–30
"critical eye" 38
cross-cultural perspectives (work–
  family interface) 175–8
Cultural Revolution 22, 27, 88,
  154, 155–7, 158–9
culture
  China 154–63
  collectivistic 141, 176–7, 206
  of gender 178–82
  gender across 180
  heritage/ideologies 171–8
  historical landscape
    154–71

Hong Kong 164–6
individualistic 141, 176–7, 206
United States 166–71

"date book" 54
daughters
   atypical fathers of 35–7
   equal value (China) 161
   learning from mothers 21–35
   –mother bond 31–2
Davies, P. G. 185
day-care (effects on children)
   108–9, 124
deep relationships 229
deferential family norms 178–9
democracy/democratization 34
Deng Xiaoping 157, 158, 162, 163
diaries 125–6
Diener, E. 18
discrimination 16, 65
   against mothers 12–15, 203–4,
   224–6
   maternal wall 117–20
   sexism 164, 168, 178–80,
   189–90, 201
   statistical 203–4
dissing/disrespect 12–15
divorce 2, 15, 64, 91, 93, 94–5,
   103, 213
Dole, Elizabeth 181
domestic help 58–60, 73–4, 76,
   77–9, 148–9, 150, 175, 208–9,
   223
Dong Jianhua 92–4, 258
Drago, R. 211
Drucker, P. 189, 190, 207
dual-career families 95–7, 133
dual-centric women 10–12, 79
dually successful women 1–2, 5–6, 9
   checklist of ideas 220–8
   finding husband/partner 212–13
   finding mentors/coaches 213–14

finding time 53–71
happiness 228–9
leadership crisis 229–30
Motherhood Mandate 211–12
motivation and self-efficacy
   209–10, 219–20
normative roles 214–18
step-by-step approach 191,
   218–20
Duehr, E. E. 184, 189
Dweck, C. S. 31–2

Eagly, E. H. 166, 190, 197–8, 202,
   213
Eby, L. D. 44–5
Eckes, T. 118
Edmundson, Lorna Duphiney
   11–12, 36, 78, 100, 175, 249
education 230
   China 160, 172–3
   Hong Kong 165, 173–4
   intelligence and 31–2
   schools (role) 42–4
   trends 2–3, 4
   USA 166, 174
Edwards, Ada 249–50
Edwards, L. 160
elder care 56, 215
elderly women 15
Ellemers, N. 221
emotional support 37, 83–4, 95,
   213, 223
employment
   maternal (effect on children)
   121–8, 215–16
   part-time 7, 9, 16, 169, 174, 211
   trends 2, 3–5
   see also job(s); work
enhancement (enrichment) 131
Ensher, E. 34, 37, 45
Equal Employment Opportunities
   Commission (USA) 168

Equal Opportunities Commission
(Hong Kong) 164, 271
equal pay
Hong Kong 164, 165
USA 168
Equal Pay Act (USA) 168
Equal Rights Amendment (USA)
168
ethical leaders 190
Eu, Audrey 28–9, 81, 269–70
European Union 3, 48
evaluation, biases in 202–3
expectations (work–life rules) 222
extended family
pressure from 85–6
support from 78–9, 127, 149–50,
177
"extreme jobs" 52, 53

Fair Labor Standards Act (USA) 48
Families and Work Institute 10
family
-centric women 10–12
deep relationships 229
dually successful lives 5, 10–12,
53–71, 208–30
extended 78–9, 85–6, 127,
149–50, 177
-friendly policies 7, 8, 169–71,
174, 211, 219–20, 222
maintaining bonds 110–15,
221–2
roles 137–42, 171–5
sequencing strategy 63–5
socialization/norms 178–9
see also children; fathers;
mother(s);
work–family; work–family
spillover
family calendar 54–5, 221
Family Medical Leave Act (USA)
170

family wage 121
Fan, Rita 90, 144–5, 166, 192–3,
270
fathers
normative roles 8, 97
patriarchal system 161, 164
role models/mentors 35–7
time on household duties 47
Fei, Barbara 36–7, 270–1
Feng Cui 43–4, 68, 150, 157, 172,
258–9
Feng Lida 26–7, 80, 153, 259
filial piety 31–2, 37, 139–40
Fischer, L. R. 31
Fish, S. 15
Fiske, S. T. 178
Fletcher, J. K. 134
flexibility 2, 7, 16, 169–70, 174,
211
Fong, Nellie 72, 152, 271
food/cooking 62, 68, 75, 111–12,
171–2
Forbes, Steve 181
Ford, M. T. 134
formal mentors 37–42
Four Modernizations 23
"Four Selfs" 160
Framingham heart study 10–11
Franklin, Barbara 54–5, 92, 188,
189, 250–1
Franklin, Benjamin 50
Friedan, B. 15
Friedman, S. D. 134, 142
Friedman, T. L. 199
Frisco, M. 213
Frone, M. R. 133, 134, 137
Furstenberg, F. F., Jr. 126

G8 meeting 18–19
Galinsky, E. 47
Gauthier, A. H. 126
Geary, D. 118

gender
  culture of 178–82
  discrimination *see* discrimination
  ideologies, culture and 171–8
  stereotypes *see* stereotypes
  *see also* men; women
gender equality 98–100, 229–30
  China 158–61, 164
  Hong Kong 164–6
gender gap
  crisis in leadership 229–30
  housework 73, 74–5, 79–82
  wages 12, 16, 39, 65
Gernsbacher, M. A. 118
Gilbert, L. A. 79, 83
glass ceiling 169, 190
Glass Ceiling Commission 169
Glick, P. 178
*Global Gender Gap, The* 229–30
globalization 206
goals 142–3, 146–7, 148, 207, 209,
  210, 212, 219
Goethals, G. R. 196
Goldsmith, M. 190
Gong, Ginny 68, 251
Gong Qiaoyu 259–60
good leaders (redefining) 214–18
good mothers 106–7, 126, 130,
  219
  redefining 110–15, 214–18
Gottfried, A. E. 122, 216
Gottfried, A. W. 122, 216
Goulden, M. 5
Government Accounting Office 16
"Great Man" theory 194–5
Greenhaus, J. H. 53, 133, 134, 142
Grzywacz, J. G. 135
Gu Xiulian 149, 176, 260
guilt 62, 109, 115, 126, 127–8,
  130, 175, 215–16
Gupta, S. 73
Gur, D. 118

Halpern, D. F. 118, 132
Hammer, L. 169
happiness 18, 228–9
Happy Homemaker model 73–105
harmony (work–family spillover)
  131–53
Hausmann, R. 229
health 56–7, 67, 144–6, 151, 170
  stress 10–12, 72, 132–3, 177
heart disease 10
Heilman, M. E. 118, 202–3
Heinen, B. A. 134
heritage, cultural 171–8
Herst, D. E. L. 134
Hesselbein, Frances 86–7, 147–8,
  176, 188–9, 190, 196, 197,
  228, 251–2
Hewlett, S. A. 5, 52, 53, 64–5,
  115, 211–12
Heydens-Gahir, H. A. 142, 148
Higgins, M. C. 45
hiring process (discrimination) 12,
  120–1
historical events, culture and
  154–71
Ho, Doreen Woo 39–41, 78, 88–9,
  126, 172, 252–3
Hochschild, A. R. 4, 52
Hofstede, G. 176, 206
Hollenshead, C. 211
home economics (new) 73–82
homework 24, 152, 173, 174, 178
homosocial reproduction 204–5
Hong Kong 154, 162–3
  women's advancement 164–6
  women leaders (biographies)
    265–77
hostile sexism 178, 179
housework
  domestic help 58–60, 73–4, 76,
    77–9, 148–9, 150, 175, 208–9,
    223

housework (*Cont'd*)
   gender gap 73, 74–5, 79–82
   Happy Homemaker model
      73–105
   husbands (role) 73, 74–5, 79–82,
      96, 178, 212–13
   SuperMom syndrome 75–7,
      125–6, 174
   time spent 47, 73, 74
husbands
   attitudes to wife's fame 89–91
   buffer against extended family
      85–6
   coach/cheerleader 86–9, 97, 213
   finding the right one 212–13
   housework 73, 74–5, 79–82, 96,
      178, 212–13
   Mr. Right myth 100–5
   normative roles 8, 95–7
   power struggles 91–5
   roles 82–100, 212–13
   sensitivities of 102–5
   supportive 98–100, 212–13
   synchronized time schedules
      54–5
   wives earning more than 17–18
   *see also* family; fathers; marriage
Hyde, J. S. 10, 118, 125

"ideal worker" 215, 227
idols 42–4
"implicit stereotypes" 117
incremental beliefs (intelligence)
   31–2, 46
individualistic societies 141, 176–7,
   206
infanticide 161
informal mentors 37–42
Institute for Women's Policy
   Research 65
integration strategy (work–family)
   60–3, 70–1, 134–6, 220–1

intellectual support/compatibility
   88–9
intelligence 31–2
"intensive mothering" 125
International Labour Organization
   48
International Women's Forum 13,
   34, 248, 267
interviewees (biographies) 5–6
   in Hong Kong 265–77
   in Mainland China 257–69
   in USA 246–56
intimacy 82–100, 101–2

job(s)
   assignment 151
   "extreme" 52, 53
   satisfaction 44, 45, 133–4, 177,
      224
   sharing 7
   *see also* employment; housework;
      work
Johannesen-Schmidt, M. C. 198
Johnson, B. T. 197
Johnston, D. D. 110
Jones, D. 32
Judge, T. A. 195

Kahn, R. L. 133
Kahneman, D. 129
Kanter, R. M. 204–5
Karau, S. J. 198
Kelloway, E. K. 11, 229
Kern, Ann 41, 143, 174, 253
Kirwan-Taylor, H. 129
knowledge 45, 140
Korean War 23
Kram, K. E. 37–8, 45
Krishnan, H. A. 201, 207, 227
Kroeck, K. G. 200
Krueger, A. H. 129
Kuomintang regime 26, 27, 155

labyrinth 166, 190, 213–14
Lai, G. 141, 177
Lam, Peggy 27–8, 85–6, 271–2
Langkamer, K. L. 134
latchkey children 150–1
Lau, Emily 76, 90, 272
Law, Fanny 84, 173, 272–3
Law on the Protection of the Rights
    and Interests of Women 160
Lawler, J. J. 206
leadership
  crisis in 229–30
  definition 190
  homosocial reproduction 204–5
  politics of 183, 199
  step-by-step approach 191,
    218–20
  style 184–90, 194–201, 217,
    219–20, 226–8
  transactional 194, 195–6, 198,
    200–1, 202, 203, 206
  transformational 194, 195–7,
    198, 200–1, 205–6, 219–20
  see also women leaders; women
    leaders (biographies)
learning
  intelligence and 31–2
  see also education
Lee, A. M. 11, 133
Lee, C. M. 16
Lee, I. C. 178
Lee, M. C. 178
Lee, Sandra 29, 42–3, 145–7, 273
Lee, Shelley 42, 273–4
legal protection (women in USA)
    168–71
"leniency bias" 118
Lentz, E. 44–5
Leung, A. 11
Leung, Sophie 62–3, 82, 86, 102,
    112–13, 274
Levine, J. A. 50

Li, H. B. 16
life expectancy 11
life management strategies 142–52
Lima, L. 44–5
line positions 223
Linver, M. R. 122
Lipman-Bluman, J. 190
Liu Shaoqi 25
Lo, S. 11, 173
Logsdon, M. C. 212
Lowe, K. B. 200
Luce, C. B. 52, 53, 211
Luk, V. 11

Ma, Mary 14, 61, 69, 70, 105,
    156, 199–200, 260–1
Ma Yuan 22–4, 67, 75, 104,
    139–40, 158, 261
McCann family 106–7
McCartney, K. 124
McDonald, D. A. 135
MacDonald, E. 18, 183
McKee, M. C. 11, 229
McKinsey and Company 5, 19–20,
    207, 213–14, 227
makeup (culture of gender) 180–2
Makhijani, M. G. 198
Mao Zedong 154, 155, 157
marriage
  age at 2
  equal partnership 79–82
  gender gap 73, 74–5, 79–82
  Happy Homemaker model
    73–105
  husbands/partners (role) 82–100,
    212–13
  power structure 17–18
  power struggles 91–5
  working hard at (fairytale myth)
    100–5
  see also divorce; family; husbands;
    wives

Marriage and Family Society of
China 17
Marshall, N. L. 124
Martinez, C. D. 50
Mason, M. A. 5
maternal employment
(effect on children) 121–8,
215–16
maternal wall 117–20
maternity leave 170, 212
Matthews, R. J. 133
meaningful work 11, 20, 126, 218,
224, 227, 228–9
media 7, 106–7, 124, 129, 180–1,
226
women in limelight 89–91
Media Mentions and Suse News
Stanford Report 166
meditation 147
Mehrain, T. 165
men
as leaders (research)
197–200
patriarchal system 161, 164
see also fathers; husbands
Mencius (mother of) 21–2
"mental schemata" 185
mentors/mentoring 205
effectiveness of 44–6
fathers as 35–7
finding 213–14, 226
formal/informal 37–42
mothers as 34–5
psychosocial 41, 45
self-confidence and 41, 42, 45
Merkel, Angela 18–19
Milkie, M. A. 73
Ming, Jenny 9, 54, 55–6, 57, 61,
76, 90–1, 111–12, 137–8, 170,
172, 175, 206–7, 212, 224,
253–4

mommy track 6–9, 211–12
"Mommy Wars" 108, 130
money 18, 228–9
retirement income 65
see also wages
Montoya, R. M. 229
Mooijaart, A. 221
moral values 42–3
Morgenstern, J. 50
Motherhood Mandate 211–12
mother(s)
–daughter bond 31–2
discrimination against 12–15,
224–6
good 106–7, 110–15, 126, 130,
214–18, 219
guilt 62, 109, 115, 126, 127–8,
130, 175, 215–16
learning from 21–35
maternal employment (effects on
children) 121–8, 215–16
maternal wall 117–20
maternity leave 170, 212
of Mencius 21–2
as mentors 34–5
mommy track 6–9, 211–12
"Mommy Wars" 108, 130
Motherhood Mandate 211–12
normative roles 8
permission to daughters 33–4
preparation for motherhood
212
pride 114, 115, 126, 128, 216,
219
as role models 21–35, 115, 126,
216
sacrifices by 21–2
stereotypical mothering 115–21
SuperMom Syndrome 75–7,
125–6, 174
time (saving/spending) 47–72

wage gap 120–1
*see also* working mothers
motivation 195, 196
  self–efficacy and 209–10,
    219–20
multitasking 69–71, 73, 74, 135,
  148
Murphy, S. E. 34, 37, 45, 132

National Association of Women in
  Law Firms 4
National Institute of Child Health
  and Human Development 108,
  123
National People's Congress (China)
  160–1
National Study of the Changing
  Workforce 49
National Study of Confidence in
  Leadership 229
National Working Committee on
  Children and Women 160
NATO 34, 248
negative work–family spillover 131,
  134
Nelson, B. J. 167
networks 213, 214
Ni Zhihua 135, 261
no (learning to say) 57–8, 139
normative roles
  changing 8, 95–7
  of husbands 8, 95–7
  redefining 214–18
  of wives/mothers 74, 85

off-ramp option 64–5, 169
Okimoto, T. G. 118, 202–3
on-ramp option 64–5, 169
"One Country – Two Systems"
  (in China) 162–3
one-child policy 161

Opium Wars 162
optimization strategy (life
  management) 142, 148
organizational strategies 221
outsourcing 58–60, 62–3, 208–9,
  223
overtime 48, 139, 148
Owen, M. T. 124
Ozanian, M. K. 18

parental leave 170, 212
parents
  filial piety 31–2, 37, 139–40
  *see also* fathers; mothers
Park, D. 201, 207, 227
Parker, K. 108
Parry, G. 133
part-time employment 7, 9, 16,
  169, 174, 211
patriarchal system 161, 164
Pelosi, Nancy 166
pensions 65
permission
  from mothers 33–4
  to pay for hired help 59
personal digital assistant (PDA)
  54
personal role redefinition 137,
  139–41
personal rules 221
Philliber, W. W. 83
Piccolo, R. F. 195
Pittinsky, T. L. 229
planning
  a family (timing and age)
    128–30, 223–4
  priorities 55–7
  strategic 40
  time management 54–5
Poelmans, S. A. Y. 176, 177
politics (of leadership) 183, 199

positive work–family spillover 131, 134, 135
Poteet, M. L. 44–5
poverty 50, 65, 122, 124, 155, 161, 190, 228
power 183, 196
    empowerment 31, 140, 227
    imbalance (childhood experience) 99–100
    structure (in marriage) 17–18
    struggles (in marriage) 91–5
"power mentoring" 34, 45
Pratto, F. 178
pregnancy 12, 128, 161, 170, 212
"prescriptive stereotyping" 117–18
pride 22–3, 114, 115, 126, 128, 216, 219
priorities 55–60, 62–3, 143–5, 147, 208
Program for the Development of Chinese Women 160
promotion 39, 45, 64, 65
protégés 39, 44, 45
Pruitt, B. H. 134
psychic dollars/benefits 15–18
psychological support 38
psychological well-being 11, 177
psychosocial mentoring 41, 45

Qing dynasty 155, 164
Quinn, R. 133

Ragins, B. R. 39
Rapoport, R. 133, 134
Rapoport, R. N. 133
reactive role behavior 137, 141–2
Rehabilitation Act (USA) 168
relationships
    deep 228–9
    see also family; marriage
Repetti, R. J. 133

resources (maximization) 223
retirement income 65
Roberts, S. 15
Robinson, J. P. 73
role expectations (traditional) 79–80
role models 105, 220
    fathers as 35–7, 80
    idols (and school) 42–4
    for men (socialization process) 100
    mentors 34–5, 37–42, 44–6
    mothers as 21–35, 115, 126, 216
    roles
    personal 137, 139–41
    reactive role behavior 137, 141–2
    structural 137–9
    work–family balance 136–42
Rosenthal, R. A. 133
Rosenthal, S. A. 229
rules
    personal 221
    work–life 222
Russell, M. 133

sacrifices (by mothers) 21–2
sandwich generation 215
Sayer, L. C. 73
Scarr, S. 108–9
Schechter, Sue 138–9, 191–2, 254
scheduling 54–5, 221
Schiller, P. 211
Schkade, D. A. 129
Schoen, R. 89
Schoenberger, C. R. 183
schools (role) 42–4
Schwartz, F. 6–7
Schwarz, N. 129
selection strategy (life management) 142–8
self-confidence 17, 72, 114, 160
    mentoring and 41, 42, 45

self-efficacy 33, 46
  motivation and 209–10, 219–20
self-esteem 34, 42, 45, 219, 220
Seligman, M. E. P. 18, 229
separation strategy (work–family)
  60–3, 70–1, 133
sequencing strategy 63–5
Sex Discrimination Ordinance 164
sex ratio (China) 161
sex selection (China) 161
sexism 14–15, 36, 164, 168, 180,
  189–90, 201
  benevolent 178–9
  hostile 178, 179
Shafiro, M. 169
Shanahan, B. 212
Shi Qingqi 24–6, 155–6, 157,
  186–7, 261–2
Short, S. A. 74
Singh, V. 3
Sino-Japanese War 22, 24, 25
Sivasubramaniam, N. 200
Slaughter, A-M. 48
sleep/sleep patterns 66–9, 102,
  142
Smeeding, T. 126
Snoek, J. D. 133
social support 83, 177, 223
socialist market economy (China)
  157
son-preference 161
Spector, P. E. 177
Spencer, S. J. 185
Staab, Valari D. 77, 95–7, 254
statistical stereotypes 203–4
Steele, C. M. 185
step-by-step leadership development
  191, 218–20
stereotypes 9, 98, 205, 214–15
  leadership 184–90, 217, 227
  prescriptive 117–18
  statistical 203–4

unconscious effects 184–90
unexamined 14, 117
stereotypical mothering 115–21
Sternberg, R. J. 38
Sone, A. A. 129
strategic planning 40
stress 10–12, 72, 132–3, 177
structural role redefinition 137–9
Sullivan, B. 211
Sun, Nora 17, 262
Sun Yuehuan 75, 104–5, 140, 172,
  187–8, 262–3
SuperMom Syndrome 75–7, 125–6,
  174
support
  career-related 37–8
  emotional 37, 83–4, 95, 213,
    223
  from extended family 78–9, 127,
    149–50, 177
  from husbands/partners 98–100,
    212–13
  psychological 38
  social 83, 177, 223
Sutton, M. 134
Swanson, D. H. 110
Swift, Jane 180

Tai, Alice 98–9, 140, 173–4, 274–5
talents (loss of) 7, 20
Tang, C. S. 11, 133
Tang, T. 11, 133
telecommuting 7, 169, 211
Thatcher, Margaret 19, 35, 82
Thomas, D. A. 45
threat (of wife's success) 91–5
time 148
  conflict 131–2, 153
  choices and nonchoices 49–51
  household tasks 47, 73, 74
  planning for children 128–30,
    223–4

time (*Cont'd*)
 spent with children (generational
  comparison) 125–6
 strategies 53–71
 working hours 47–9, 52–3, 73–5,
  133, 169, 177
"time famine" 53
time management 51–3, 72
 priorities 55–60, 62–3, 143–5,
  147, 208
 scheduling/planning 54–5, 221
 sequencing 63–5
 strategies 60–3
"time use diaries" 125–6
Time Use Survey 47
Title VII (Civil Rights Act) 168
"toxic leaders" 190
transactional leadership 194,
 195–6, 198, 200–1, 202, 203,
 206
transformational leadership 194,
 195–7, 198, 200–1, 205–6,
 219–20
trust (domestic help) 77–9
Turner, N. 11, 229
Tyson, L. D. 229

"unconscious" stereotypes 117
unemployment 122
"unexamined stereotypes" 14,
 117
United Nations 33, 34, 68, 144,
 224–5, 248
 Convention on the Elimination of
  All Forms of Discrimination
  against Women 168, 259
United States
 legal protection for women
  168–71
 women leaders (biographies)
  246–56
 women's employment 166–8

Van de Kamp, Andrea L. 60–1,
 101–2, 111, 132, 142, 254–5
Van Engen, M. 198
Van Steenbergen, E. F. 221
Vandell, D. L. 124
Vannoy-Hiller, D. 83
Vinnicombe, S. 3

wages 9, 50, 52, 74
 after career break 8, 64, 65
 discrimination 12
 equal pay *see* equal pay
 family wage 121
 gender gap 12, 16, 39, 65
 motherhood wage gap 120–1
 psychic dollars/benefits 15–18
 unpaid leave 170
Waldfogel, J. 121
Waldron, I. 133
Walumbwa, F. O. 206
Wan, O. C. 164
Wan, P. S. 164
warmth, competence and (rating)
 118–19
Warner, J. 106–7, 120
Warr, P. 133
water molecule metaphor 153
Weddington, Sarah 38, 56–7, 92,
 191, 218–19, 255–6
Wei Keizheng 103, 186, 263
Weinick, R. M. 89
Weisell, R. 50
Westwood, R. 165
Wheaton, S. 180
"whispers of our lives" 147, 228
Williams, J. 14, 117–18, 215, 225
Williams, K. 213
Wisner, K. 212
wives
 fame (husband's attitude) 89–91
 normative roles 8, 74, 85, 95–7,
  214–18

power struggles (and threats)
91–5
success (husband's sensitivities)
102–5
see also childcare; housework;
marriage; mother(s)
Wolfe, D. M. 133
women
career track 6–9, 211–12
dual-centric 10–12, 79
dual success see dually successful
women
education (trends) 2–3, 4
employment (trends) 2, 3–5
gender equality see gender
equality
legal protection (USA) 168–71
Mommy Track 6–9, 211–12
rights of (China) 158–62
scarcity of (at the top) 4, 18–20
see also mother(s); wives; women
leaders; women leaders
(biographies); working
mothers
women leaders
business (advantages) 200–1,
205–7
career paths 190–4
disadvantages for 201–5
dual-centric 10–12, 79
dual success see dually successful
women
finding time 53–71
influence of mothers 21–35
numbers 3–4
research 197–200
role of mentors 34–5, 37–42,
44–6
scarcity 4, 18–20
step-by-step development 191,
218–20
stereotypes 184–90, 217, 227

style 184–90, 194–201, 217,
219–20, 226–8
women leaders (biographies) 5–6
in Hong Kong 265–77
in Mainland China 257–65
in USA 246–56
Women's Commission 164, 267,
271, 274
Wong, Rosanna 33, 77, 275–6
Woo, Marjorie 181, 263
work
-centric women 10–12
harder and smarter 65–6
–life rules (expectations) 222
meaningful 11, 20, 126, 218,
224, 227, 228–9
see also employment; housework;
job(s)
work–family
balance 6, 132–52, 220–8
conflict see work–family spillover
integration strategy 60–3, 70–1,
134–6, 220–1
interface 70–1, 134, 142, 153,
175–8
separation strategy 60–3, 70–1,
133
transitions (personal rules) 221
–work (sequencing) 63–5
work–family spillover 12
balance 132–6
life management strategies
142–52
negative 131, 134
roles (redefining) 136–42
time conflict 131–2, 153
working hours 7–8, 11, 133, 177
extreme jobs 52, 53
flexible 2, 169–70, 174, 211
on household tasks 47, 73–4, 75
international comparisons 47–9
overtime 48, 139, 148

working mothers
  effects on children 108, 121–8,
    215–16
  good 106–7, 110–15, 126, 130,
    214–19
  guilt 62, 109, 115, 126, 127–8,
    130, 175, 215–16
  -hate 106–9
  planning a family 128–30,
    223–4
  stereotypes 115–21
World Bank 18, 261–2
World Economic Forum 1,
  229–30
World Values Survey 224–5
Wu Qidi 88, 151, 263–4

Xin, Julia 97, 264

Yang, J. 74
Yang, Marjorie 13, 55, 163, 166,
  204, 276
Yang, N. 141, 177
Yau, Carrie 58, 139, 148, 172,
  276–7
Yeung, W. J. 122
York, Margaret A. 12–13, 67–8,
  87–8, 127, 168–9, 193–4, 256
Young, C. E. 222
Yuen, Betty 89–90, 143, 166, 173,
  277

Zahidi, S. 229
Zhang, J. S. 16
Zhang Xin 1, 99, 135–6, 207, 224,
  264–5
Zhu, W. 229
Zou, Y. 141, 177